Publishing coordination
Giancarlo Calcagni

Art director • Graphics
Arianna Monti

Matteo Editore s.r.l.
Via E. Mattei, 17
31030 Dosson di Casier (TV)

MARK KOSTABI

and the East Village Scene 1983-1987

photographs and text by

BAIRD JONES

Forward by Enrico Baj

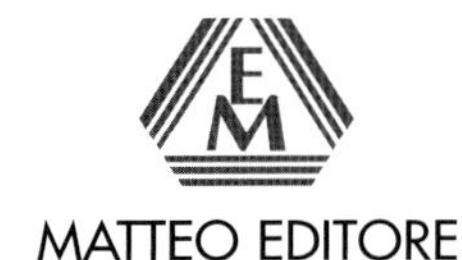

MATTEO EDITORE

Special thanks to

Molly Barnes

Paul Bridgewater

Ronald Feldman

Peter Frank

Lawrence Horn

Tama Janowitz

Michael McKenzie

Marc Miller

Alan Moore

Once upon a time, in a gigantic metropolis, there was a magic neighborhood, much like Montmartre in Paris during the early twentieth century, the era of the Bateau Lavoir of Picasso and company. This neighborhood, rendered picturesque by the presence of countless artists and frequented by many visitors, had taken shape when — in a kind of suspension of our largely technological and speculative behaviors — expression, desire, and the imaginary had provisionally reoccupied the minds and sensibilities of painters.

A minimalism made up of formal emptiness and of museum celebrations was newly countered by a fullness made up of participation and emotion — a fullness that contained figurative messages of immediate

A LOST ART

brutality: such as those of FA-Q or, for a while, Van Gogh.

Passersby were attracted to and intrigued by thousands of tiny galleries, often ephemera that lasted for only a day. These exhibition spaces opened up throughout that magical neighborhood known as the East Village. From the early 1980s to 1987, New York experienced a period of fantastic and spontaneous creativity. Many East Village buildings were — and perhaps still are — abandoned, windowless, with store windows and entrances shattered and even blackened by the smoke of fires.

Virtually emerging from caves, dens, and burrows, the imaginations of these "Situationist" (1) painters pitched camp everywhere,

multiplying and puffing up like expanding plastic foam. Their imagina-
tions entered the cafes and eateries such as the Life Cafe and the
Pharmacy, venturing beyond Tompkins Square Park all the way to
Avenues C and D. And they moved across those barriers toward the
Lower East Side and circles worthy of Dante's Inferno.

In these areas, on Stanton Street, we can still find an active
art center founded in 1968 by the painter Shalom: Fusion Art, which is
currently showing a transgressive group of artists and poets called the
Unbearables.

Near the corner of Rivington Street and Forsyth Street, another magic garden emerged: the Sculpture Garden, which likewise fell into a state of neglect. It was during that period that I first met Mark Kostabi, who is now showing with the Unbearables. Several years later, in 1991, Mark visited me in Italy, and we very rapidly collaborated on some forty paintings and some hundred drawings.

Our inspiration was our memories of the East Village.

ENRICO BAJ, May 2002

Translated from Italian by Joachim Neugroschel

1. In France during 1957, the Situationists founded a political and literary movement aimed at creating "situations" in opposition to the triumphant Society of Spectacle.

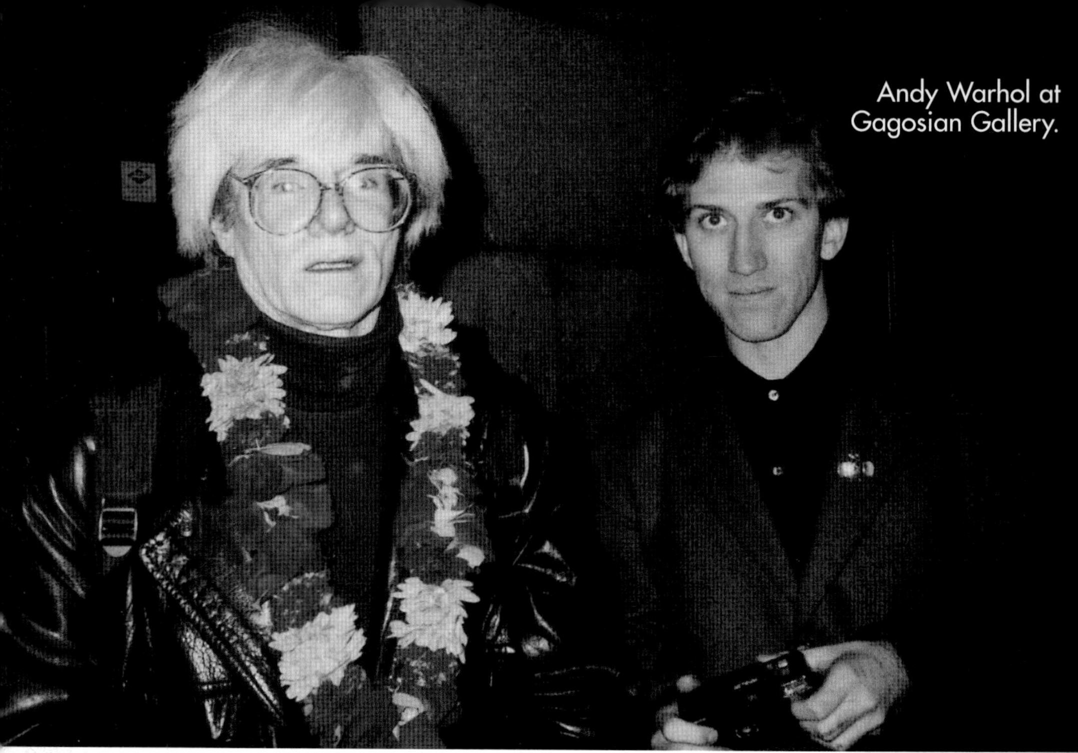

The East Village scene first coalesced as a nightclub party crowd. Mark Kostabi's name was seen for the first time in New York in 1983 when it started popping up on invitations at clubs such as Danceteria, Zippers, the Underground, and Kamikaze. Mark was mentioned for the first time in the New York Post's Page Six as Mark "Kastabi" as late as Oct. 22,1984 for being discovered at Zippers while his friend, painter

MARK KOSTABI
AND THE
EAST VILLAGE SCENE
1983-1987
BY BAIRD JONES

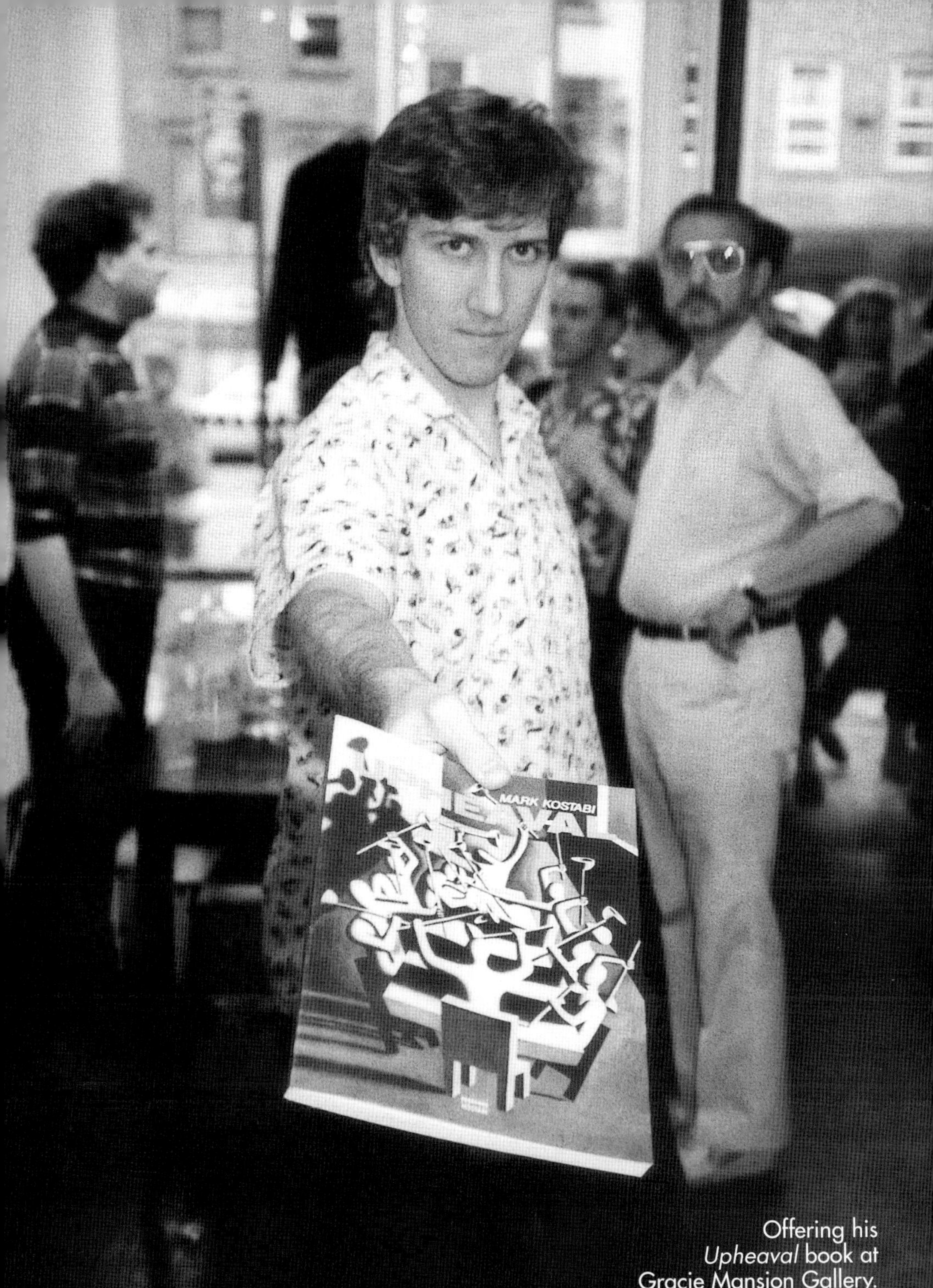

Offering his *Upheaval* book at Gracie Mansion Gallery.

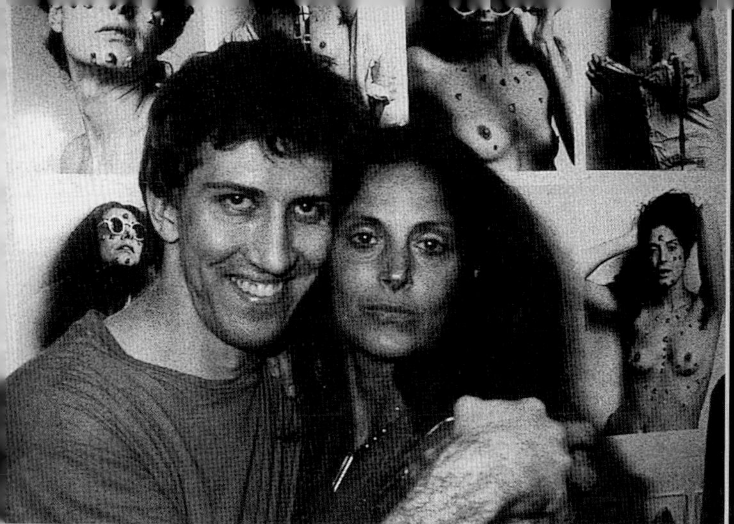
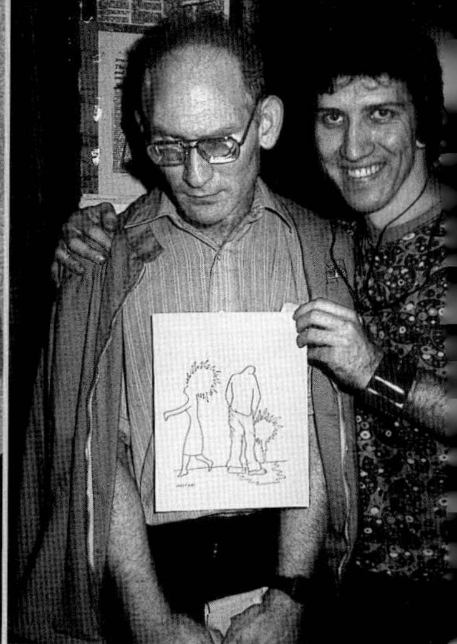

Artist Hannah Wilke in front of her self-portraits.   Art critic Peter Frank at Cuando.

Martin Wong, according to the Post, was first noticed by Soho's Semaphore Gallery owners at Danceteria. The same Post article noted that "Carl" (meaning Carlo) McCormick had just curated fourteen consecutive shows at the Limbo Lounge with a different artist each night. But the East Village club circuit had been in full swing a full year earlier and the major museums were already acquiring works by the Alphabetland painters left and right. The myth and hype of the 80s East Village scene was that you could buy Keith Haring's art on the cheap if you had just gotten there first. In fact, those bargains always seemed to disappear by the time the big names like Haring and Jean-Michel Basquiat filtered into the mainstream. Mudd Club owner Steve Mass said that the legendary anecdote about his doorman Keith Haring in the early 80s painting whole room installations for "25 bucks and a can of black paint" were completely false. Mass once confessed to me, "Keith never did wall paintings at the Mudd Club, he was way beyond that by then - Keith did the door for me and otherwise did curations. He got Jean-Michel Basquiat to paint a wall once, but Keith only organized the shows rather than tag the space directly." (The Mudd Club is now the downstairs two floors of painter Ross Bleckner's digs on White Street). In many ways, the East Village explosion was always about trying to find the next Keith or the next Jean-Michel, and for many collectors and press hounds that search, in the end, came up empty.

Andy Warhol and Jean-Michel Basquiat at the Mary Boone Gallery.

Mark remembers one of his first shows with the East Village clique was June 5,1983 at the *Night of a 1000 Balloons* curated by Liz*Val at Danceteria where the artists all permitted their art to be destroyed by letting the works fly away attached to helium balloons. And why not? The

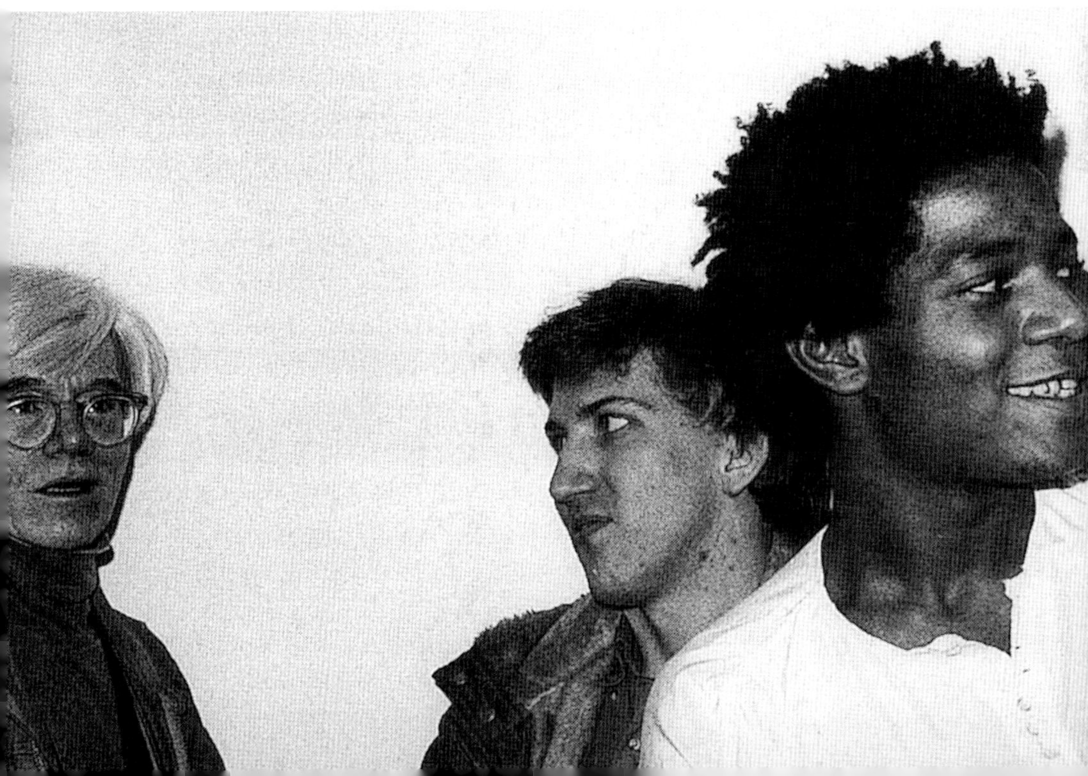

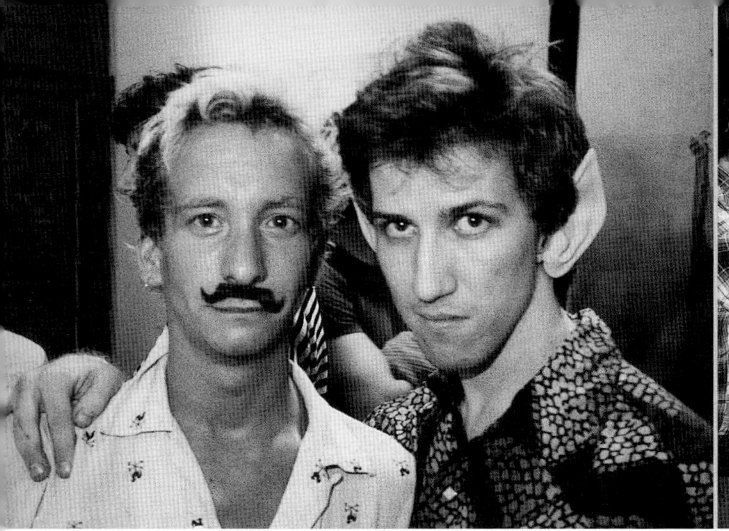

Civilian Warfare Gallery co-owner Dean Savard.

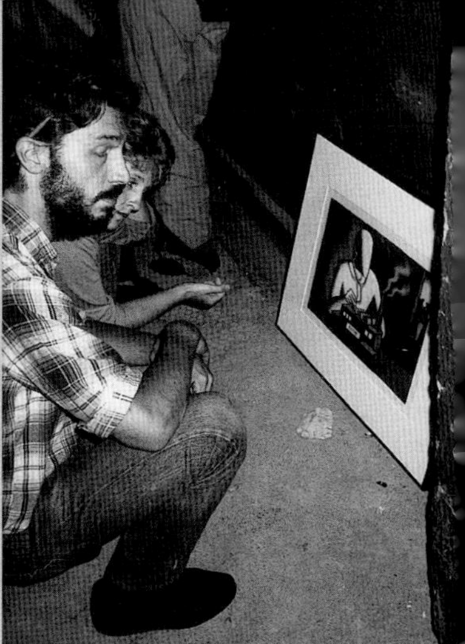

A group show reception in a hallway at ABC No Rio.

artists who showed at these massive group exhibits hardly expected to sell their work. At the Balloon show Mark claims he was virtually the only artist who showed any hesitation about losing an artwork. Apparently the other artists such as Walter Robinson just thought the whole mass destruction was a hoot. The Balloon show was supposedly inspired by Warhol's silver, helium-filled pillows which floated in a gallery. For Warhol the pillows symbolized his paintings floating away — because at that time Warhol claimed to be retiring from painting to just make films. Danceteria's owner Rudolf told me that he was obsessed that Andy Warhol never came once to Danceteria but showed up at all the clubs nearby (like Zippers, where he was a regular). Getting the artists to throw away their art was not going to do the trick because Andy never made it to the Balloon show either.

Andy Warhol went to the East Village art shows regularly once they were hyped, just as Andy chased every trend. However, Andy never made it out to the South Bronx for the graffiti exhibits. Andy was always warning me not to let my parties get too black when I was throwing my disco bashes around town in the early 80s. But then a little later when graffiti got hot he was hanging with "the homies" all the time. I used to rib Warhol about his previous racism and he would just dodge it like always with his favorite statement which was "wha, wha, wha." In general the East Village had less to do with Andy Warhol than one might think.

Mark's installation at the Cuando festival.

Andy's stock had declined a great deal. In a way, Andy died of neglect. In the end, his apathetic assistants just let him down. I was trying to hook Warhol up with a new assistant, Allanby Singleton-Green, the week Andy died. Andy should have had someone staying up with him when he was in the hospital in addition to his nurse. But Andy was being treated like he had become a nuisance. Everyone just wanted to get rid of him.

At Warhol's funeral service at St. Patrick's Cathedral the only person, other than his older brother, who really seemed to show any sincere grief was Mark Kostabi. Everyone else was rubber-necking to see which celebrity was arriving. When the service ended there was a mad rush to get to the door to angle for an invite to the after-party which was just a

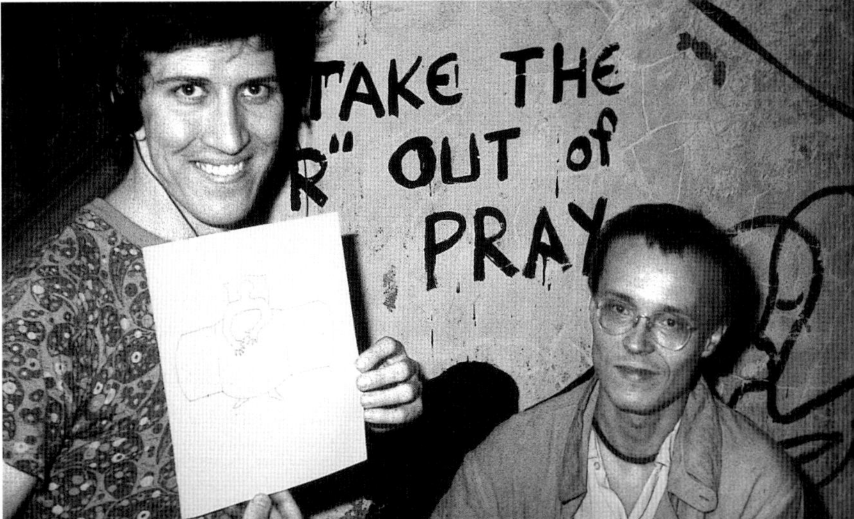

Abstract painter Bernd Naber at Cuando.

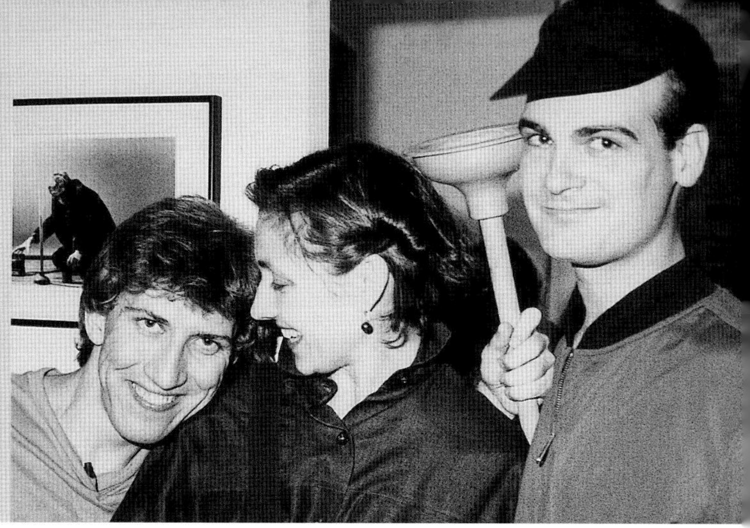

A plunger is not a very romantic accessory. Artist Laren Stover and gallerist Steven Style.

few blocks away. Only Mark was walking around in a stupor too caught up in his own inner turmoil not to care about crashing the after-party. Mark later told me, "Warhol's memorial at St. Patrick's Cathedral was the first memorial I had ever attended. I was shocked to see people flamboyantly posing for photos outside the church steps immediately after the service. People tried to take my photo too but I just walked away as fast as possible. I was sad and I just wished Andy hadn't died. To me he was a symbol of possibility and making dreams come true. He represented a lot of what I came to New York for."

Mark and Andy hung out a few times. In May, 1984, Mark ran in to Andy at Jean-Michel Basquiat's opening at the Mary Boone Gallery.

After the reception Mark and Andy walked up West Broadway together and Andy asked Mark if he wanted a ride to his next destination, probably assuming it was a few blocks away where Andy would drop Mark off and continue heading uptown. But Mark said he'd like to go uptown and stayed for the whole ride and they chatted away. They spoke about nervousness. Andy told Mark that the way Andy combated his nervousness was to drink booze. Few people at that time realized how much Warhol drank but I remember at my parties at Studio 54 Andy used to always order straight vodka and then just chug it down. The rest of the taxi ride Andy pointed out to Mark the uptown buildings and public sculptures he liked. Then, at the end, Andy gave Mark a twenty for the ten dollar ride so

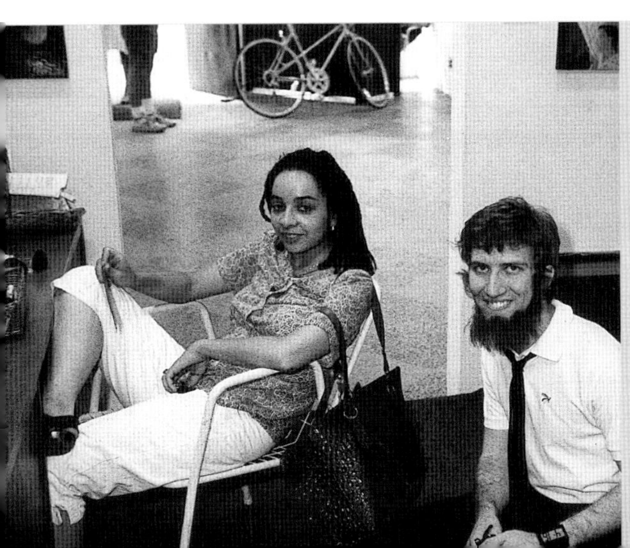

Writer Yasmin Ramirez-Harwood relaxes in the office of one of Mark's East Village galleries, Semaphore East, in 1985.

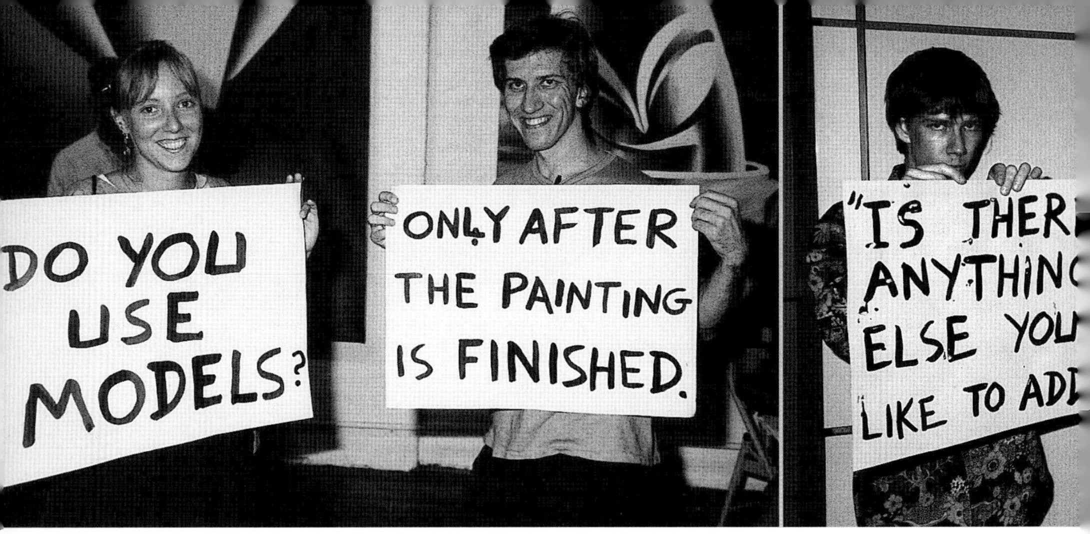

Artist India Northrop at Mark's housewarming party in Tribeca in 1985.

obviously Andy had figured out that Mark really wasn't going anywhere uptown but had just made that story up to spend time with Andy. Mark told me he went a few blocks more in the cab, then got out and took a subway back downtown, deliriously happy that he had spoken with Andy for so long one on one.

Later many critics drew a connection between Mark and Andy Warhol. In 1985, while Andy was still alive, the East Village critic Carlo McCormick told me, "Mark's whole notion of posterity is tied to a Warholian notion of fame. Mark's part of a whole generation who got their values wrong and Mark is the most extreme which also makes him the most interesting. It's like Grade B Hollywood trash. I'd say the whole East Village is screwed up along that path. It's more process than product. That someone would put everything from friendship to anything else, just towards a career, that success, fame and fortune would became his number one aspiration. But Warhol is about packaging while Mark is basically about consumerism."

With Mark's work, the factory assembly line, the media fanaticism, the courting of fan ambivalence, the emphasis on greed and cynicism, Warhol is everywhere. Right at the end, Mark and Andy were starting to gel. Otherwise, when Andy went out he was being met with near universal contempt. I remember Warhol walking around parties trying to hand out

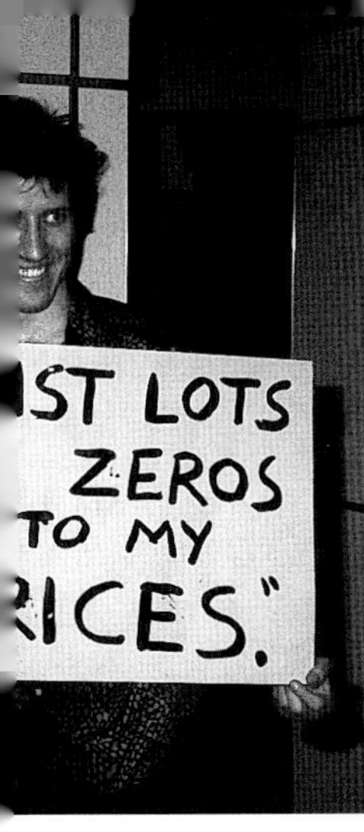

Younger brother Paul Kostabi who was known as Ena during the 1980s.

Gallerist Patti Astor at the legendary Fun Gallery.

six-month-old Interview magazines and people just contemptuously looked at him with his ugly complexion and smears of Clearasil botched all over his face. I thought Andy must have been completely numb until I read

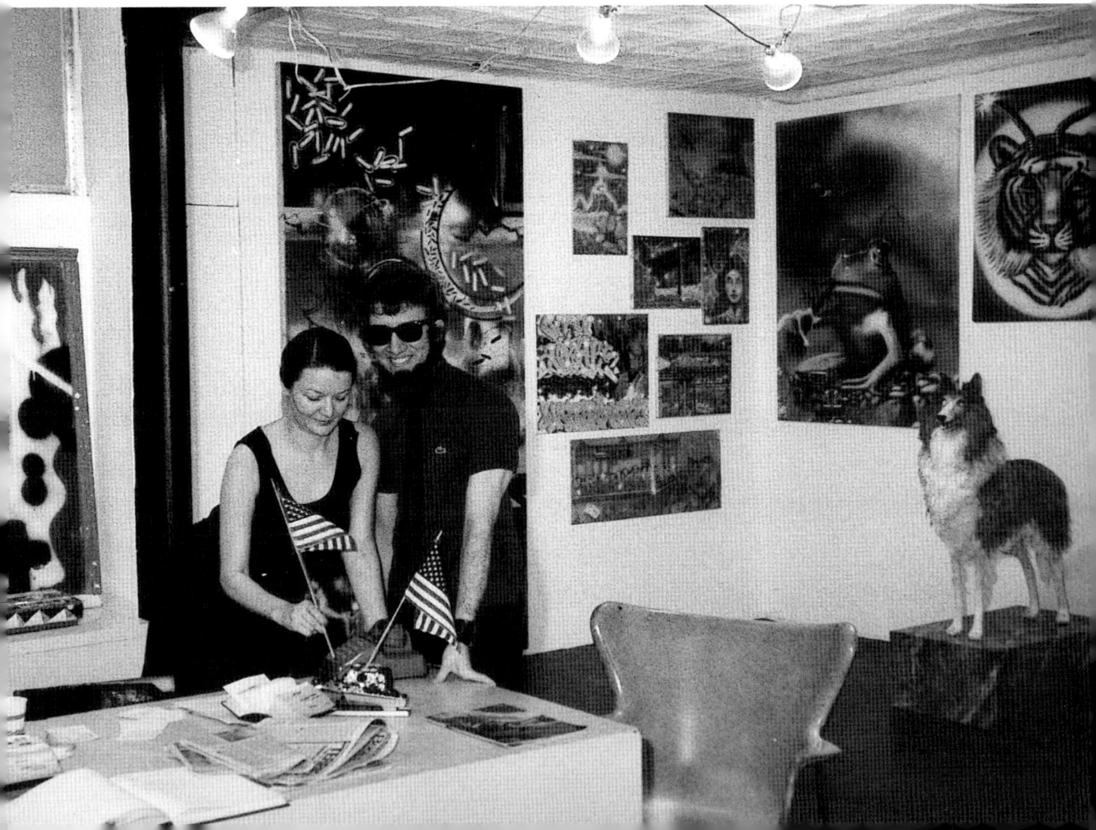

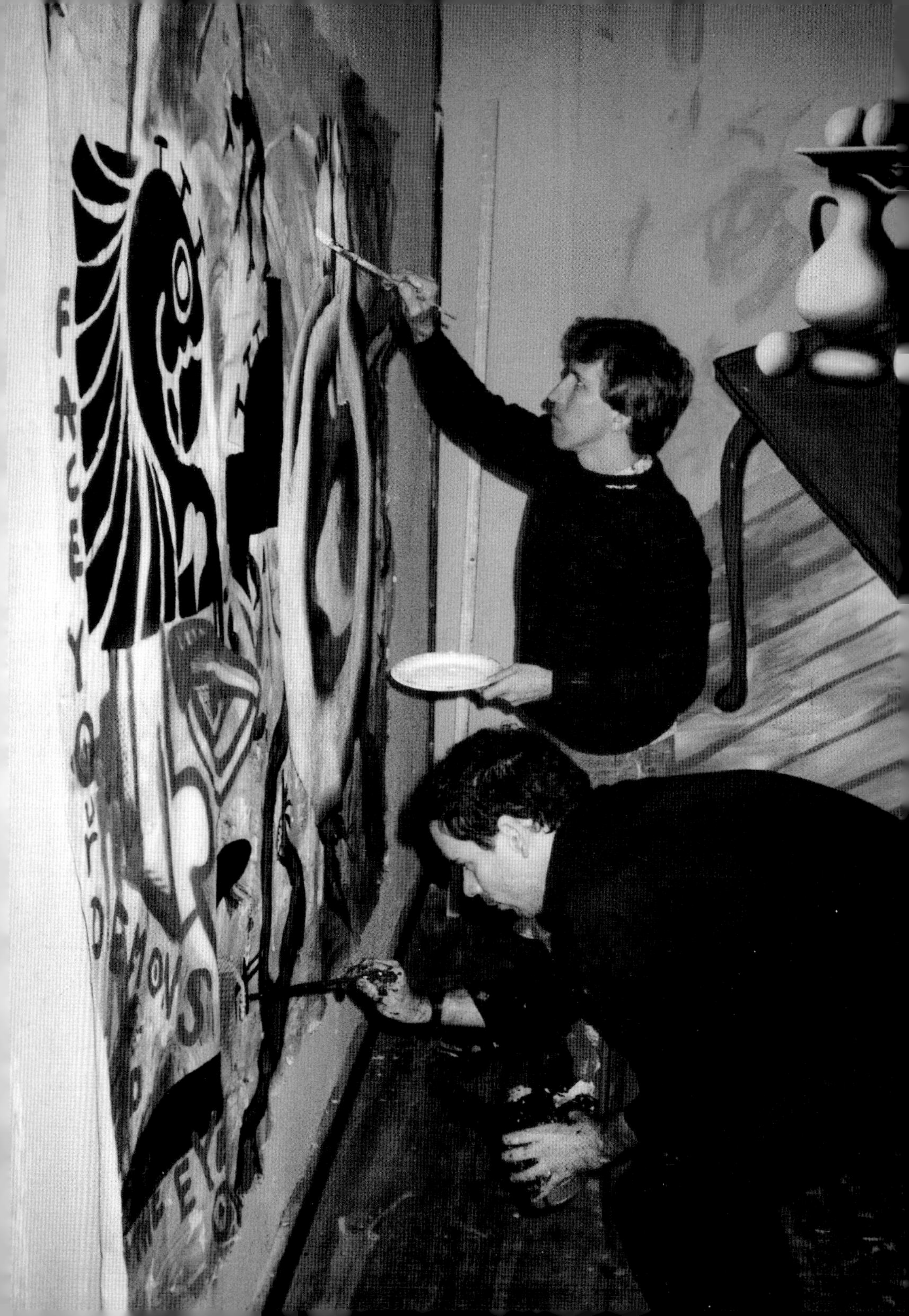

FUCK YOU
DEMONS

his *Diaries* and realized he keenly felt and remembered those snubs. I went to a dinner party at the Area disco where they handed out Warhol's serigraph *Cowboys and Indians* as a party favor. The guests were really top like Diane von Furstenberg, Steve Martin, Fran Lebowitz, Paul Simon, Huntington Hartford, Chris Reeve, Tom Hulce, Boy George and Michael and Diandra Douglas. When I left, I noticed that almost all the guests had just dropped their prints in the trashcan on the corner. But there was one worse step below *Cowboys and Indians* yet to come for Warhol. It was his collaboration with Jean-Michel Basquiat in 1985 which was deemed a failure for both artists. The East Village was no more a lucky place for Warhol than anywhere else.

In 1983 Basquiat was still known as SAMO. He was selling color Xerox postcards for a dollar in front of the Museum of Modern Art. At night he would go down to the Mudd Club where Keith Haring was the doorman. Basquiat would try to get picked up by either a guy or girl so he could hustle a place to stay for the night. The other East Village artists weren't selling their work so insurance at the East Village oriented shows in those days wasn't a problem. That attitude with nightclub art would change. By 1986, the Palladium art shows were constantly derailed by artist claims of damage. Buster Cleveland, at 50, then the oldest of the Gracie Mansion Gallery stable, even got a $5,000 payout from Palladium owner Steve Rubell when a clubgoer removed a dollar bill from one of his collages

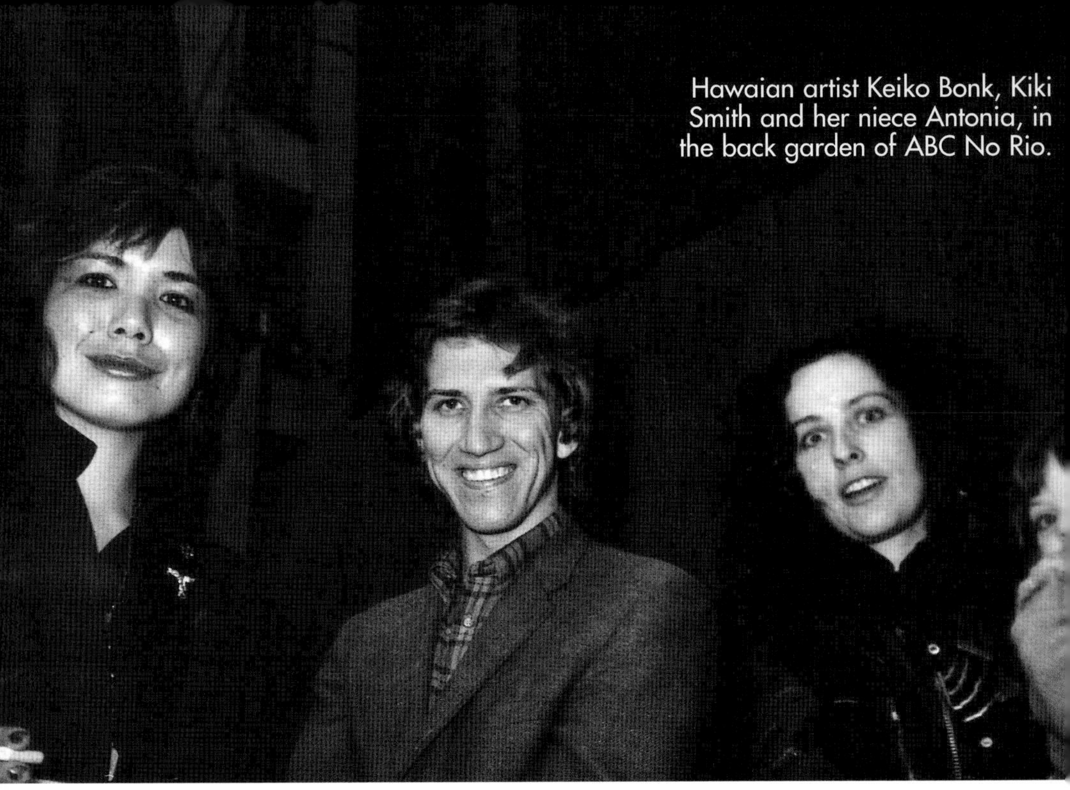

which was on display in a group show. Cleveland self-righteously claimed the artwork had been destroyed and he could not just replace the missing bill. Cleveland insisted that the only proper recourse was for the damaged artwork to be purchased by Rubell, ergo the five grand. Rubell, already dying of AIDS (and whose brother Donald was a major buyer of avant-garde art) did the right thing, bought the collage, and cancelled all future Palladium art curations a few weeks later, forlornly opting to turn the mammoth disco into a guido cash cow from then on instead.

But in the early days, the downtown painters were on the cusp of getting hot and they were young and wild and typically pretty good looking, even if they didn't shower much. In those days, no one called that clique "East Village." "East Village" connoted heroin users. I remember the nightlife impresario Rudolf fleeing a party at the 14th Street poolhall (next door to the Palladium) waving his arm in dismay, exclaiming, "It's just too East Village," although Matt Dillon was one of the pool players. When asked what he meant, Rudolf replied that the crowd was too sallow and

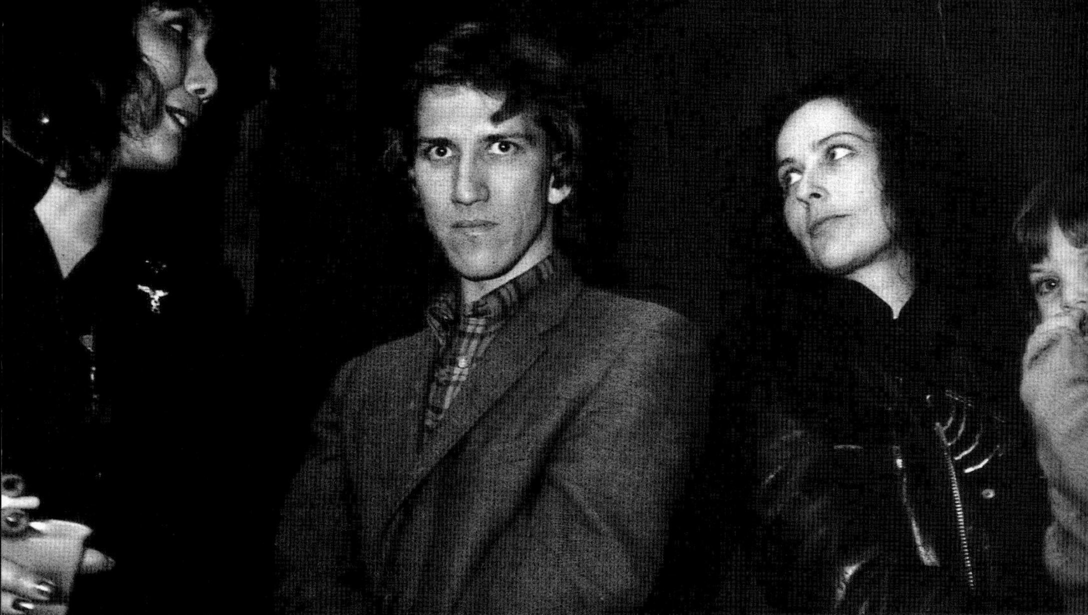

pasty-faced, looking like drug addicts to him. In an omen of hype to come, photographer Patrick McMullan made his debut amongst the In Crowd that night shooting for the gay magazine 212.

One reason the nightclub roots of the East Village scene are forgotten is that a prime curatorial group was then called Anonymous Productions (Jeanette Iannuci, Micheal Gormley, and Victor Mendolia), who also ran Limbo Lounge, a gallery/club which shifted locations several times, always heading east. The Anonymous Group did a dozen important eclectic nightclub shows in 1983. They, along with Fun Gallery, Civilian Warfare, Piezo Electric, 51X, Nature Morte and Gracie Mansion were among the pioneers of the East Village in 1983-84.

Tony Shafrazi can lay claim to being the source of two points of origin for the East Village. Not only did Keith Haring work for Shafrazi in his gallery before becoming famous as a graffiti writer but gallerist Patrick Fox was also a Shafrazi underling. Patrick Fox told me, "I was working for Tony Shafrazi when he was still at 88 Lexington Avenue up

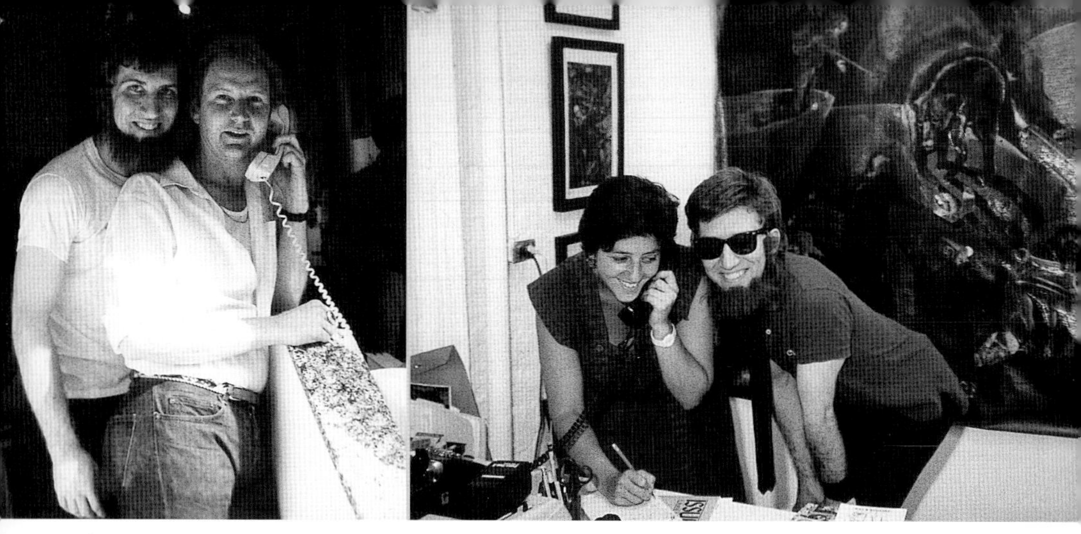

Alan Barrows at Civilian Warfare Gallery. PPOW Gallery co-owner Penny Pilkington.

on 20th Street. I was the assistant at his gallery right after Keith Haring had quit to become an artist. Tony was just about to make his big move down to Mercer Street. This was in 1983. I opened up the Anderson Theater Gallery on 2nd Avenue and 4th Street in October 1983 just at the same time as Civilian Warfare Gallery. I showed George Condo, Sue Williams, Vincent Gallo and Greer Lankton in a group show that was co-curated by Edit deAk. I did shows there for around a year and then I switched over to the space on Bleeker Street that I ran until 1986 with Dean Rolston, whom I really grew to hate. I thought he was such a monster. Then I left New York. I'd had enough. I was showing George Condo before Pat Hearn."

Gracie Mansion Gallery had a head start because it was already known, having had an 80 person group show entitled *Famous* on St. Marks Place before shifting over to Avenue A. Jeanette Iannuci later said that by calling themselves "Anonymous" the curatorial team had made a horrendous mistake because it made everyone rapidly forget them, but at the time it seemed compellingly anti-heroic. They frequently not only put Mark Kostabi in their shows, they also used his catchy drawings as invitation artwork. Even Mark Kostabi's harshest critics have allowed that he has a skill at witty drawings (and for that matter amusing slogans and titles). It's fair to say that if Mark had just stayed in that genre he

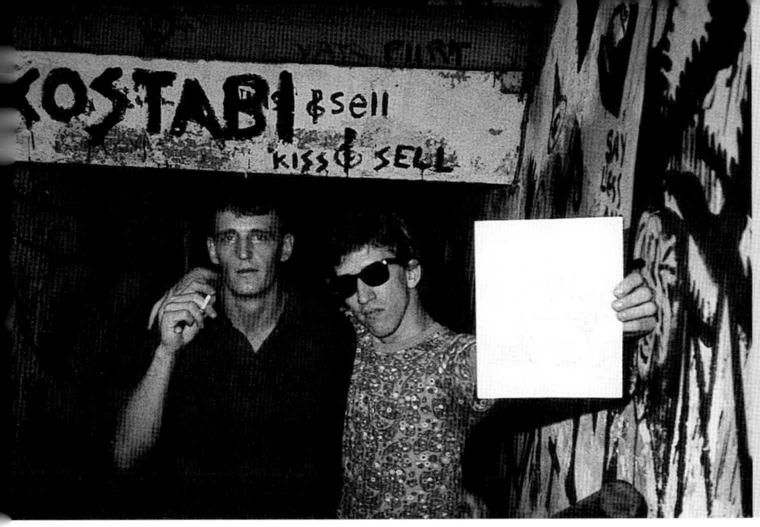

Print-maker extraordinaire Donald Sheridan. Sheridan was Andy Warhol's print-maker. He also printed numerous serigraphs for Mark, including *Close Call* which was acquired by the Museum of Modern Art and *Climbing*, acquired by the Brooklyn Museum.

could have possibly made a niche in modern art perhaps at a par with Saul Steinberg or Al Hirschfeld. In the early phase of the East Village it was his drawings, published in the New York Times or used as artwork on invitations, which drew Mark public attention.

Before Mark moved to New York in January, 1982, he had already caught the eye of gallerist Molly Barnes in L.A. for his provocative line drawings. The day after meeting Mark, Molly Barnes began selling his drawings to many top Hollywood producers who were struck by their parodic humor about the corporate world. Mark has always felt grateful to Molly Barnes for getting him started. He once told me, "Before I came to New York, Molly Barnes already sold my drawings to many of L.A.'s

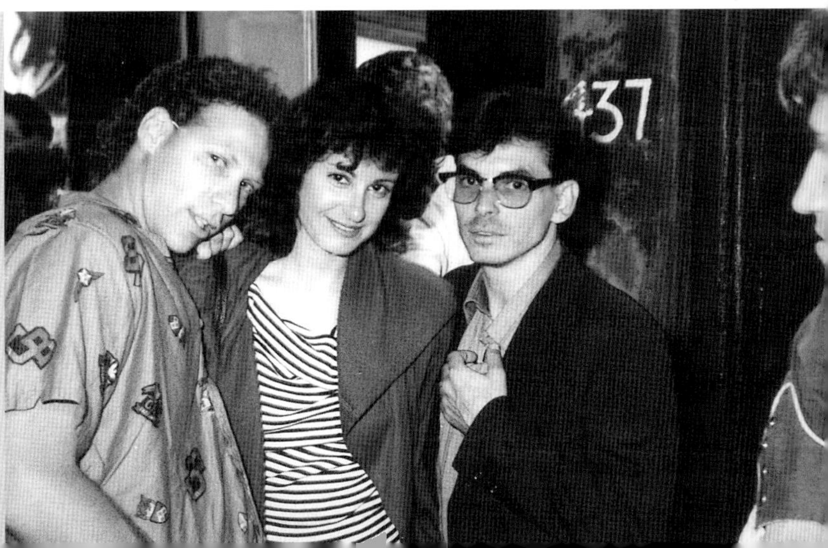

Photographers Bob Berg, Hope Sandrow and Jimmy DeSana at Gracie Mansion Gallery.

top collectors: Norman Lear, Billy Wilder, Ray Stark, Douglas Cramer, Dan Melnick, David Begelman, Herb Allen and others. After David Begleman was convicted for forging a ten thousand dollar check he returned my drawing of a board chairman holding the members heads as they sit waiting for the meeting to start. He thought the drawing was inappropriate and exchanged it for another. I think Molly Barnes deserves more credit than any other dealer I've ever worked with, because I was TOTALLY unknown when she signed me and it was only based on seeing the work, whereas all the rest used their ears." When Mark came to New York in 1982 in many ways it was a giant step backwards. He was broke

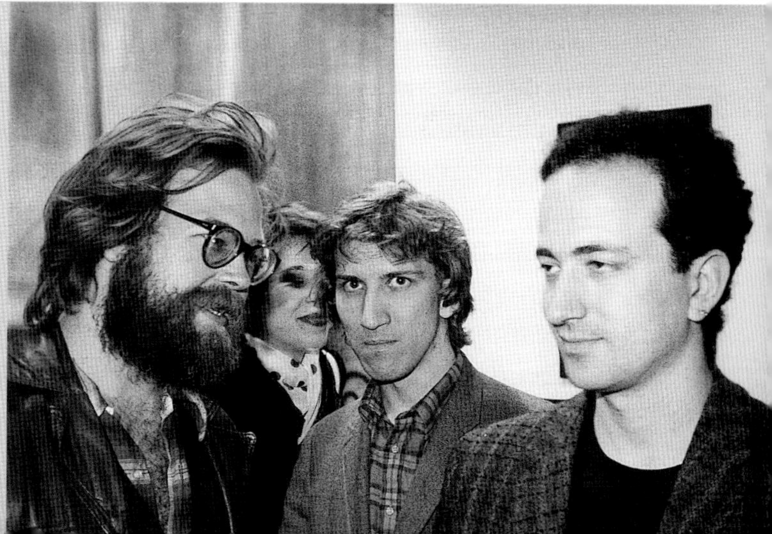

Painters John
Bowman and
Louis Renzoni.

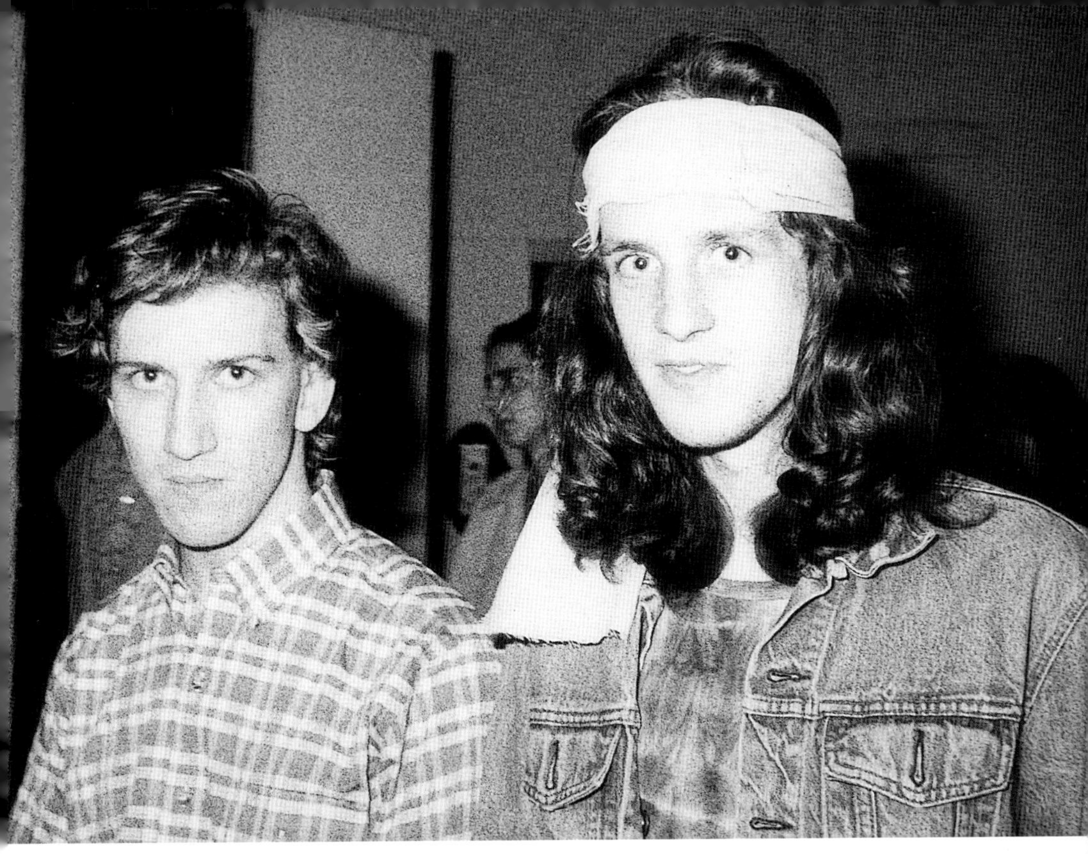

and until Evelyne's restaurant owner Paul Bridgewater bought one of his paintings for a thousand dollars all of Mark's endless pavement pounding just exhausted him. Bridgewater simply said: "I thought Mark was a great colorist." After being rejected by scores of galleries, Mark finally began networking socially in SoHo and the East Village. Mostly the East Village.

But in 1982 and early 1983 the East Village artists were really only a nightclub networking phenomena. To a certain extent this left Mark out of the circuit since he does not drink or do drugs. His geek style is not made for a swinger attitude. In the earliest phase of the East Village art movement, the nightclubs used the downtown artists mainly for their knack at drawing a large crowd. Certainly few painting sales were made, and bar or door revenue was never expected from these threadbare urchins. When Keith Haring had his first solo show at Club 57 on St. Marks Place, the event assured that club a place in history, but photos from the night make one wonder how anyone escaped without being mugged, the crowd

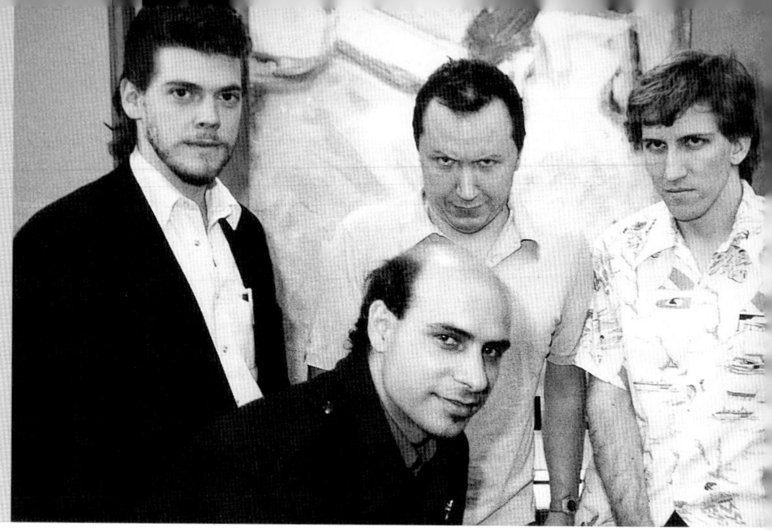

looked so seedy. Open bars were few and far between, and the parties were typically squeezed into slow nights like a Tuesday or Wednesday. The invites were low budget and the painters shared the billing with films and bands. Only later would the painter Rusty Buckingham morph into Russell Buckingham and then to Russell Joseph Buckingham. I can remember one show I curated for R. Buckingham at the Underground on 18th Street and Union Square in the terminal phase where he spent the entire night at a pay phone frantically trying to reach his guests to disinvite them because he felt the other customers coming into the club (who were not even there for his section of the club where the art show was) weren't good enough and he did not want to shame his friends even if they only temporarily mixed with this hoi poloi. That was when he had become Russell Joseph Buckingham III.

During this period in shows around town, Mark started to show up in reviews up against the remnants of the fading European group. Simplistically, as the American economy surged out of the recession of the 70s, it swept away the Italian and German artists who had been fueled primarily from abroad. Collectors and critics started to cultivate new, young, homegrown talent. Surprisingly, Mark's name popped up in positive statements in ARTnews and other staid publications in otherwise negative reviews of groups shows. Often Mark was taking on fading stars who had previously found favor among the European clique like Jedd Garet.

Oddly, Mark started getting noticed by prim reviewers who adamantly refused to mention his name but reluctantly pointed out his work as being nonetheless noteworthy, in a sort of final, old guard dam bursting before the onslaught of the East Village hordes. Occasionally moralistic critics

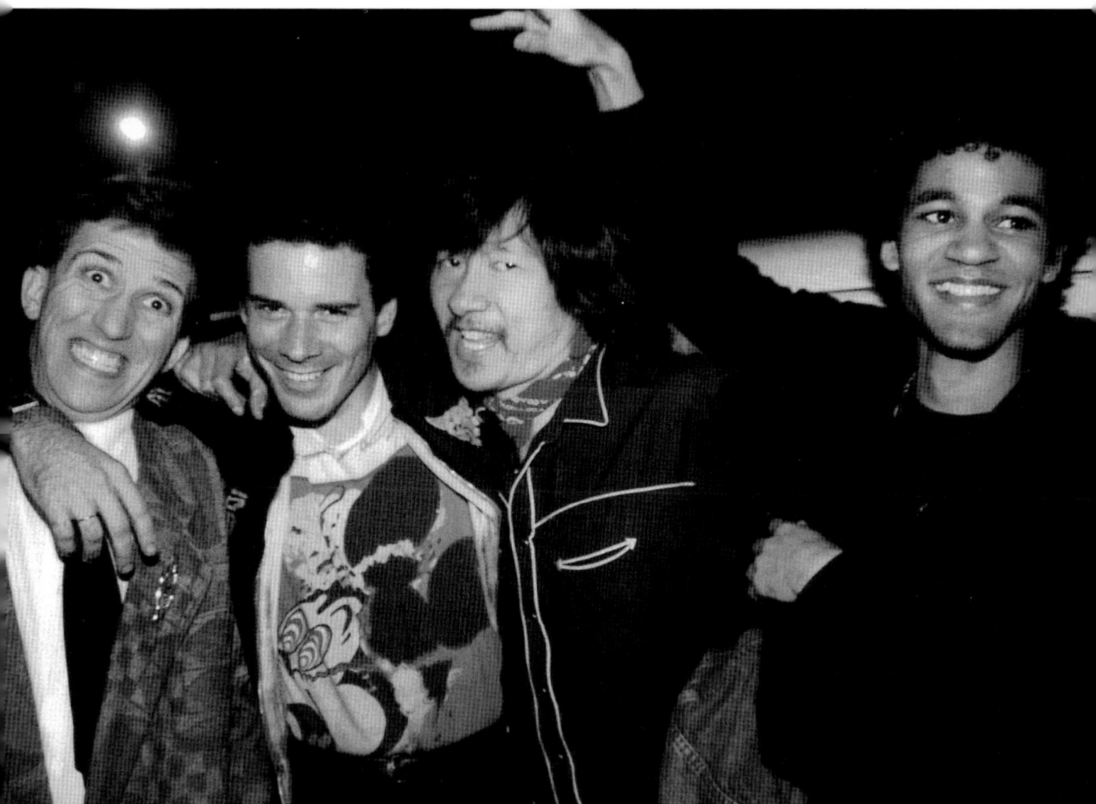

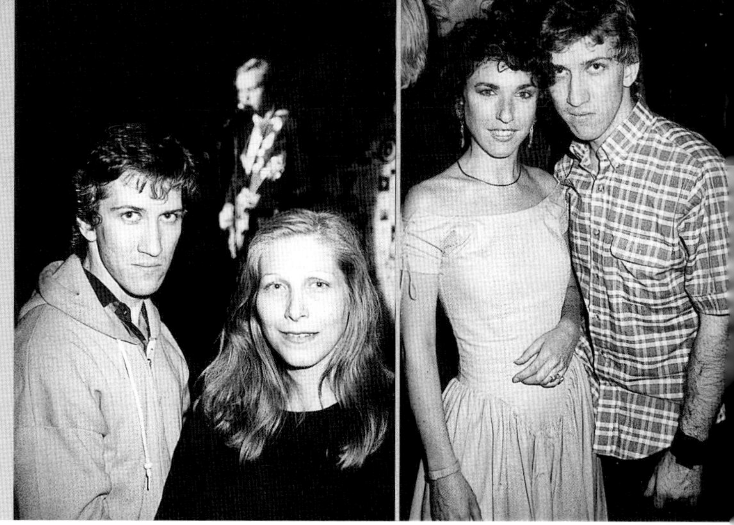

would single out his work in positive group reviews but then refuse to mention Mark's name because they objected to his "shameless amorality," which only served to draw more attention to him because such un-naming is so rare in art magazine reviews. Just a few years ago I saw the revered art critic Arthur Danto in the Nation continue to do the same "I won't say his name because I disapprove so much" approach to Mark in a review. Essentially these writers are scolding Mark for his blatant careerism. In a "return of the repressed," their hinting at Mark's true identity just makes the masked reference into a loud "blind item," and draws all the more attention to the censorship, giving Mark the reward that the critics sought to avoid. But Mark did not need to patiently climb the rungs of the art

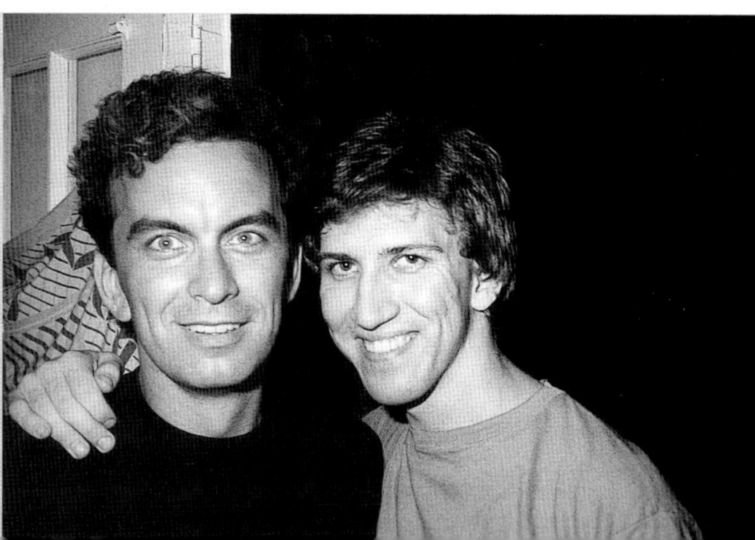

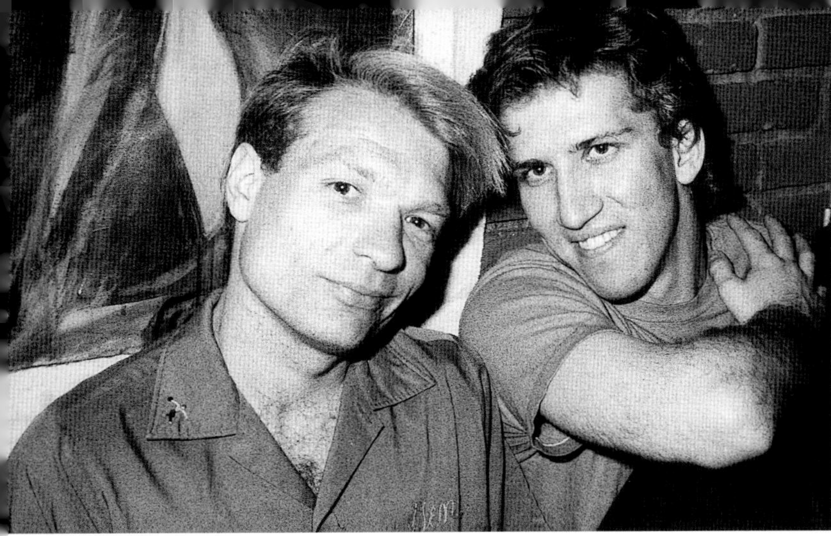

Kicking back with Darinka Club owner Gary Ray.

world hierarchy because he soon caught the wave of the East Village that came out of nowhere in 1983.

The real surge of the East Village art movement occurred in late 1983 after the police mounted "Operation Pressure Point" against the drug dealers in the area. Immediately the area became much safer and gallerists rushed in to sign leases for the cheap storefront spaces. Almost all critics agree that there was a real estate basis for the art boom in Alphabetland. There were aesthetic factors leading to the East Village as well. Graffiti had been hot in early 70s, disappeared and then suddenly come back on the scene. Jean-Michel Basquiat and Keith Haring had taken off career-wise and other graffiti writers were jostling to be next in line. Yet, in a surprising counter-move, some of the best young painters seemed to renounce their own artistic careers to become known as gallerists, feeling that wearing two hats would detract from being taken seriously and hurt their chances at selling paintings. Prior to the hype phase that began in early 1984, Gracie Mansion and Sur Rodney Sur showed their paintings at the various nightclub group shows and other large group shows that surfaced in Tribeca. But that ceased once they opened their gallery together on Avenue A. The critic and curator Steven Kaplan also stopped showing his paintings. Tim Greathouse stopped showing his photographs after 1983 opting to concentrate on managing his photography gallery on 10th Street. Ditto Steven Adams

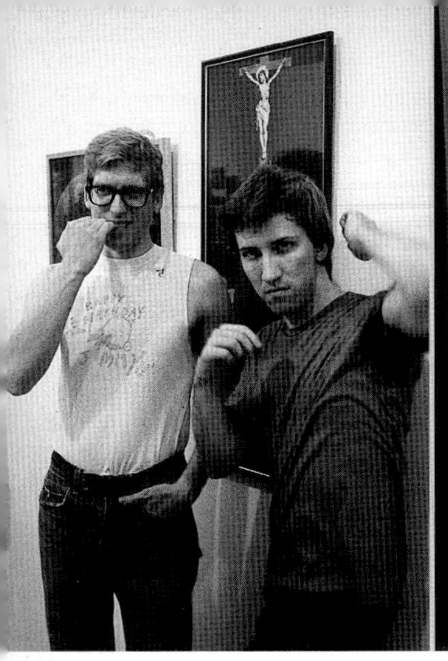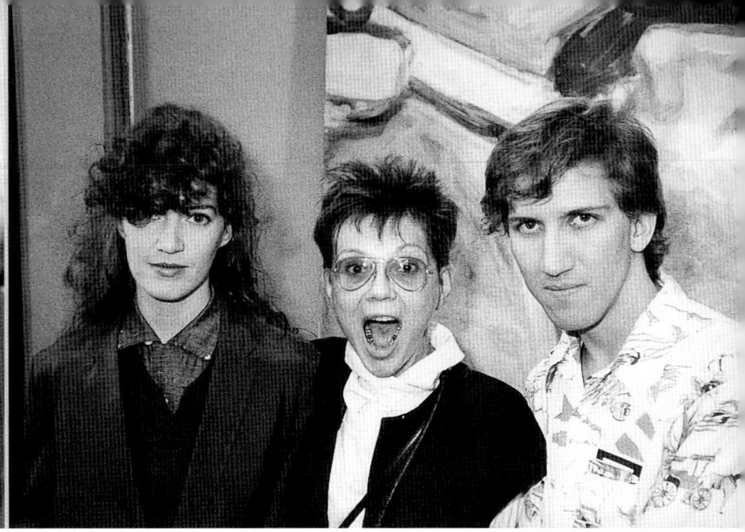

At the *Crucifix Show* with painter
Mike Cockrill, Piezo Electric Gallery.

Ena Swansea and Mary Beth Edelson.

who had stopped showing his paintings to open the Steven Adams Gallery. In a similar manner, Karen Finley was a regular showing artwork in the Anonymous Group shows but then ceased doing anything but her performance pieces.

Steven Style who had been showing his paintings as Steven Holden (he is actor William Holden's nephew) dropped his last name when he opened his gallery, Sensory Evolution, a Tenth Street gallery that consistently garnered reviews and sold paintings by the third tier of East Village painters like Kim Keever, Jim Radakovich and Hedy Klineman who ventured down from Park Avenue. Style, with his partner Stacie Teele, were the best nightclub curators, first at Kamikaze in 1984 (where Teele dated Kamikaze co-owner Kirk Walsh) and then later at the Palladium in 1985-86. Style told me that, at the Kamikaze shows, he was able to sell thousands of dollars of art per show. By contrast, at nightclub art shows in the 90s when the East Village movement had passed, except as an historical oddity or as a fillip meant to attract censorship, no art at all was sold. The curator Ron English told me that in the late 80s he was only successful selling art at the shows he organized when the sucker was drunk and English managed to walk the guy directly to an ATM. But during the East Village heyday the collectors tried to be the first on line at the door to get the bargains with prices ranging from $500 to several thousand per canvas.

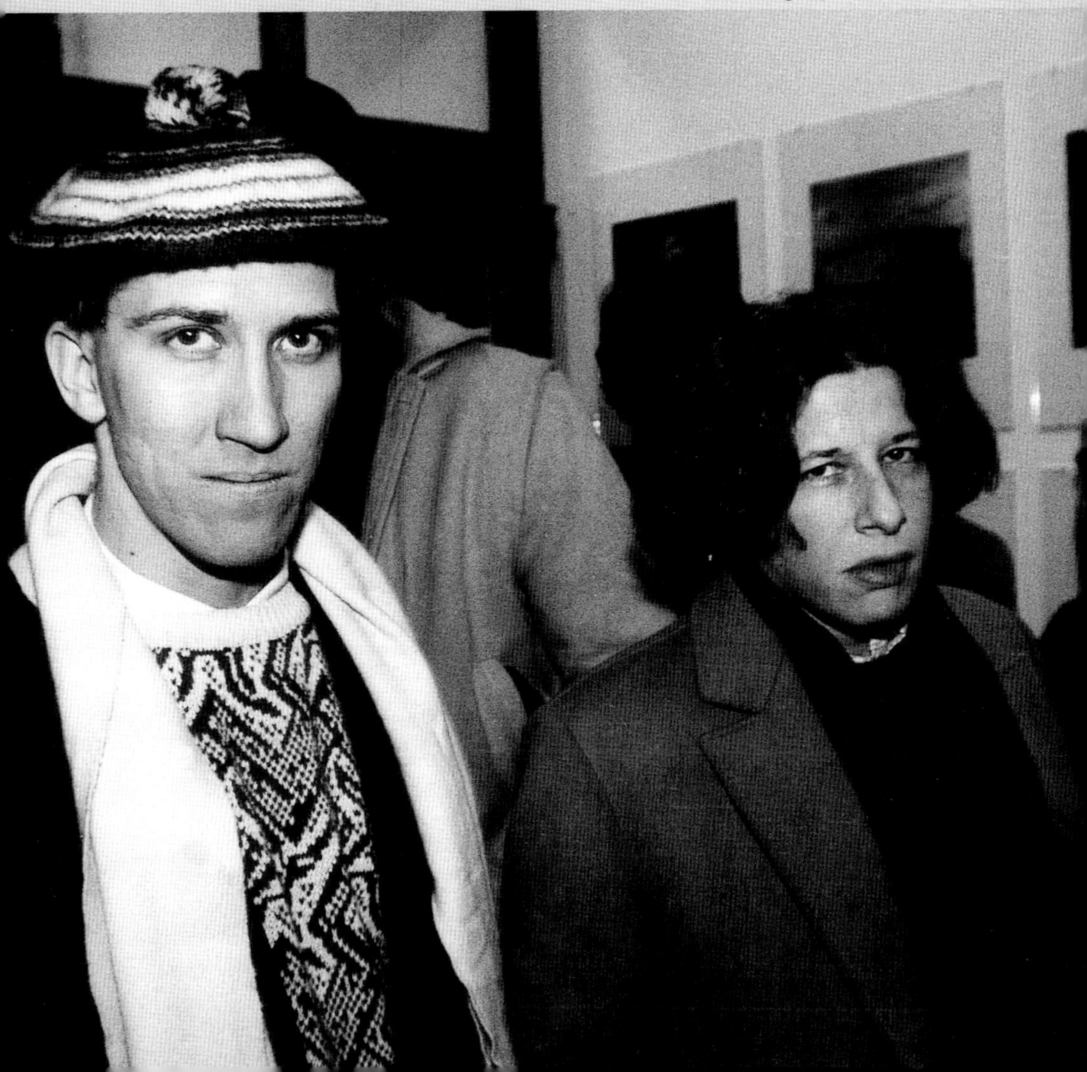

Fran Lebowitz at Gracie Mansion Gallery. Mark's cap once belonged to Julian Schnabel.

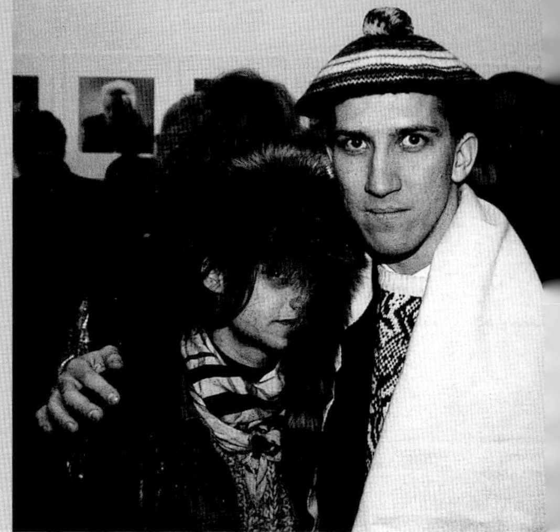

Jeanette Anonymous
who co-owned the
Limbo Lounge.

Painters Luis Frangella and Kim
Keever are pressed into hype service.

At the shows I curated at the Underground at that time we regularly had catalogues with essays by writers such as Carlo McCormick of the East Village Eye and Mark Frisk of Arts Magazine (RIP). Carlo had special significance because it was his essay, co-written by Walter Robinson

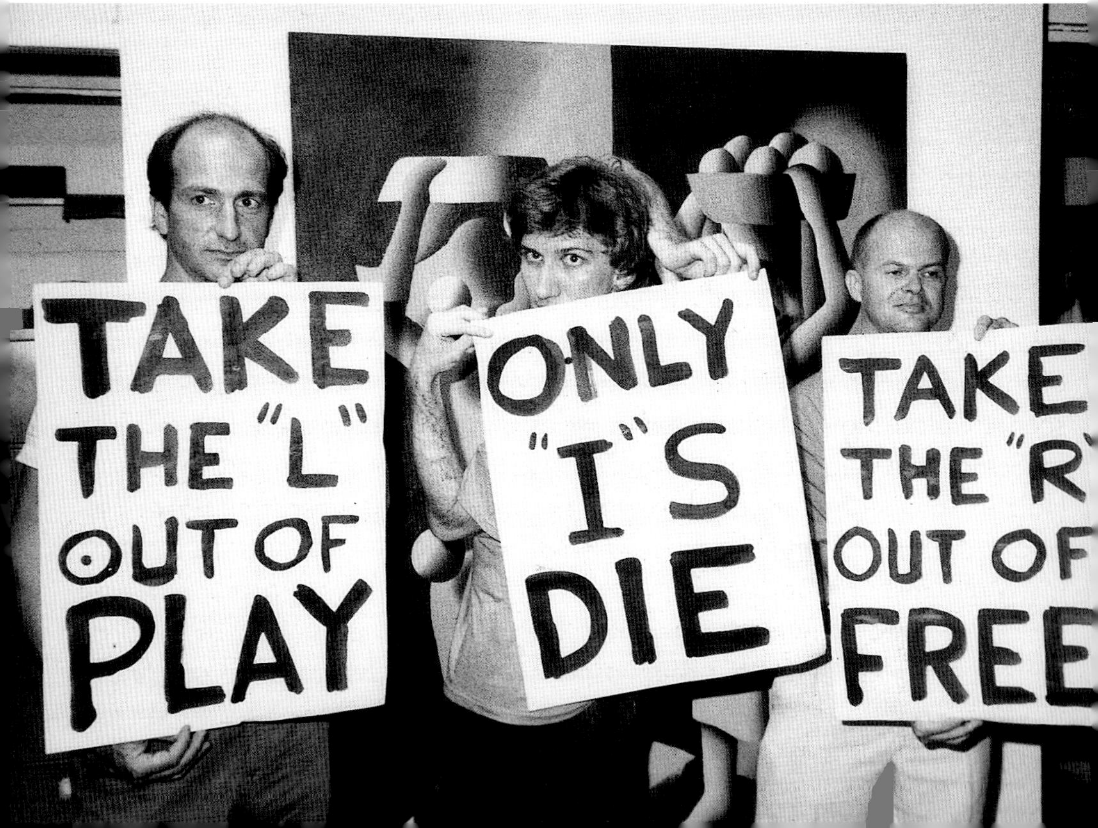

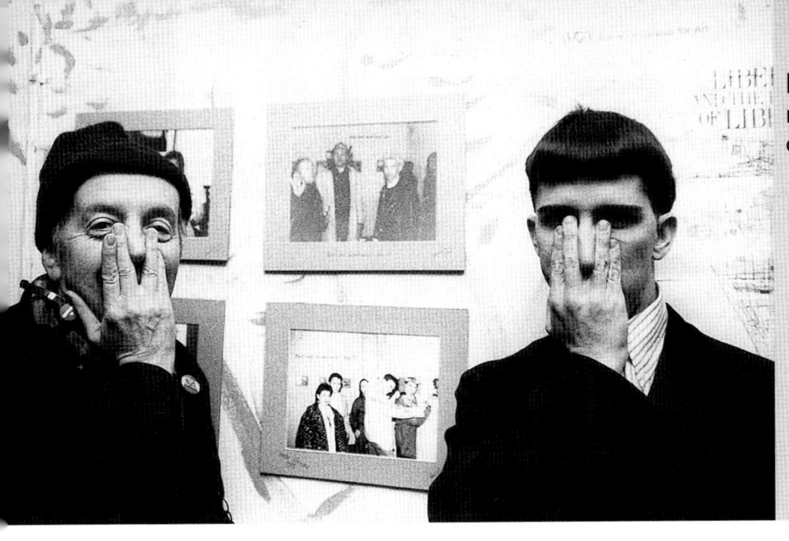
Poet Taylor Mead makes an appearance at a Kosthappening.

in Art in America in the summer of 1984, *Slouching Towards Avenue D,* that had set off the collector/critic stampede towards the East Village. That article has remarkably withstood the test of time. For instance, their essay included the figurative painter George Condo who continues to attract a cult following and defies an easy categorization in the East Village group.

If the words East Village were the mantra of the mid-80s, Colab was the abracadabra of the early 80s. Actually the radical artists group had wanted to call itself "The Green Corporation" but that name was taken, so they chose instead the name "Collaborative Projects." Colab had actually begun in 1977 with a $6,000 grant from the National Endowment for the Arts. Initially their principle activity had been avant-garde film screenings. Perhaps the best known film to come out of the Colab group is Charlie Ahearn's *Wild Style,* about the early graffiti scene. Colab regularly mounted a series of important small group exhibits in SoHo and Tribeca including *The Manifesto Show* curated by Jenny Holzer. Their legendary climb began on Jan. 1, 1980 when they broke into a long-shuttered, city-owned storefront on Delancey Street at the foot of the Williamsburg Bridge to inaugurate *The Real Estate Show.* The art Colab showed was always easily understood by poor folk as part of the accessibility that the group espoused. So in *The Real Estate Show* a huge "anti-form" pile of empty cigarette packs gathered from the

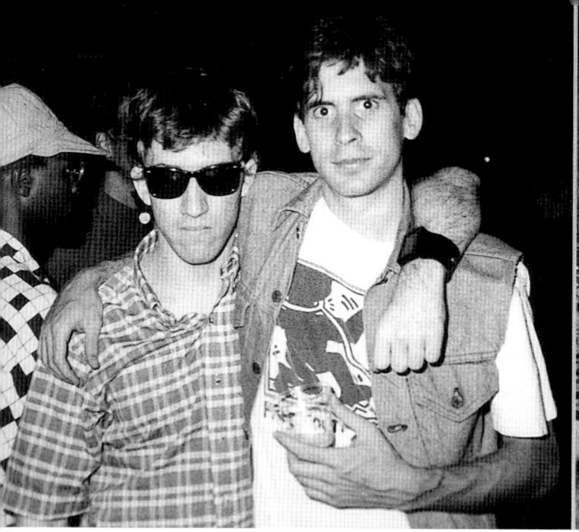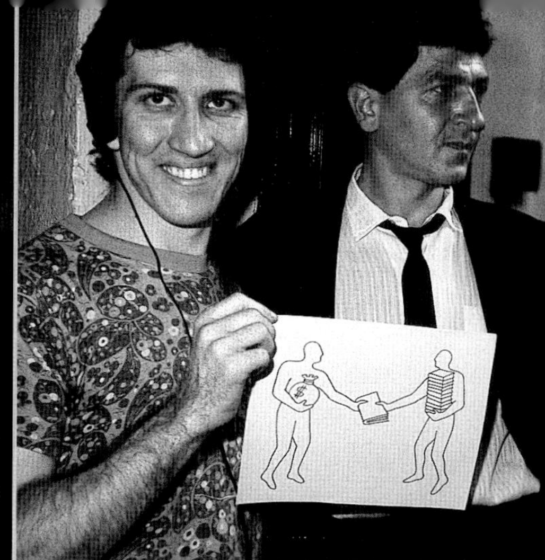

Embracing writer Steve Hager at one of Vito Bruno's outlaw parties in the summer of 1984.

German painter Peter Grass.

surrounding neighborhood by the artist Bobby G (Goldman) represented the way that global corporations extracted money from the impoverished neighborhood without investing anything back. Bobby G was an odd Colab member because he chose to leave NYC for Cologne in 1983 just when the scene took off and only returned after it had crashed. Surprisingly, the famous German artist Joseph Beuys showed up. Gallery owner Ron Feldman, who later represented Mark Kostabi, told me, "Joseph Beuys happened to be at my gallery, because we were showing him, when I got a phone call that the police were getting very close to a confrontation with the artists during *The Real Estate Show*. Beuys had been led out in handcuffs from his classes at the Academy at Deuseldorff for letting too many students attend. That was against the strict German rules about limited classroom occupancy. So Beuys identified with the Colab members. Beuys wanted to get over to *The Real Estate Show* immediately. When we got there he spoke with the police at length. He found out that many of the cops were actually from the neighborhood and had sympathies with the artists. I have no doubt that Beuys' intervention was critical in defusing the tension that afternoon because the mood had become extremely tense. It really wasn't that far away from becoming a riot." Mark always venerated Beuys, perhaps because of Beuys' manipulation of the artist persona. When Beuys died in January, 1986,

Outside Gracie Mansion Gallery
with artist Rodney Alan Greenblat.

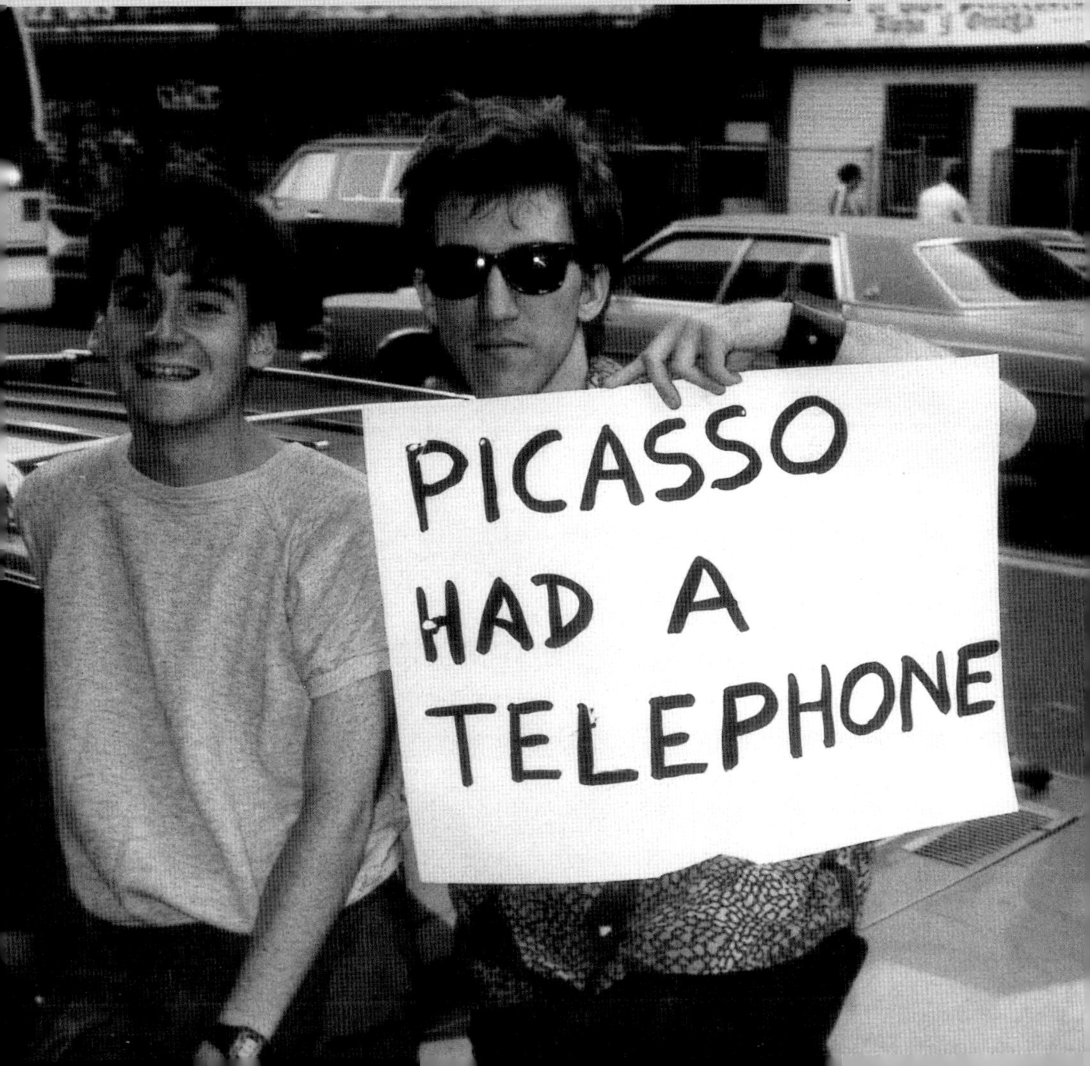

I curated a Kostahappening, *In Memory of Joseph Beuys*, which drew six writers from People Magazine as well as the usual East Village artists. Mark danced a mad gyrating gig to a bagpiper, a funereal homage to Beuys' early role in putting the East Village movement on the map. The fact that the Williamsburg Bridge location is technically part of the Lower East Side, while the East Village starts a bit to the north at Houston Street, was always blurred by the artists since Loisaida was where the poor people were, and the painters loved to identify with that group. *The Real Estate Show* extravaganza ended when the NYC Department of Housing came to reclaim the space. The Department of Housing then gave Colab a different city-owned storefront nearby on Rivington Street, a storefront

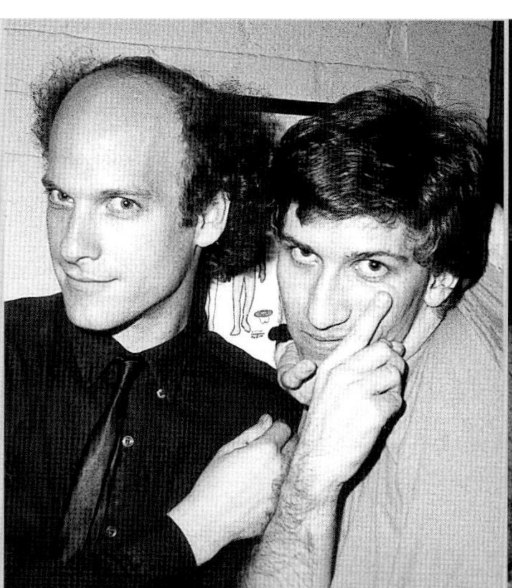

A contortion with portrait photographer Timothy Greenfield-Sanders.

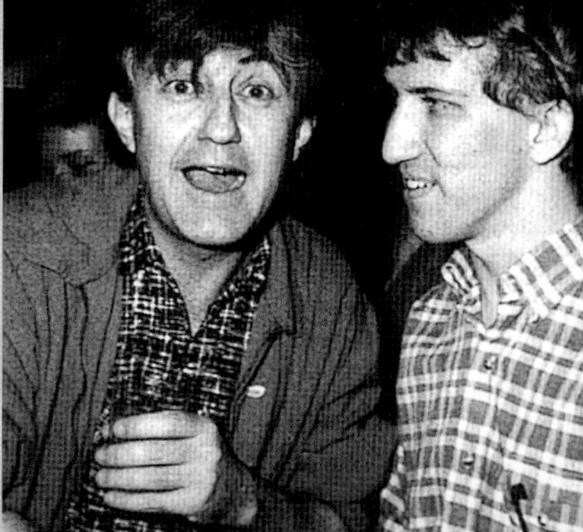

"Enough already!" shouts Stephen Saban who wrote a very influential monthly scenester column for Details Magazine during the 80s.

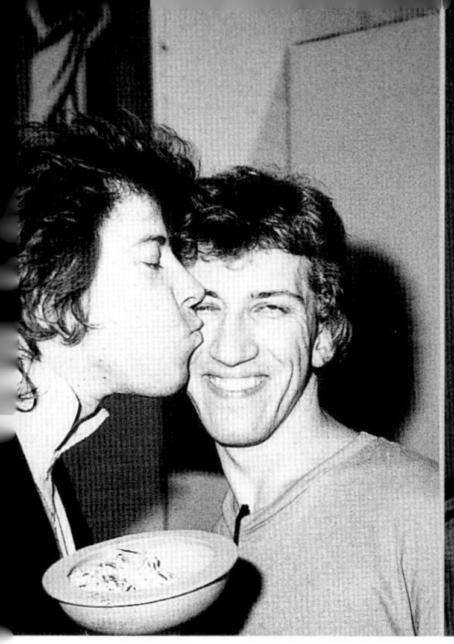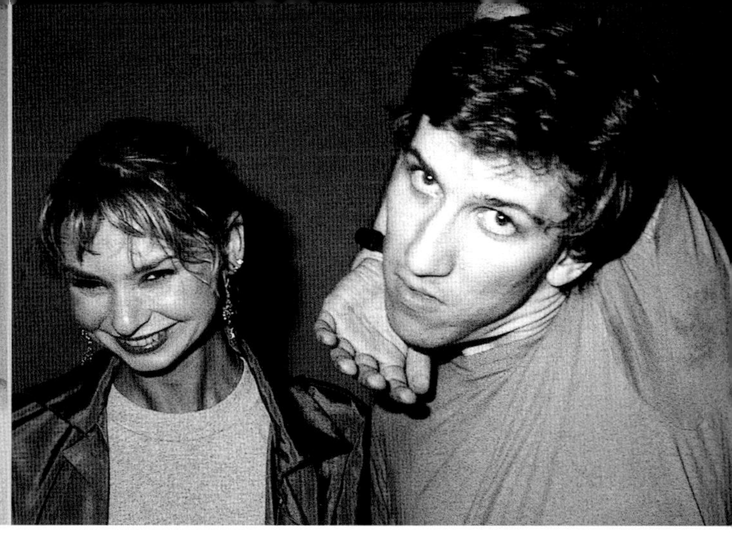

Painter Meta Madsen was Richard Hambleton's girlfriend when this photo was taken in 1985.

that was transformed into ABC No Rio. ABC No Rio was later the subject of a book, *ABC No Rio Dinero*, which served almost as a bible of how to raise scarce fundraising money in the mid-80s. Document! Document! Document!

Colab soon moved on to *The Times Square Show*, mounted in a two-story former massage parlor at 7th Avenue and 41st Street in the summer of 1980. This exhibition was principally organized by Tom Otterness and John Ahearn (who surprisingly had gone to Choate prep school). The show was co-produced by Fashion Moda, the art organization founded by Stefan Eins who ended up running an alternative space in the South Bronx but who actually started in SoHo at 3 Mercer Street in 1978. The Times Square Show was where Keith Haring and Jean-Michel Basquiat (still going under the moniker SAMO for "Same Old Shit") first showed Jeffrey Deitch in Art in America wrote of the show, "Colab at *The Times Square Show* proposed not just a change in imagery or even in structure but also a change in intent. Most of the art in the show had a concrete rather than an abstract purpose, be it entertainment, sexual statement or communication of political messages." Other Colab projects were the *New Cinema*, a movie house opened on St. Mark's Place, *Potato Wolf*, a public-access cable TV show, and exhibitions, such as *The Batman Show* held in Robin Winters' SoHo loft

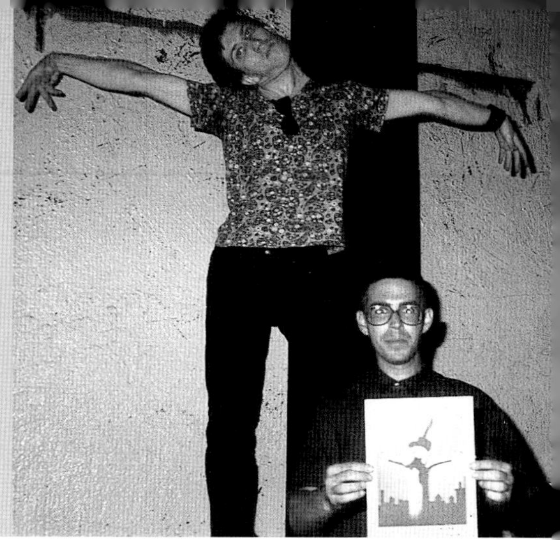

Stephen Klein, who worked for Mark as a business manager in 1985.

in 1978 to *The Buffalo Artists Open* in 1982 at Hallwalls in Buffalo. Probably the best known artists to come out of this group are Jenny Holzer and Kiki Smith. In October 1980, Group Material, an artists' collective founded by Tim Rollins, opened with a storefront space on East 13th Street. Rollins would later migrate to the South Bronx to found "K.O.S.," (Kids of Survival), a group of underprivileged children who made art which drew critical raves and which was to ultimately outlast the East Village movement by a decade.

In many ways the Colab clique was the older generation of the East Village scene, and it probably helped fuel the E.V.'s intensity that the Colabers had punk roots. The art critic Alan Moore told me, "For the early history of the East Village scene, the punk rock music movement was of indisputable importance. Colab's early art exhibits were called 'punk art.' The punk rockers took on the mainstream music industry, started their own labels, and opened their own clubs. They lived in the East Village, and the punk/new wave connection to visual culture, photography, and film as well as art was dramatically showcased in the show *New York New Wave* that Diego Cortez organized for P.S. 1 in 1981. This show, which traveled to Italy, had a far larger international impact than *The Times Square Show*." Critic and curator Marc Miller recalled to me: "In 1978 when my friend Alice Denny asked us to find something new for the Washington Project for the Arts, we jokingly suggested 'Punk Art.' The

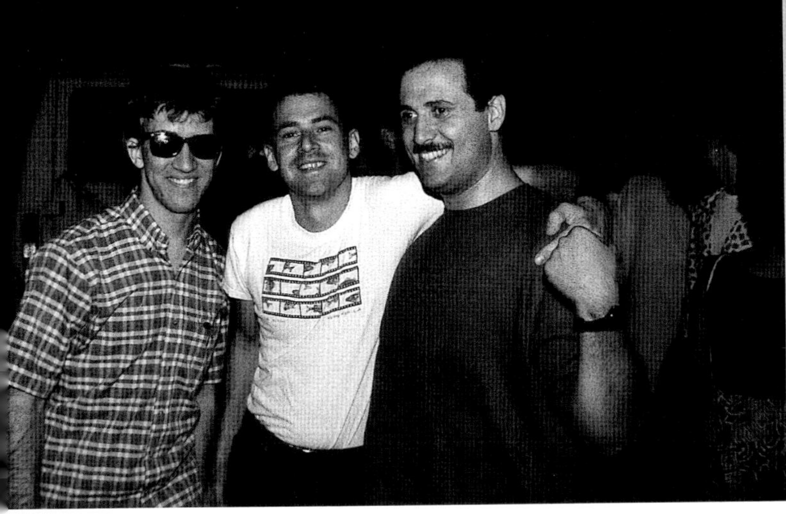

East Village Eye editor Leonard Abrams and party-giver Vito Bruno.

show never could have been organized in New York. Half of its appeal was that we were an invading army out to shake up our nation's boring Capital. The 'world's first Punk Art show' opened with bomb threats, police lines and saturation worldwide press coverage. Highlights included Alan Suicide's light sculpture along with a film by Walter Robinson and Edit DeAk based on Suicide's musical saga *Frankie Teardrop*, Neke Carson's rectal realist portrait of Andy Warhol, Ruth Marten's live tattoo performance, a group of Colab artists assembled by Alan Moore, destructive kinetic sculpture by Steven Kramer - then married to Patti Astor who would go on to found the Fun Gallery, drawings by Joey Ramone and paintings by Ramone's art director Arturo Vega, Marcia Resnick's

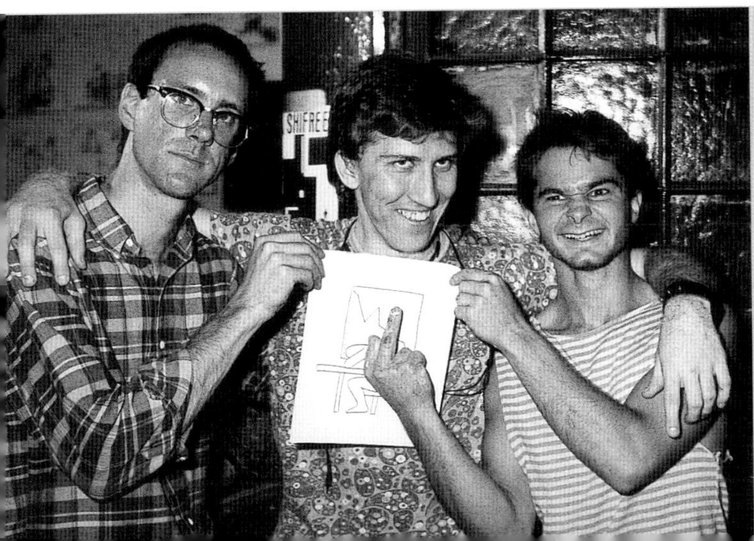

Photographer Tom Warren and sculptor Linus Coraggio.

41

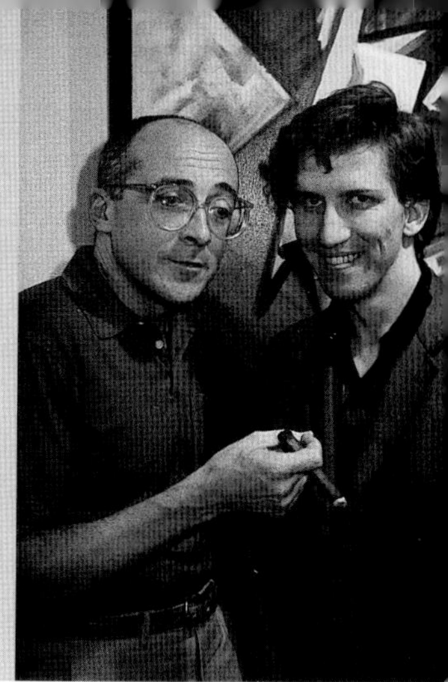

Artist FA-Q at Mark's home.

photographs of *Bad Boys*, a Punk fashion show by Animal X, and a battle of the Bands between Punk and Disco that ended in bottle throwing. Police were called again when Legs McNeil led a group intent on throwing McDonald's hamburgers at the Russian Embassy. *Baltimore Night* featuring John Waters, Divine, & a band fronted by the egg lady Edith Massey

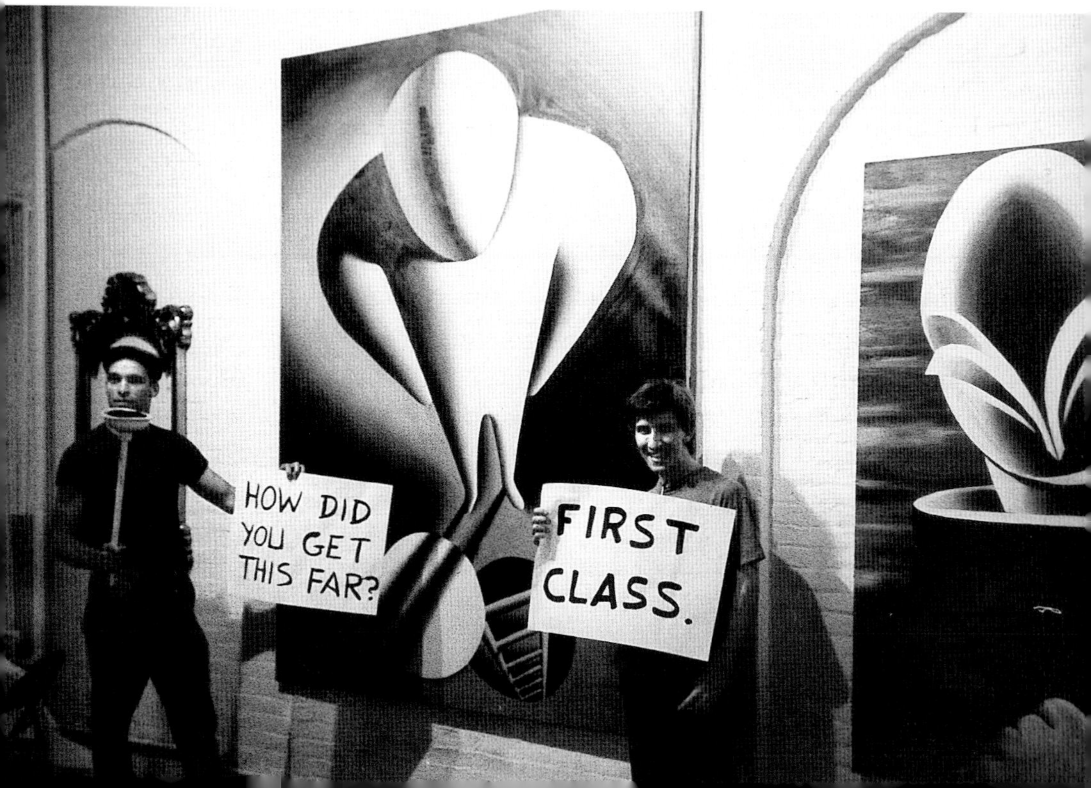

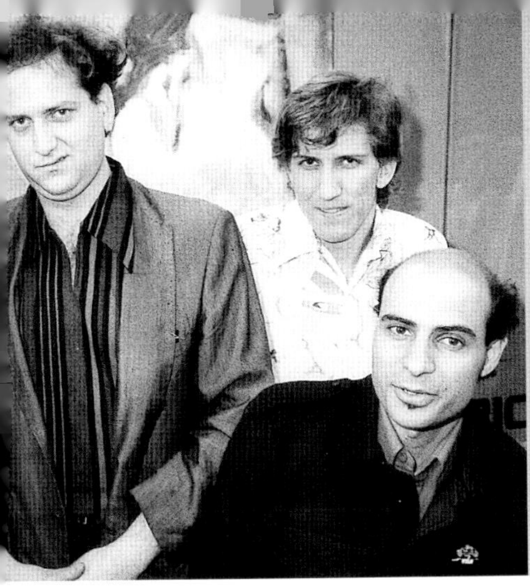

Abstract painter David West and a bent over
Franc Palaia at Sensory Evolution Gallery.

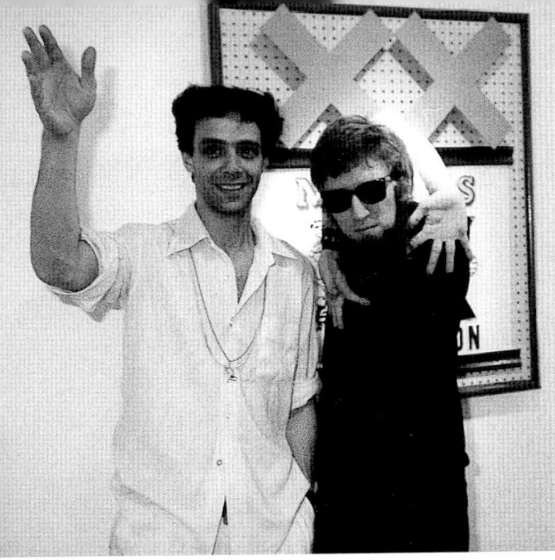

The fake beard look in front of
Colin DeLand's gallery Vox Populi.

ended in disaster when Carson's rectal portrait of Warhol was stolen. Fortunately it was returned after a local radio station made it a cause celebre. My biggest curatorial mistake was at the last moment eliminating Tom Otterness' *Dog Shot* film. I had seen how angry it made people when it debuted in New York! Tom's film is included in the 30 page catalogue along with Jimmy De Sana's nude self-portrait hanging from a noose, entitled *Rope*, and an interview with Andy Warhol. Multi-media theme shows in unlikely locations were soon the rage and set the tone for the emerging East Village scene. A few months after the Washington show closed, Bettie Rigma and I organized a one night multimedia event at the School of Visual Arts in November, 1978. Diego Cortez now joined the cast as did Robert Mapplethorpe who showed his film of Patti Smith and slides of his most extreme photographs. Among those in the audience was SVA student Keith Haring who soon was organizing similar shows at Club 57 and the Mudd Club. Edit deAk curated a show at the Kitchen adding The Funky Four plus One More to the mix, which was probably the first time rap was seen by downtown artists. Alan Moore and others then organized *The Real Estate Show*. Tom Otterness organized *The Times Square Show*. Diego Cortez organized *New York New Wave* at PS1. Patti Astor soon founded the Fun Gallery. The East Village would grow from there."

Colab was part of the tight family context that formed the

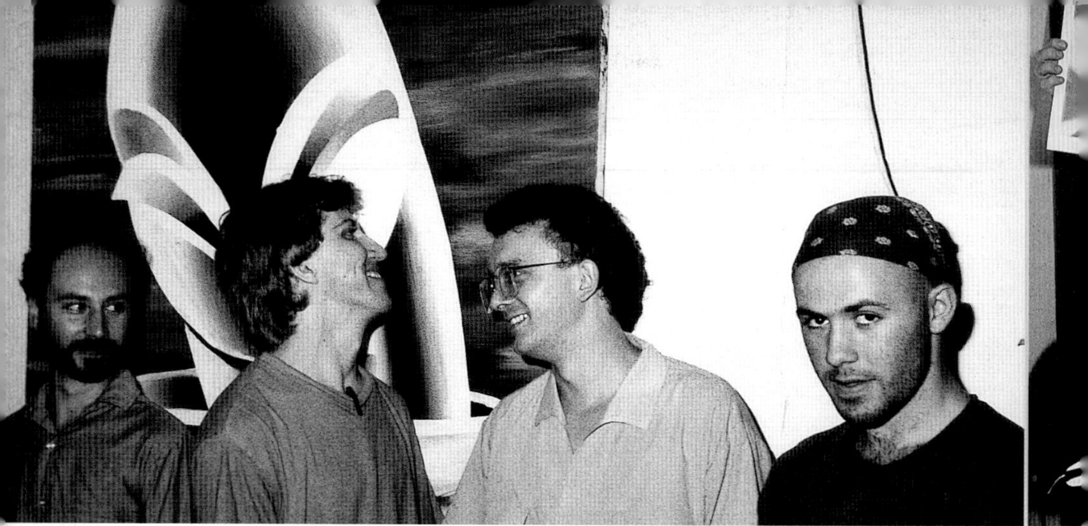

A&P Gallery owner Paul Castrucci, M-13 Gallery co-owner
Bruno Meziere and A&P Gallery owner Andrew Castrucci.

early core of the East Village scene. Many of the artists were doing work that was sort of an insider joke, you had to get it. Mike Bidlo copied other artists work. You had to know that he had done it as a performance piece, typically in a gruff manner and not in a particularly accurate or detailed manner. When Art in America criticized him for not duplicating Modigliani's brushstroke with sufficient authenticity in 1986, Bidlo told me that they had completely missed the point of what he was trying to do. He had meant to do it in his own rushed style, not in blind imitation. In a sense, Bidlo was the butch boy of the Gracie Mansion stable (although ultimately he was to show in the Leo Castelli basement with his Picasso

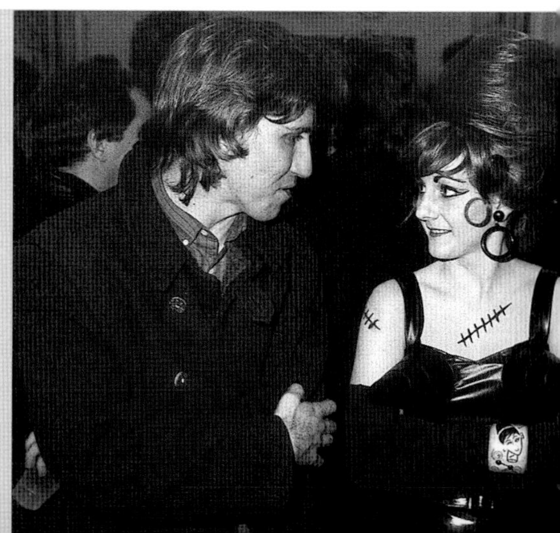

Meeting the punk look:
Caren Scarpulla, the
owner of B-Side
Gallery.

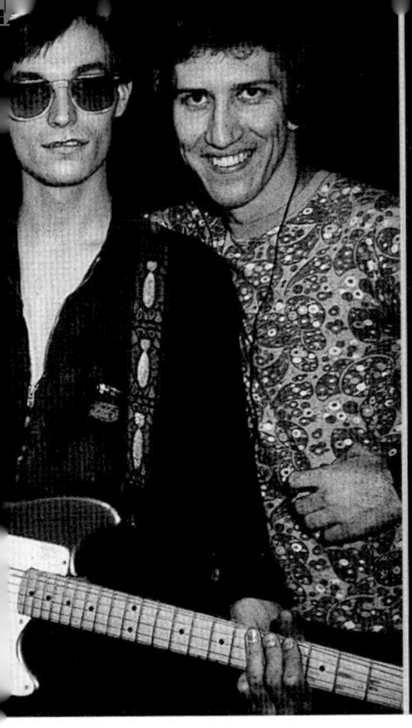

ocker Tom Coté at Cuando.

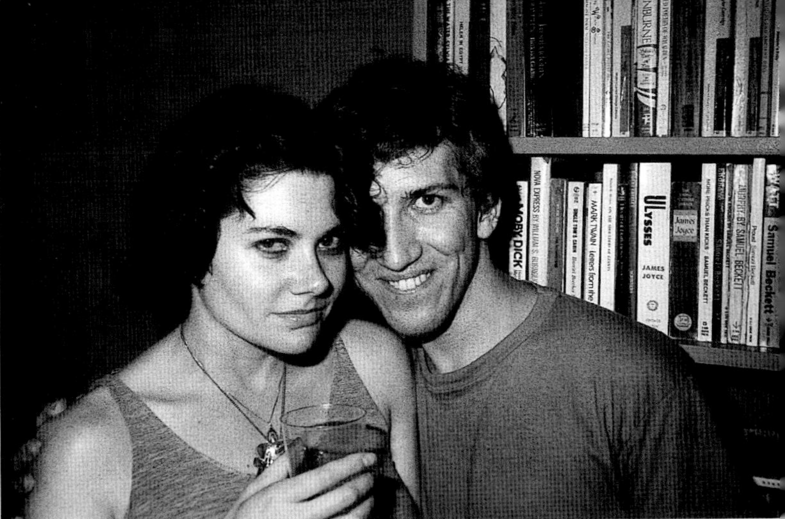

Musician Emily XYZ.

knockoffs in 1987 as the East Village scene whimpered out). Mark Kostabi remembers a story that illustrates the tough guy persona Bidlo developed, "At first Bidlo was a bully, making tough guy condescending remarks towards me, calling me a sad sack, because I didn't smile when he thought I was supposed to. At a party he once aggressively grabbed me and pried my mouth open with his hands and forcefully poured a shot of vodka into it."

It may be though that Mark had a nerdish quality that invited bullies to victimize him. Mark told me this story which took place at the Palladium disco in 1986, "Once I tried to strike up a friendly conversation with the successful SoHo artist Donald Baechler. He responded by discretely spilling the entire contents of his wine glass on my stomach, all over my clothes, in a way so no one else could see what he had done. I almost never get mad but this infuriated me and I began yelling at him, which made me look like a rude, intrusive, trouble making loser, harassing the then-more-famous SoHo artist. All his friends, who were well-dressed attractive women just dismissed me as an annoying jerk. They were all within five feet of me when Donald deliberately spilled his drink on me but they couldn't see the act because of the near darkness and Donald's clever manner. He tricked me and I felt like a freshman in high school falling for a senior's mean prank."

The first gallery credited to have started the East Village movement

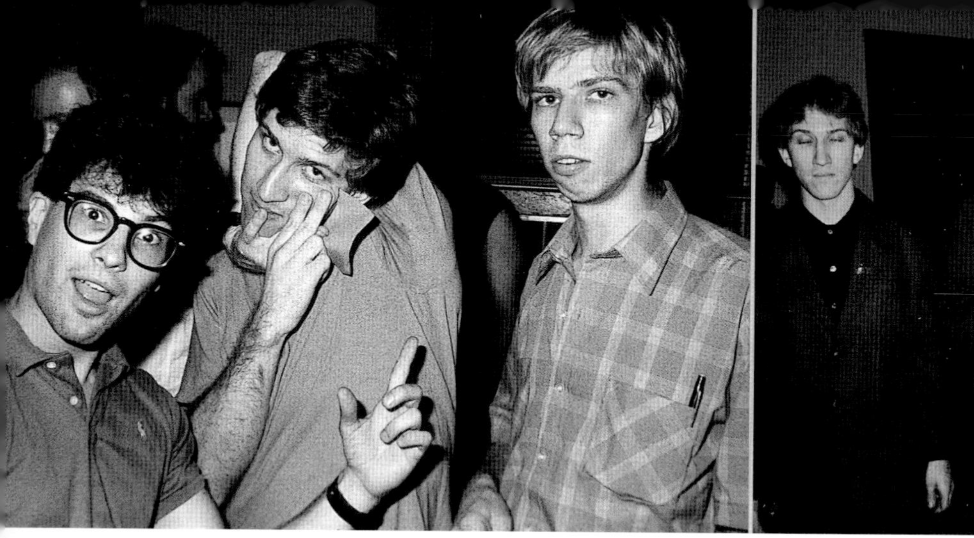

Gallerist Frank Bernarducci and Paul Kostabi.

A&P heir, millionaire Huntington Hartford.

was the Fun Gallery begun by Patti Astor on East 10th Street in October, 1981. Astor claimed, "I just wanted a place to show art and didn't want to bother with filling out grant forms." The gallery didn't even have a name until the third show when Kenny Scharf came up with the name. Many of the East Village galleries sprang up spontaneously, with no planning, often in a person's living room. Mark's younger brother Paul Kostabi told me how the Nada Gallery had its origin in the "Rivington School" group based on seedy Rivington Street: "It was called Casa Nada but all lower case, I do believe, thus 'casa nada.' I didn't even know what that meant at the time in Spanish 'nothing.' Later it became known as Casa Nada Gallery or 'Jim C's Casa Nada Gallery.' I think I actually suggested he, Jim C, could have a gallery instead of a party pad. The date had to be sometime in late 1984. It took me a day to pick up about 200 beer bottles and candy bar wrappers. I had to take out an old refrigerator and sink, mop, broom the place, then paint the walls white. There was some girlfriend there making potato stamp art with Jim C the whole time. They thought I was insane cleaning up 'Jim's Place.' I am pretty sure they were very drunk and stoned by 1:00PM or even from the night before. For my show, I had about 20 oil stick on canvas paintings that people compared to Basquiat a little at the exhibition. I remember vividly Basquiat coming over to 7 Rivington Street and trading drawings for pot and cocaine. The

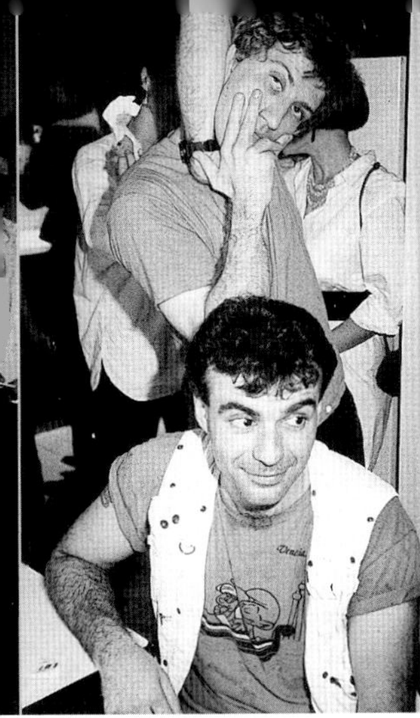

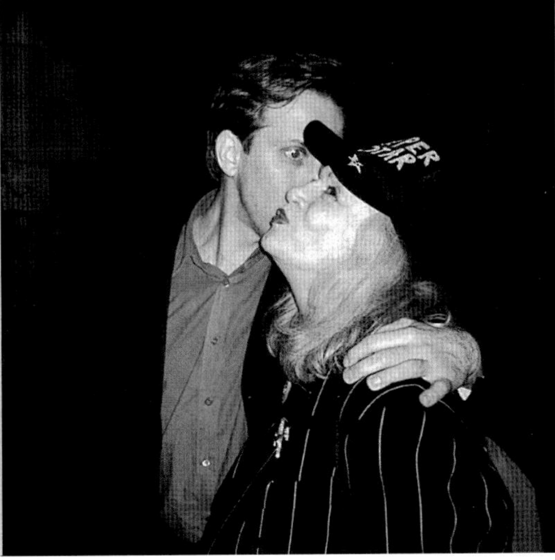

Sylvia Miles checks out the scene.

Doing contortions behind a bemused painter Ronnie Cutrone in 1984.

dealers were across the street. Richard Hambleton all dressed in black was also there on his bike. There were no collaborations with Mark in the show. Nothing sold but all had a nice time. I think this was at the beginning stages of 'Scum Rock,' that I was peripherally involved with somehow by having a rehearsal studio next door at 8 Rivington Street. Again, I was not accepted because these people were 'Scum' and my clothes were too clean and I was the brother of Mark Kostabi so how could I be a 'scum rocker.'

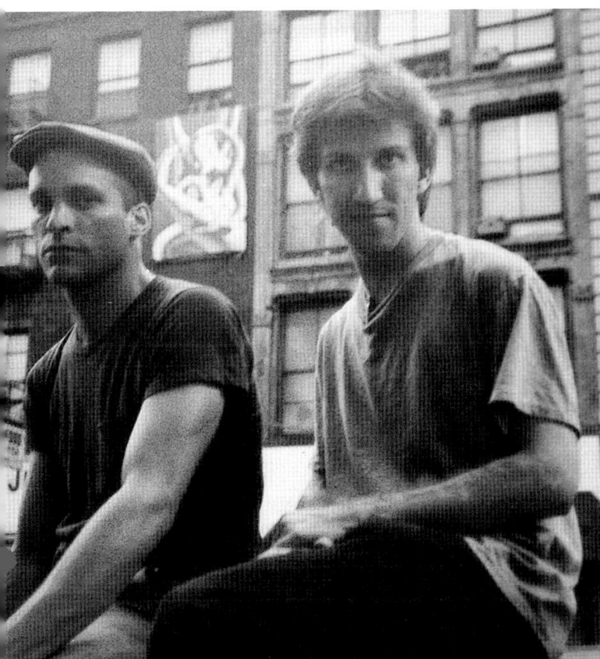

FA-Q in front of Mark's Tribeca building wall installation. In the typical spirit of his unbridled self-promotion, Mark hung a giant painting on the outside of the building on West Broadway where he lived and worked. The painting covered one of his windows and faced the popular art world restaurant, Odeon.

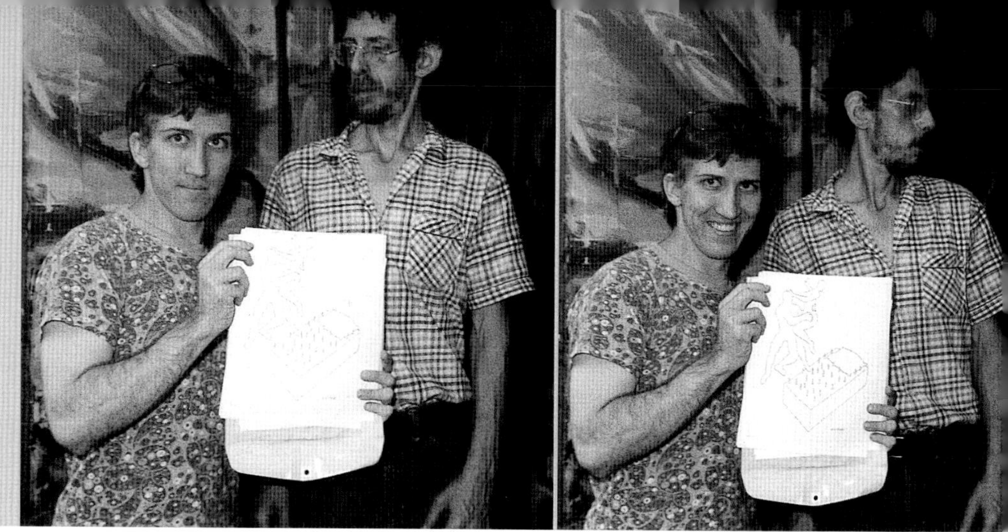

Installationist Alan Sarat trying to deal with Mark's endless self-promotion.

I created a group called White Zombie and released a record in 1985, *Gods On Voodoo Moon*. Then in 1986, the 'Rivington School' was created. None of the 'Rivington School' artists lived on Rivington Street, similar to how most of the East Village artists lived away from the East Village."

In 1983 painter Ronnie Cutrone was the object of enormous expectation. He had just left Andy Warhol's employment after decades of being Andy's right hand man. Not only did Ronnie do much of the silkscreening but sculptor Dennis Oppenheim said that when he traded art with Andy once in the late 70s it was Ronnie who did all the negotiations for Andy and that Cutrone was a tough bargainer. There was always

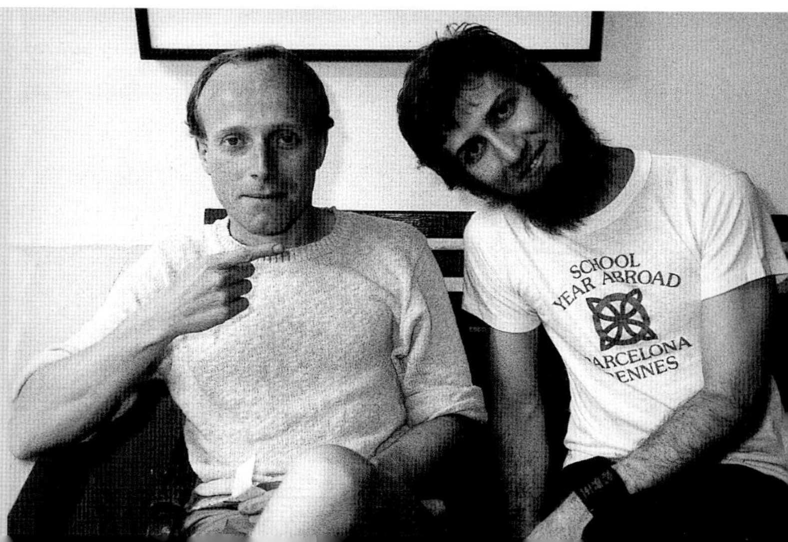

Gallerist Tim Greathouse reacts to Mark who is wearing a School Year Abroad T-shirt.

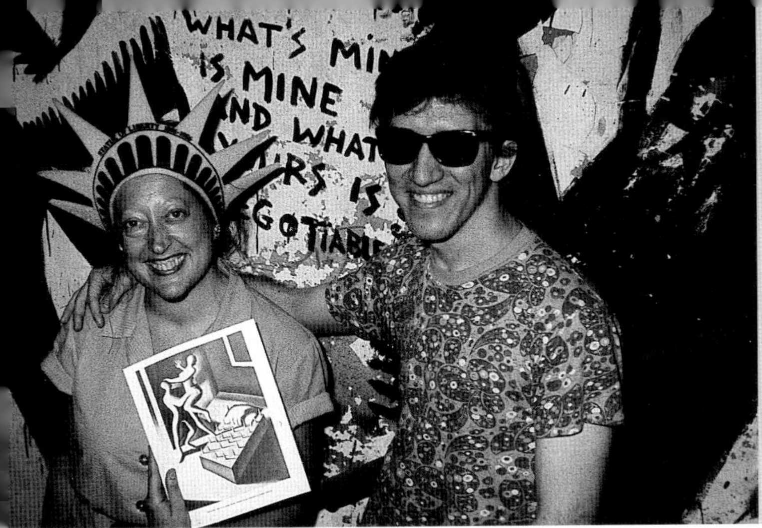

Martha Wilson of the Franklin Furnace alternative space (RIP), one of the original Tribeca art spaces.

the assumption that Ronnie had been the creative force behind many of Andy's major silkscreening efforts since Andy maintained such a passive persona. In retrospect, Andy was probably much more active in private and Ronnie's involvement in making the silkscreens actually had a "hired hand at the command" nature to it. But no one knew that fact back in 1983. To the East Village painters, having Ronnie Cutrone show up at a party was like having Andy Warhol's real creative spirit walk in the door. Ronnie said that he left the Warhol team because he wanted to establish his own reputation. At first, his cartoon style was enticing, marketable and it fit right in with the fun style of graffiti that was then all the rage. Actually Ronnie and Andy had become quite estranged. Ronnie had dated downtown novelist Tama Janowitz through 1983. Tama told me that whenever they saw Andy at a party, Andy would just say hi and move on. Andy and Ronnie had virtually no interaction. Later after Ronnie and Tama had split up and Tama had become friends with Andy, Tama told me all Andy ever said about Ronnie was, "How could you have gone out with him? He killed cats." But the East Village clique did not know that Andy wasn't following Ronnie Cutrone through the door, so everyone expected Saint Andy to make an arrival whenever they saw Ronnie. Actually it was Tama Janowitz who brought Andy into the scene later in 1984 and in 1985 when she resurfaced with her Interview Magazine clique. The Interview set included Andy, Andy's closest friend Paige Powell,

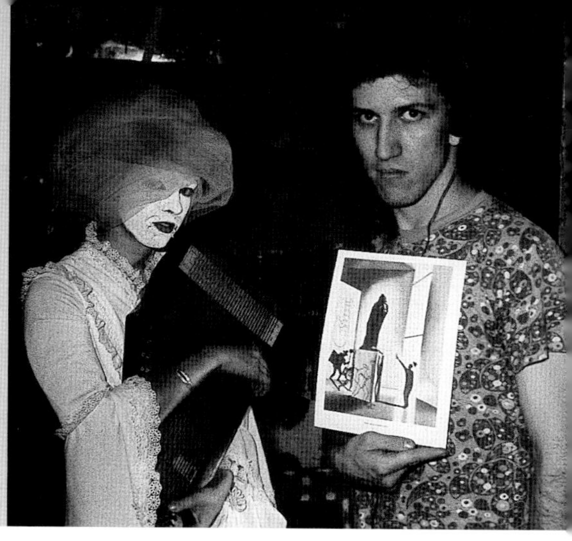

Musician Rachel Garniez who dated Jim C. of Nada Gallery on Rivington Street.

who at one time was dating Jean-Michel Basquiat, and Jeff Slonim. Slonim opened the East Village gallery that held the record for briefest duration, the Silver Limo Gallery, which only lasted one weekend, although it showed powerful Haitian painting. Jeff Slonim's older brother, painter Hunt Slonem (with a differently spelled last name, apparently for numerological reasons) was a favorite of Metropolitan Museum curator Henry Geldzahler, an art trend setter still with a powerful reputation in the 80s. But after Andy Warhol died, Ronnie Cutrone's luster faded. Ronnie went through a succession of less pretty girlfriends and his painting style became numbingly repetitive. The New York Post even stated at one point that Ronnie had given up making art and that he had become a film-maker. Yet as many of the other Lower East Side figures fell away, Cutrone's prices and critical reputation remained steady. Ronnie Cutrone's hype contribution to the East Village art scene was remarkable at the beginning of the movement and then remained amazingly enduring.

Richard Hambleton exploded on the scene virtually on a par and at the same time and even on some of the same streets with Keith Haring and Jean-Michel Basquiat, yet few now remember Hambleton. Hambleton was from Canada and hitchhiked across the USA anonymously sketching outlines of bodies for his *Mass Murder* series from 1977 to 1979. Then from 1980-81, Hambleton anonymously painted shadows in remote sections of cities (as distant as Rome) which looked like muggers about to pounce. Ultimately he focused on doing these menacing figures, which gave everyone a fright, only in NYC. He also painted squirrels on trees in various parks throughout New York. Finally, Hambleton admitted that he was the one who had been doing them, but he still stoutly refused to sign the works even when they were on detached door frames and signing them could have brought him thousands of dollars. Years after the East Village scene was over, Mark finally got him to sign one of the mugger shadow works in return for money when Hambleton was totally broke

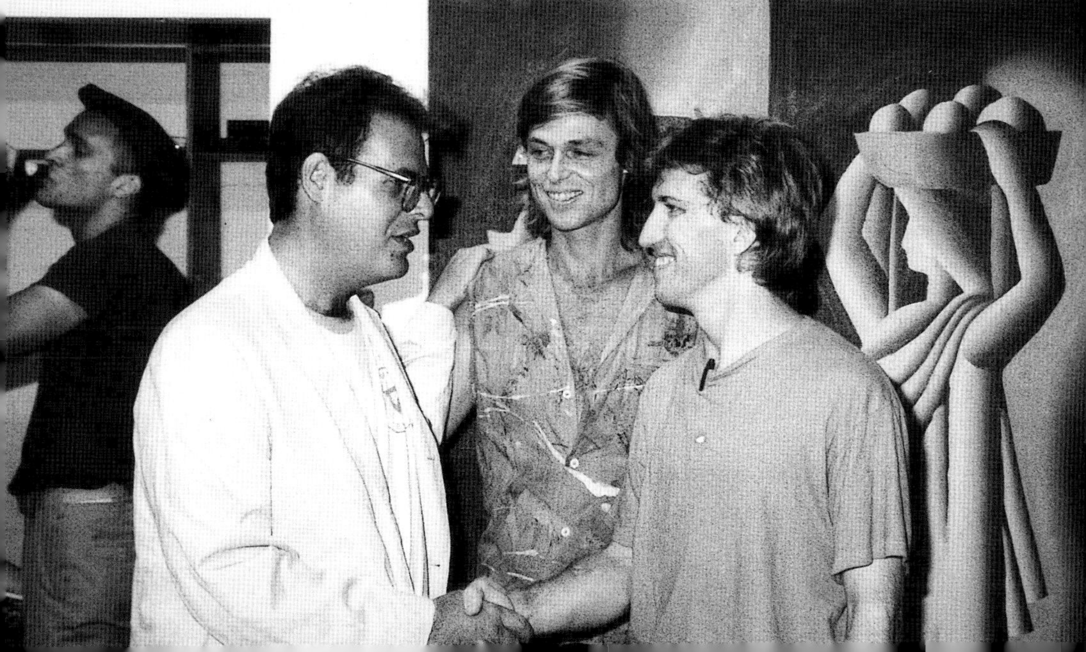

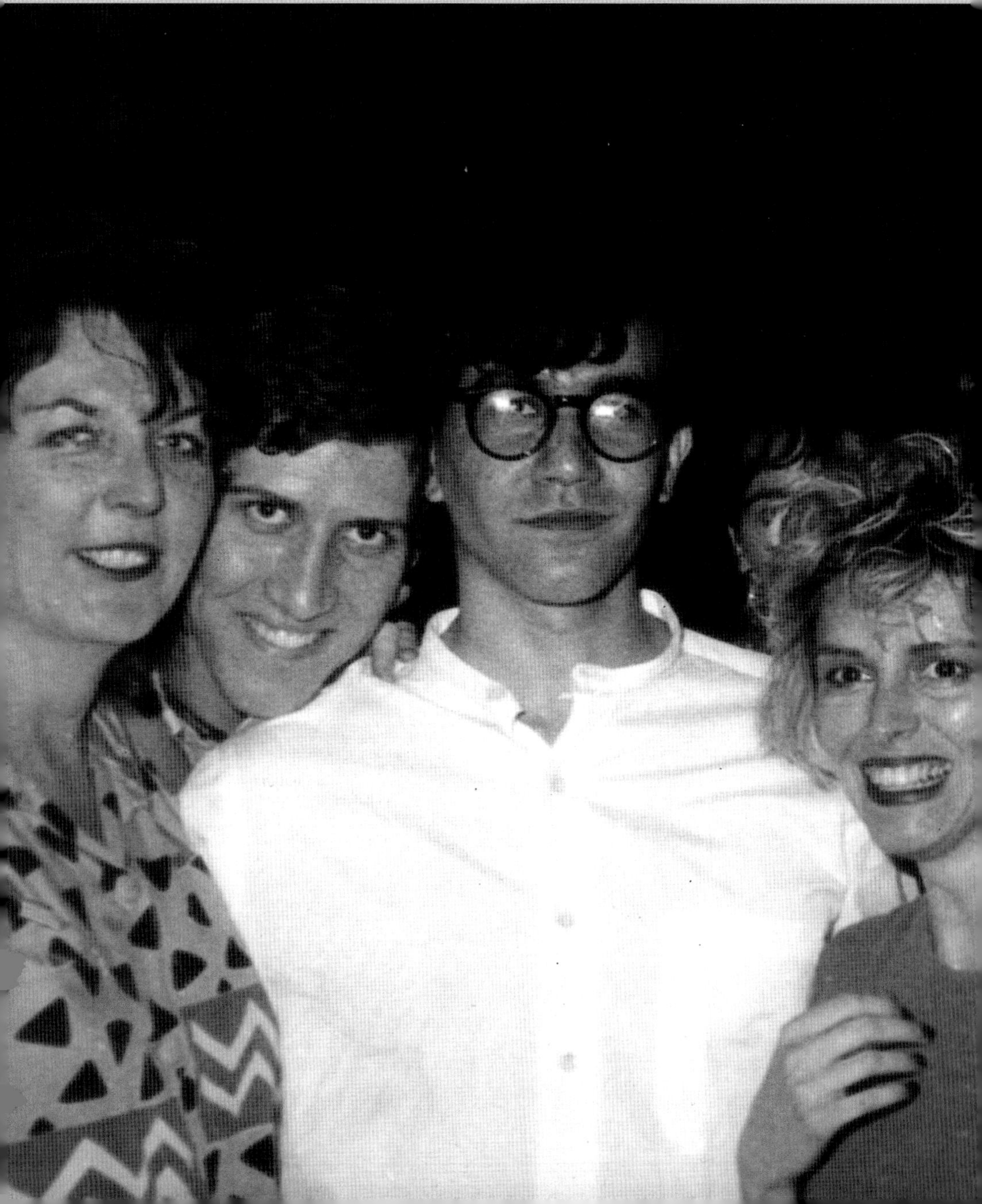
Artist Marilyn Minter, Jim Radakovich (who now works as an assistant to former East Village painter Hedy Klineman), gallerist Ellen Donahue, Sensory Evolution owner Steven Style, artist Christof Kohlhofer and gallerist Willoughby Sharp on the 4th of July, 1984 at a rooftop party.

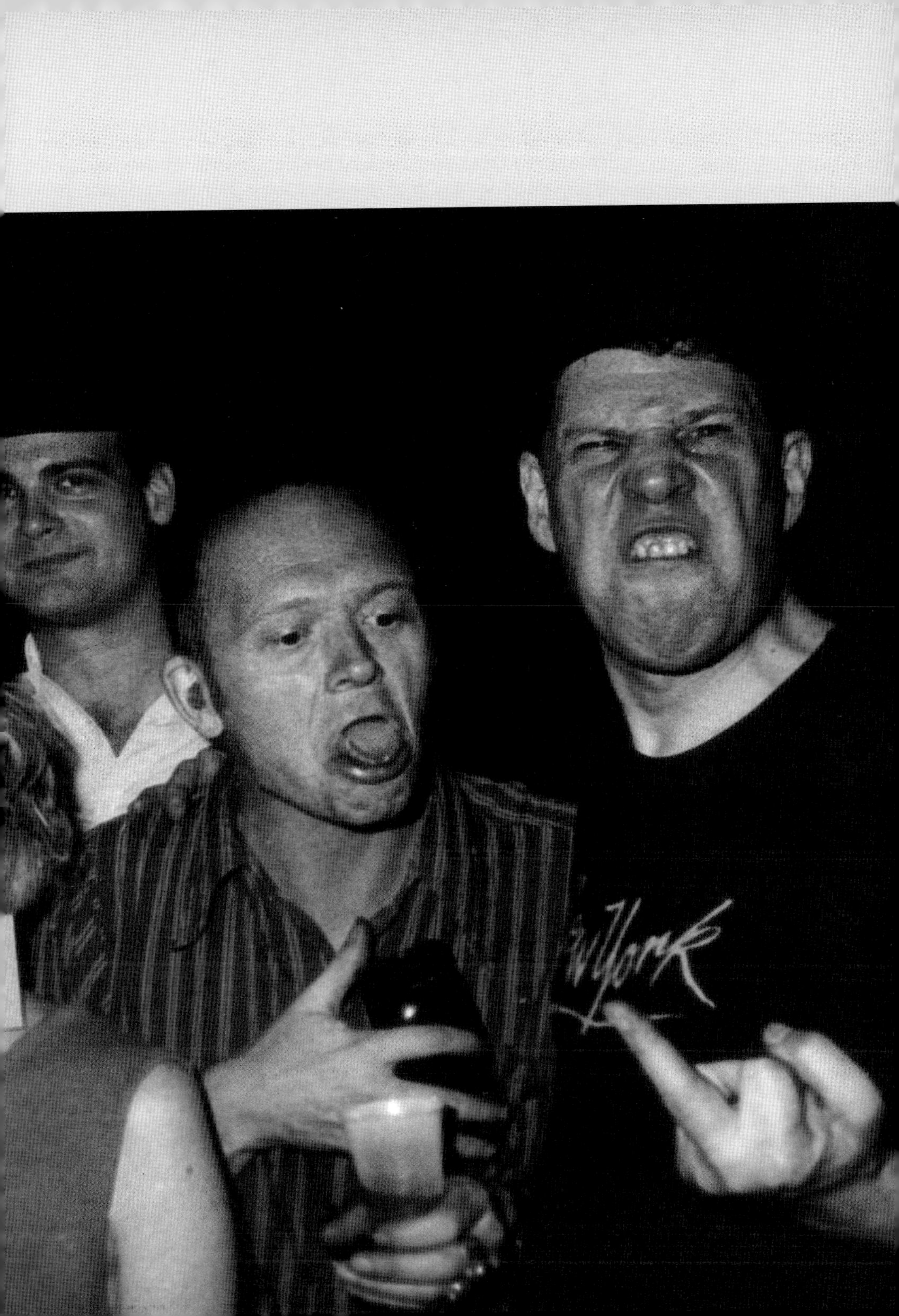

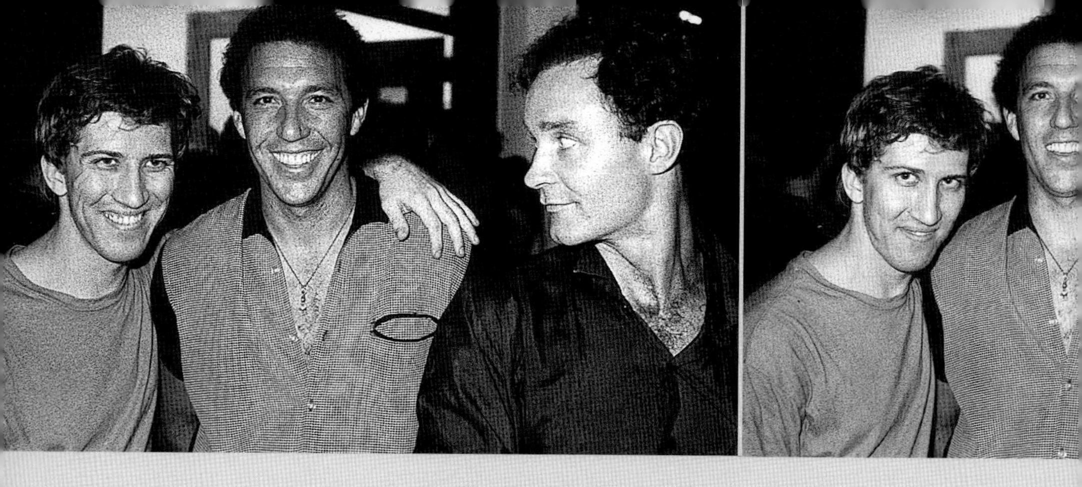

and fishing food out of street corner trashcans. Hambleton was completely opposed to taking credit for his work. As a student he had specialized in earthworks. Perhaps Hambleton was antagonistic towards signatures of any kind. Whatever the reason, he soon succumbed to the pressures of success, becoming a completely strung out addict. By 1984 critics murmured that Hambleton was turning out "junkie art," bland paintings coated with an odd, waxy substance that for some reason Hambleton adored. Yet in 1984 his *Marlboro Man* series, and a few of the splashed paintings that

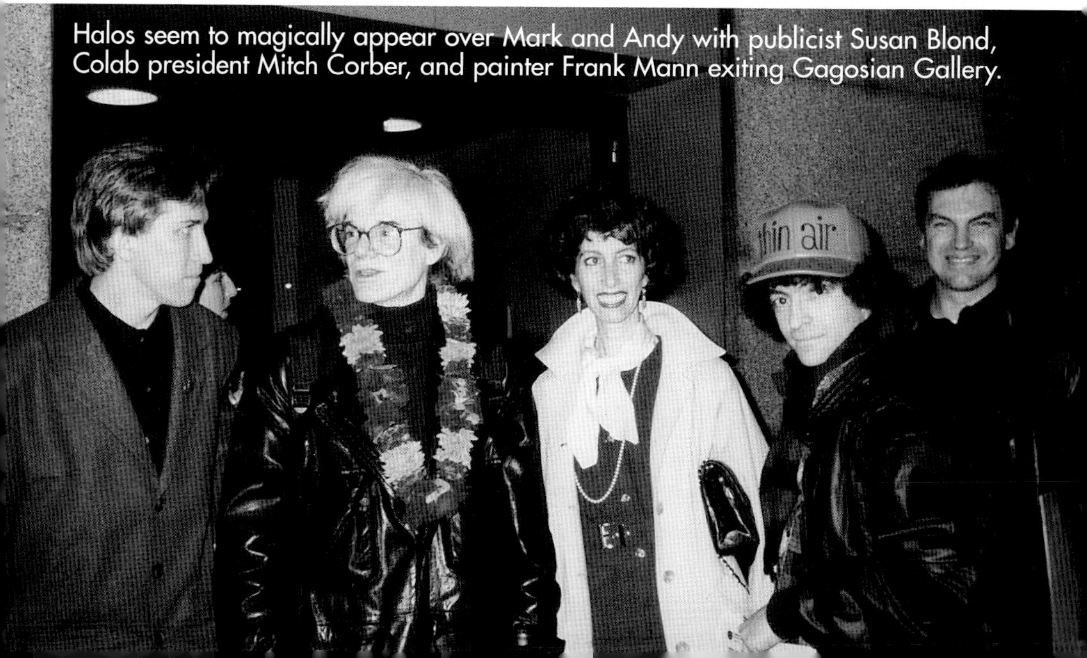

Halos seem to magically appear over Mark and Andy with publicist Susan Blond, Colab president Mitch Corber, and painter Frank Mann exiting Gagosian Gallery.

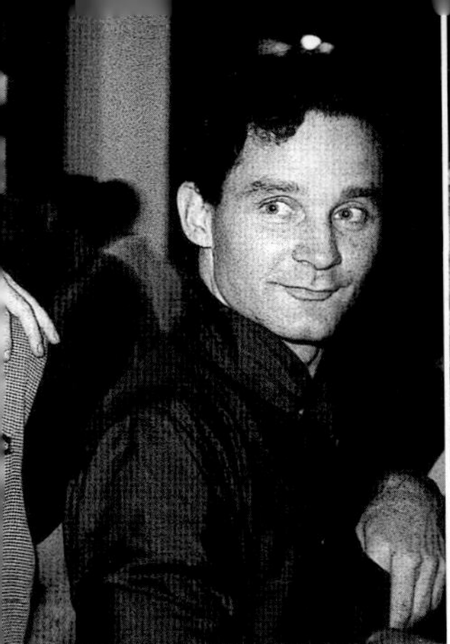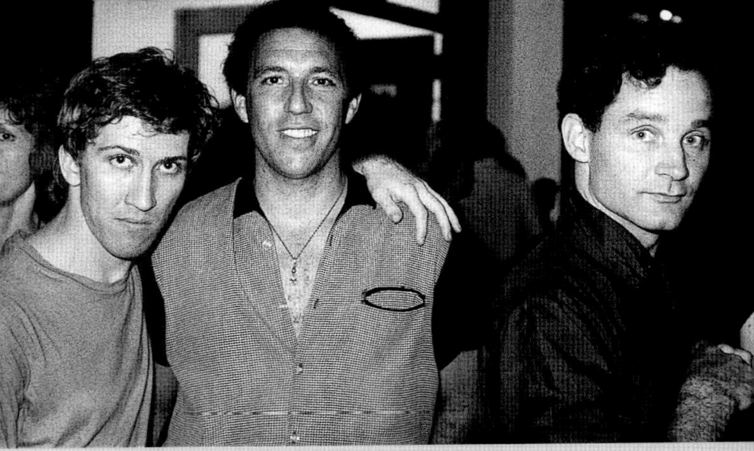

Artist Richard Gins and a fleeing Richard Hambleton at Piezo Electric Gallery in 1984.

had some connection to his menacing figures still had some appeal. I showed Hambleton's painting at the Stamford Museum in an historically oriented group show of East Village painters in 1987. I wanted to show one of his shadow mugger paintings from the early years. Hambleton indignantly refused saying that he never showed these for his own private reasons. All I could get from him was a Marlboro Man. Gallery owner Ron Feldman told me, "I wanted to meet Richard Hambleton in 1984 and in 1985 because I was certainly aware of his work. His art was the real thing and had an edge to it. But it was difficult tracking him down." Hambleton was represented in 1984 by the Milliken Gallery in SoHo, a lightweight establishment. His heroin problems took him out of the real world just as he was being lauded with a museum solo show in Holland. Hambleton was a classic case of someone who did one or two projects incredibly well and then would never go back to them even though the art market rejected his newer works. Some people used to say that about Julian Schnabel and how Julian no longer does plate paintings until they find out that in fact Schnabel still does plate paintings, he just only does them as expensive commissioned portraits.

When I started photographing Mark Kostabi, we had Richard Hambleton targeted in June 1985 on the hierarchy of East Village gods as the one niche ahead of Mark that we could realistically see Mark dislodging. When Hambleton would see Mark coming he would nervously start rolling

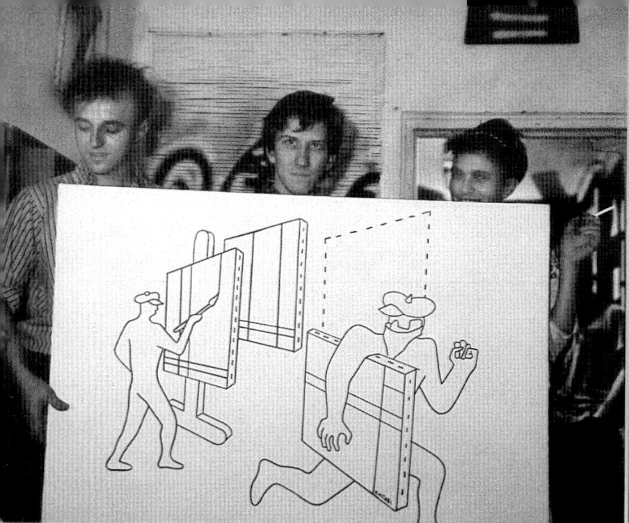

Nada Gallery owner Jim C with the painting *Amateurs Imitate - Professionals Steal.*

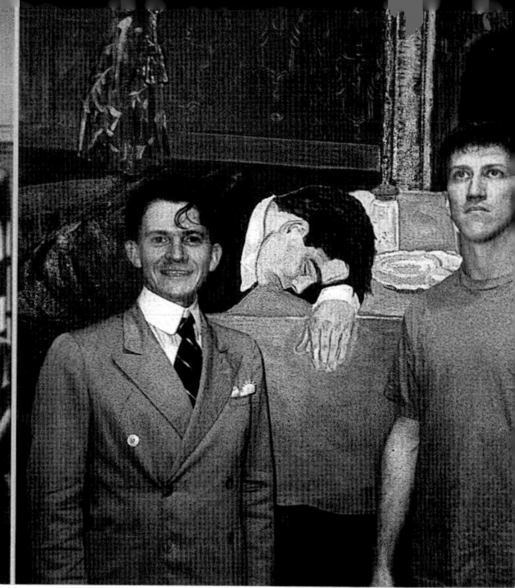

The dandy tradition in the East Village was exemplified by David McDermott.

a cigarette on his nose to absorb the sweat and then after a few minutes would just bolt for the door. Paul Kostabi recently bought a mugger painting from Hambleton for twenty dollars on the street at the same time that an uptown gallery was actually trying to sell a similar work for eight thousand dollars. What an indication some twenty years after Hambleton's heyday of the gap between his highwater mark and his current state. But in 1984 his inspiration to a generation of young hustling East Village painters was keen. Hambleton seemed like the success who had made no concessions. His peers had seen Basquiat, Haring, and Kenny Scharf rapidly become wealthy and famous. In the mid-80s, others in the downtown clique like Madonna and performance artist Ann Magnuson were becoming stars. In the summer of 1985, with Richard Hambleton in his sights, Mark Kostabi seemed about to make it just as quickly.

Mark had been one of the first of the *nouveau arrivistas* to pop up in Alphabetland in 1983. The art critic Carlo McCormick told me in 1985: "Mark Kostabi sort of attached himself to what was going on in the East Village in the summer of 1983. He was suddenly everywhere. Everyone was out then: Bobby G, Kiki Smith, Walter Robinson, Doug Milford, Dean Savard, Keiko Bonk, Stephen Lack, Gracie Mansion, Ed Higgins. There weren't a lot of spaces to go to. Limbo had just opened up. Mark personifies how things have become. That's what's so scary. The complete

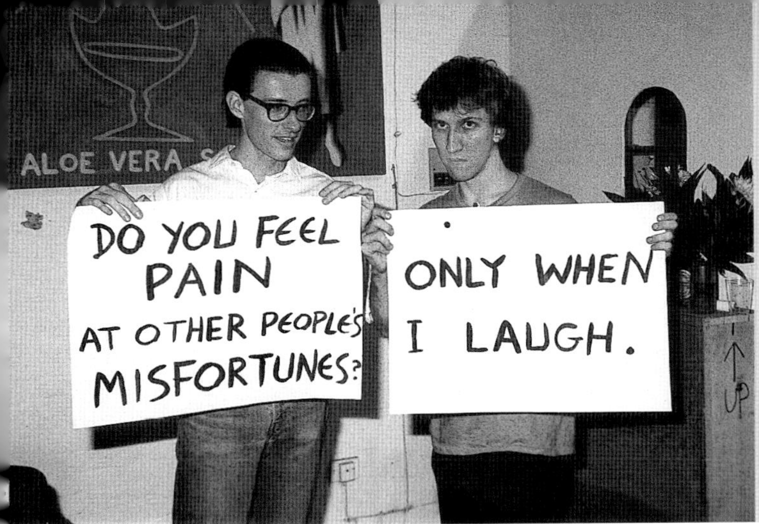

Art critic Jack Bankowsky became the editor of Artforum after Ingrid Sichy left to become the editor of Interview Magazine.

misplaced values of the young artist. All his aphorisms point to something which is really pathetic as a philosophy for an artist to have, to be consciously amoral. There's a certain psychological deformity to it." Carlo added, "Mark was not very good at disguising his intentions (in 1983). He'd have a way worming up to a conversation and sticking his ear in between the people to listen in, or say very little and always listen. He would just stand close by and collect info. He was trying to soak up the bureaucracy of the art system. He was listening to the dealers talking about who was selling and was not and people bad mouthing each other. He was raised in Whittier and he would always joke about, 'It's also the home of Nixon, another famous eavesdropper.'" About Mark's art Carlo had this to say at

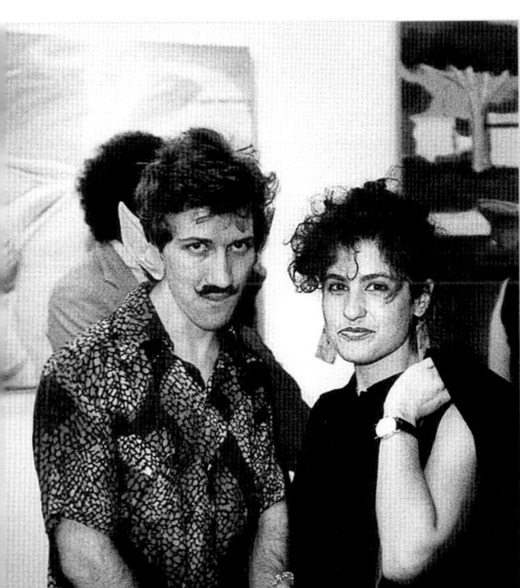

Painter Kathy Ruttenberg, who went to Chapin grade school on the Upper East Side, migrated downtown to the East Village, when the scene got hot.

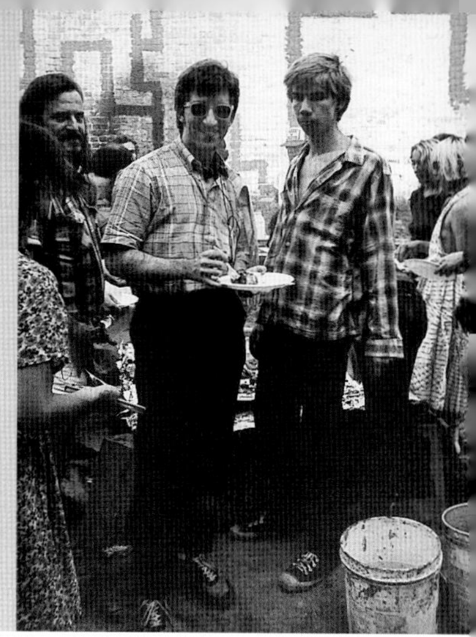

Translator extraordinaire Joachim Neugroschel and Paul Kostabi at the 4th of July Pigfest which was sponsored by the nightclub 8BC in a vacant lot.

the time: "Mark's paintings draw you in with their charm and prettiness as a trap and then make some mean joke on it all. They have a cruel, mocking cynicism and a conceited immorality. A bravado and sloganeering absence of self-consciousness, a comic strip disingenuousness." The critic and East Village painter Walter Robinson told me in 1985 of his memories of Mark in the early 1983 scene, "I soon became aware of Mark's really excessively odd behavior at social situations. He was always very quiet, always listening, always watching. Kostabi would come up and not say anything, openly voyeurize the situation. Everyone said that it struck them as creepy." The now L.A.-based art critic Peter Frank recalls, "Mark was becoming quite studied in his ambition by this time, and I was put off by this behavior, as I was subsequently by his notorious modus operandi. For a while I would even try to avoid him in social situations, especially if there were someone with a camera. Still, I went to Mark's Semaphore Gallery shows, and recognized, although regretted, his importance to the discourse."

Perhaps the East Village scene of the mid-80s was a sociological force, disguised and hyped as a pretentious arts aesthetic. Peter Frank believes, "The East Village art movement — which was more a sociological development into which a confluence of art tendencies flowed — was an avant-garde and rear-guard reaction to the commercialization of artistic discourse in NY. In this it followed in the wake of conceptual and

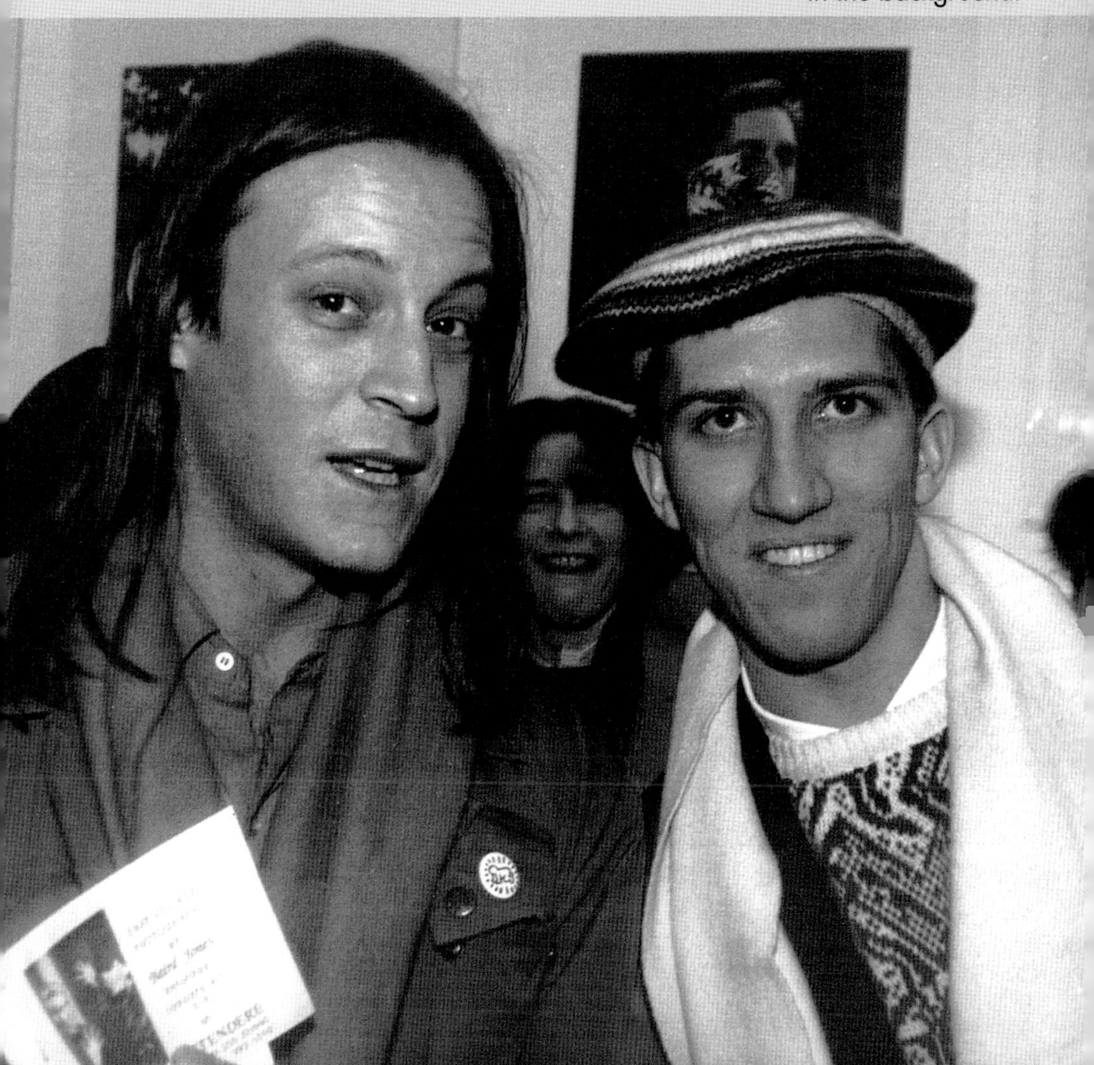

Photographer Patrick McMullan flashes Kosthappening invites at Gracie Mansion Gallery with a beaming Fran Lebowitz in the background.

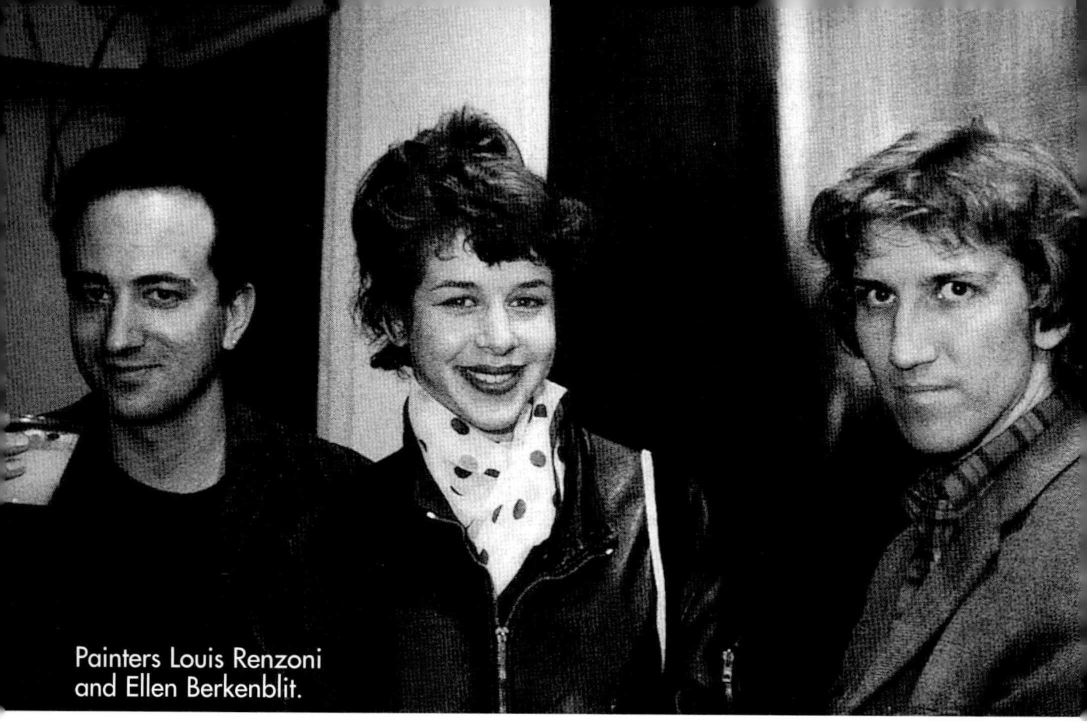

Painters Louis Renzoni
and Ellen Berkenblit.

performance art, especially in the do-it-yourself, artist-run ethos but it valorized traditional media such as painting, sculpture, and nontraditional, lowbrow formats such as graffiti, fashion, craft and furniture, even souvenirs along with anti-commercial high-art approaches. It also formalized the bohemian-gentrification cycle, repeating the Greenwich Village/SoHo pattern but doing so deliberately, self-consciously and quickly. In effect, the East Village phenomenon bespoke the emergence of a whole generation

Keily Jenkins at
Barbara Braathen
Gallery.

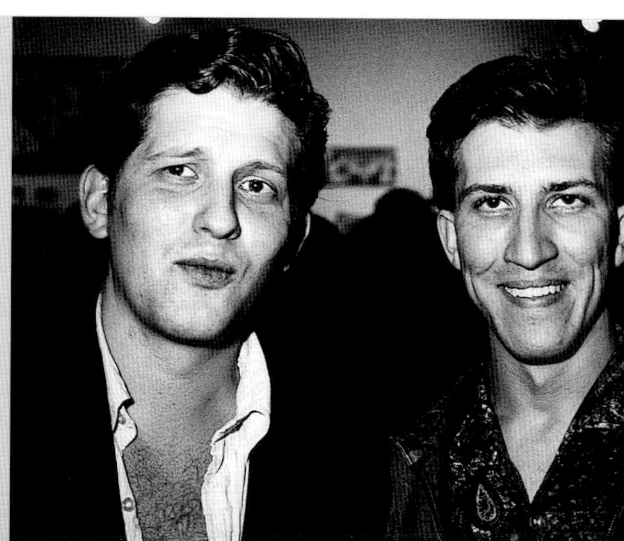

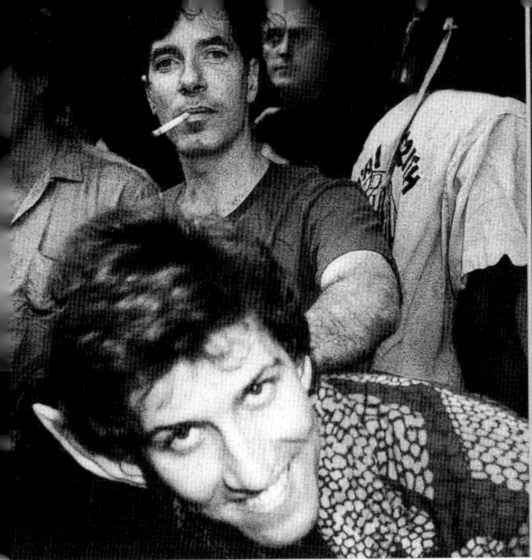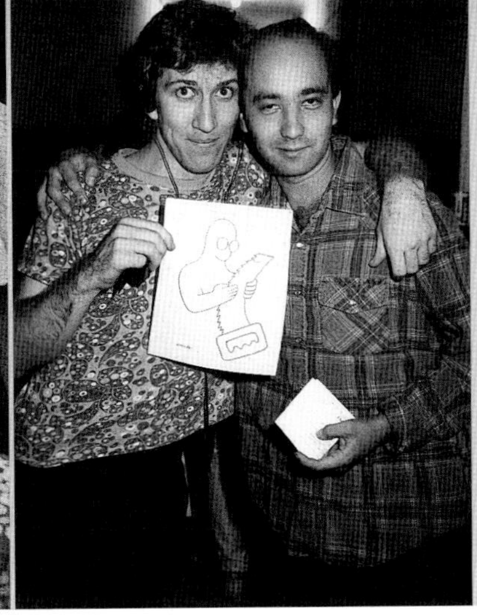

Painter Stephen Lack's success as an actor in the movie *Scanners* in 1981 was rumored to have bankrolled the Gracie Mansion Gallery's early days.

Bookseller Richard Armijo at Cuando.

of young people who valued being hip so that however bohemian it was the East Village was not a minority phenomenon, as was the beat thing or even the hippie movement, but the leading edge of majority taste. How Post-Modern is that?"

But by 1985 the floodgates had opened for all the newcomers wanting to join the posse, and they were desperate to be seen as old school East Villagers. The young painter Ivan Jenson arrived from Long Island, brazen publicist in tow. Mark Kostabi told me in 1984 that in the East Village, Ivan Jenson was the only artist he considered absolutely worthless, the only one Mark really did not want being put in a group show with. Yet in 1985 at the height of the East Village boom yuppies were paying $5000 for Ivan Jenson paintings that could not fetch fifty dollars now. More amazingly, Jenson was Absolut Vodka's ill-fated choice as one of its official artists after Keith Haring, Andy Warhol and Kenny Scharf. At that time, Absolut's talent search had begun to resemble the casting build-up for for Scarlett O'Hara and *Gone with the Wind*. Everyone was waiting to find out who it would be since the Absolut selection seemed guaranteed to make the artist into an instant star. Mark Kostabi was Absolut's first choice. Mark told me: "I was to be the fourth artist to advertise Absolut Vodka, after Andy Warhol, Keith Haring and Kenny Scharf. They

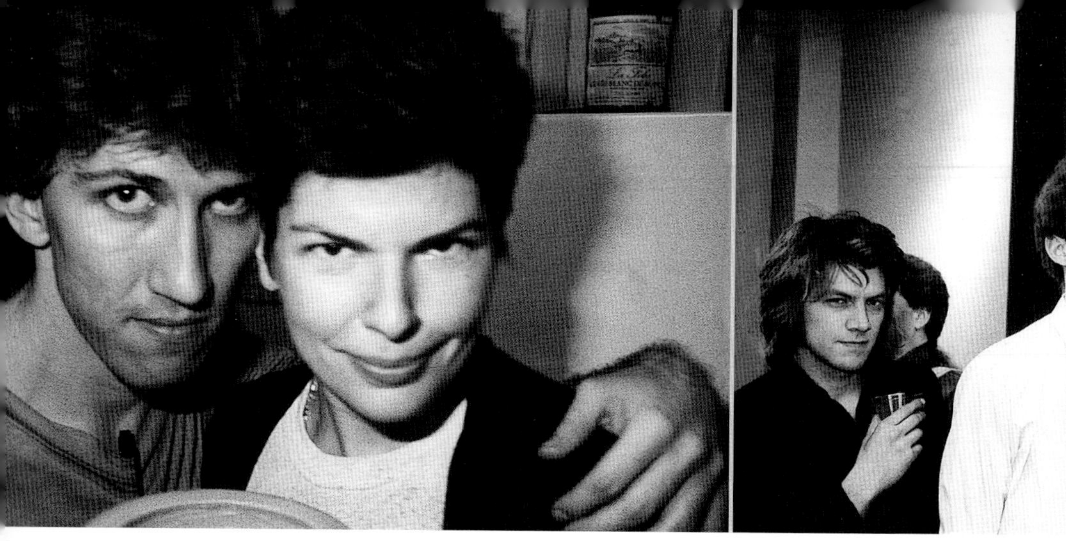

A plunger photo with critic and curator Ronnie Cohen.

Painters James Romberger
and Edward Brezinski with

agreed to pay me $60,000 which is what they told me Andy and Keith got. They came on strong at the beginning but then became flakey. Maybe they were not comfortable with the $60,000 price that they agreed to. I recall them implying that in a way I was getting more than Warhol because he gave them four original paintings as part of his $60,000 deal while I only had to give one. People said Andy would have done it for free, just for the exposure. Who knows, maybe Kenny Scharf or Keith Haring objected. Kenny and Keith were very cliquish and protective of their connection with Warhol. I remember one night I began talking with Andy Warhol at some club and Keith suddenly appeared and just butted in between me and Andy and stole Andy's attention. I felt like Keith treated me like a beggar who wandered into an upscale restaurant and he was the manager who quickly ushered me out."

It doesn't seem that Mark was just imagining Keith Haring's rivalry with him. Haring's hostility towards Mark became obvious later in 1987 when Haring was quoted as saying, "I don't like what Kostabi does at all for a lot of reasons. I think the paintings and drawings themselves are basically boring and the fact that he is having other people paint them is making it worse." Keith Haring was so extraordinarily successful at that time that for him to go out of his way to be critical of another painter illustrates a real mean-spiritedness and competitiveness.

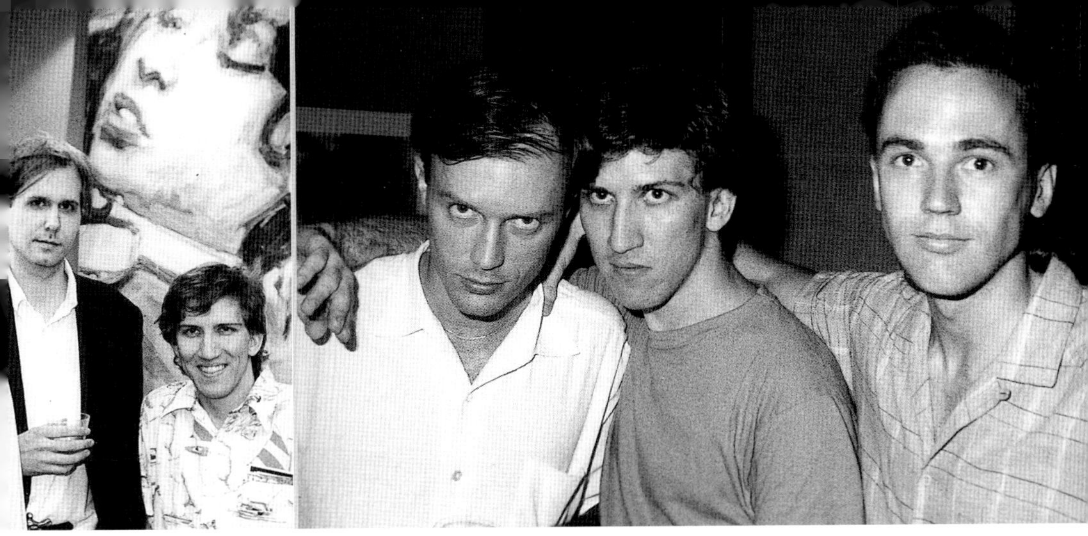

musician/gossipist
Tony Heiberg.

Publisher Roland Hagenberg and painter Peter Drake. Hagenberg took
off permanently for Tokyo when the East Village scene collapsed in 1988.

Mark continues on his dealing with Absolut: "At the same time I was negotiating with Absolut I decided to stop drinking, having never drank much anyway. I decided it's better that they were reneging on the deal because, as a famous artist, I should be a better role model and not support alcohol companies. So I mischievously placed an item in Page Six of the New York Post saying that the only reason I agreed to do an Absolut Vodka ad was so I could insert hidden anti-alcohol messages in it. They went ballistic. I was then surprised that a few years later Michel Roux, the president of Absolut Vodka who created the famous artist ad campaign,

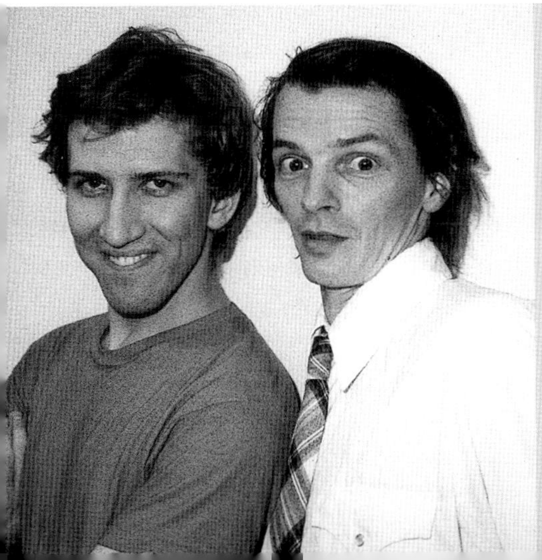

High strung painter Noel
Mapstead left New York for
California in 1988.

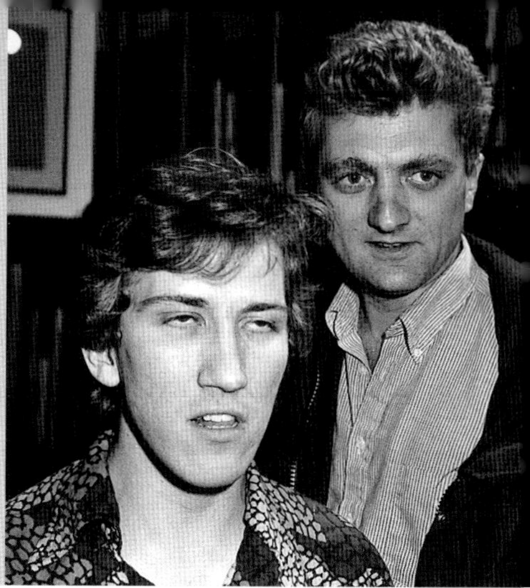

Walter Robinson met Mark in 1983 when Mark called out of the blue and said: "I like your work and I'd like to meet you." (Mark did this with several of his favorite artists in the 1980s, like George Segal and Robert Longo. Both Segal and Robinson later wrote catalogue essays for Mark, Segal for *Office Suite* and Robinson for *Upheaval*.) Robinson exhibited pulp-illustration inspired paintings of people kissing at Metro Pictures in the 1980s. He also anticipated Damien Hirst's spin paintings (which Hirst worked on with David Bowie) by over 10 years. For over a decade, he was an editor for Art In America. Today Walter Robinson is the editor of the online magazine of Artnet.com, for which Mark writes an artworld advice column called *Ask Mark Kostabi*.

agreed to pose nude in a photo book I was putting together. He even let my collaborator Linda Mason paint his penis red, while I painted a background of a prison yard, implying that he was a convict. Absolut went on to use hundreds of other artists, most of them unknown. I heard they all got $1,000 each — a far cry from the $60,000 that the first few artists got."

Mark's anti-alcohol stance alienated a number of people although it presaged his leadership skills at Kostabi World years later where a party atmosphere of any kind could have led to disaster. Given the importance of liquor sponsorship behind so many cultural promotions, Mark has paid dearly for his ideals, an interesting side note for those who criticize him for his cynicism in other matters.

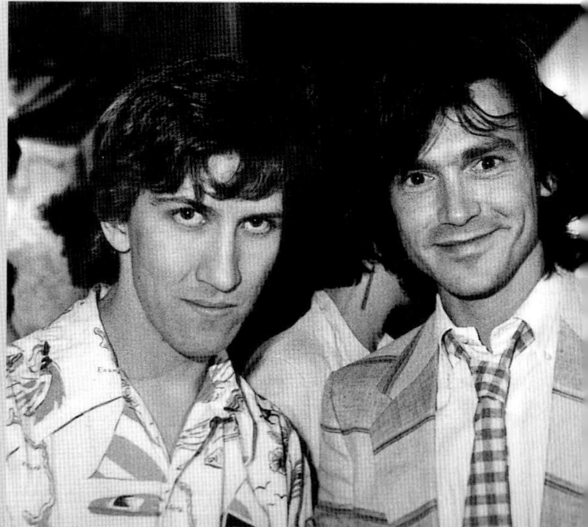

Painter Duncan Hannah, who was part of Warhol's inner circle. The very polished, well dressed Duncan Hannah, with his narrative figure paintings, was the star of Semaphore Gallery until Mark agressively joined the group. Mark quickly became the best selling artist in the gallery even though he refused to agree to an exclusive contract. It was well known that Duncan was jealous of Mark, who exhibited none of Duncan's personal sophistication or style, yet became the gallery darling overnight.

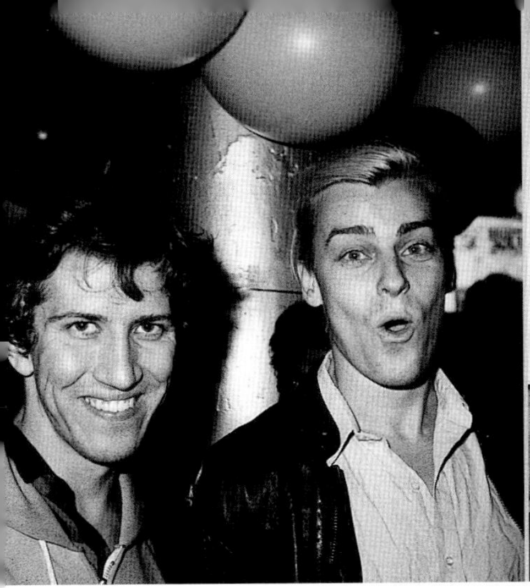
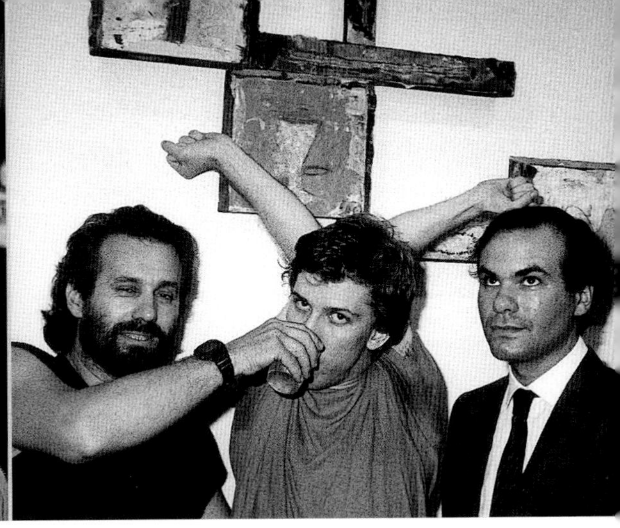

Performer John Sex at the Pyramid Club on Avenue A. Sex was featured in People Magazine as part of Madonna's crowd.

Painters Dragan Ilic and Hunt Slonem at the *Crucifix Show* at Piezo Electric Gallery.

So the $1000 Absolut endorsements started being given out to all the newcomers but it became "winner take nothing." It seemed like every day there was hype for a new Keith Haring, a new Jean-Michel Basquiat, a new Robert Mapplethorpe, a new Cindy Sherman, a new Jenny Holzer, a new Julian Schnabel, most of whom ended up working soon enough at Kostabi World for close to minimum wage. The hype machine was in overdrive, but in fact no new stars were being discovered as artists from everywhere just poured into the East Village.

Nicolo Naimo came over from Italy and joined Frank Bernarducci's 17th Street and Broadway gallery for a few years. Bernarducci was always a classic downtown gallery owner case. Since his space was located too far north and was too far west it was ridiculous for him to claim to be an East Village space. The diminutive Frank put the best face he could on it and claimed to have East Village inspiration. Frank had done graphic work in advertising but knew next to nothing about art history. For instance, he had never heard of Picasso's *Les Desmoiselles d'Avignon* and it did not matter a bit to him that he was so ignorant. The man had enormous confidence and soon brought in a cartload of second rate talent from the Lower East Side. This was understandable because by 1985 the East Village gallery glut had reached such plague-of-locusts proportions that

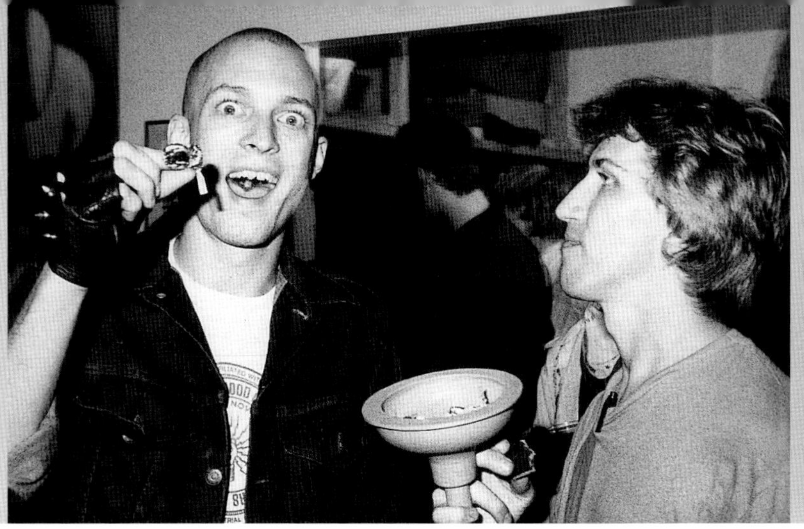

Painter
Craig Coleman.

any legitimate EV artist was being courted by a dozen nouveau galleries. Bernarducci plugged the painter Joe Davis to anyone who would listen, betting that images of Times Square seen from an East Village perspective would be the next big thing but that vista never clicked and Davis soon disappeared along with the rest. Frank slept in the backroom like most of the downtown gallerists and felt like he was on top of the world for a few years. But the gallery made few sales and soon closed. Poor Nicolo Naimo gave up and went back to Italy. But Frank Bernarducci learned his trade and went on to own a 57th Street gallery which today does excellent business.

A bunch of artists came in from San Francisco, ran around optimistically for a few years and finally went back when the scene collapsed. Ex-Marine Louis Lopes came over, opened the shoebox-size Nite Gallery, always painted the same murky, muddy geometric icon, and then departed after a few years to pursue cross-country bus trips which focused on mud baths. The S.F. artist Karen Kaplan walked around the East Village galleries handing out these wonderful abstract color postcards which drew gasps of awe until one looked closely and noticed that she had painted herself naked in the middle of each, arms outstretched. Karen did discover the Paterson Museum in New Jersey. In 1987, it seemed like dozens of painters from Paterson, NJ had joined the Avenue A cadre. There was a certain quid pro quo trade-off going on since the Paterson Museum was open to showing East Village painters. That artist exchange

Artist and Fashion Moda
co-founder Joe Lewis.

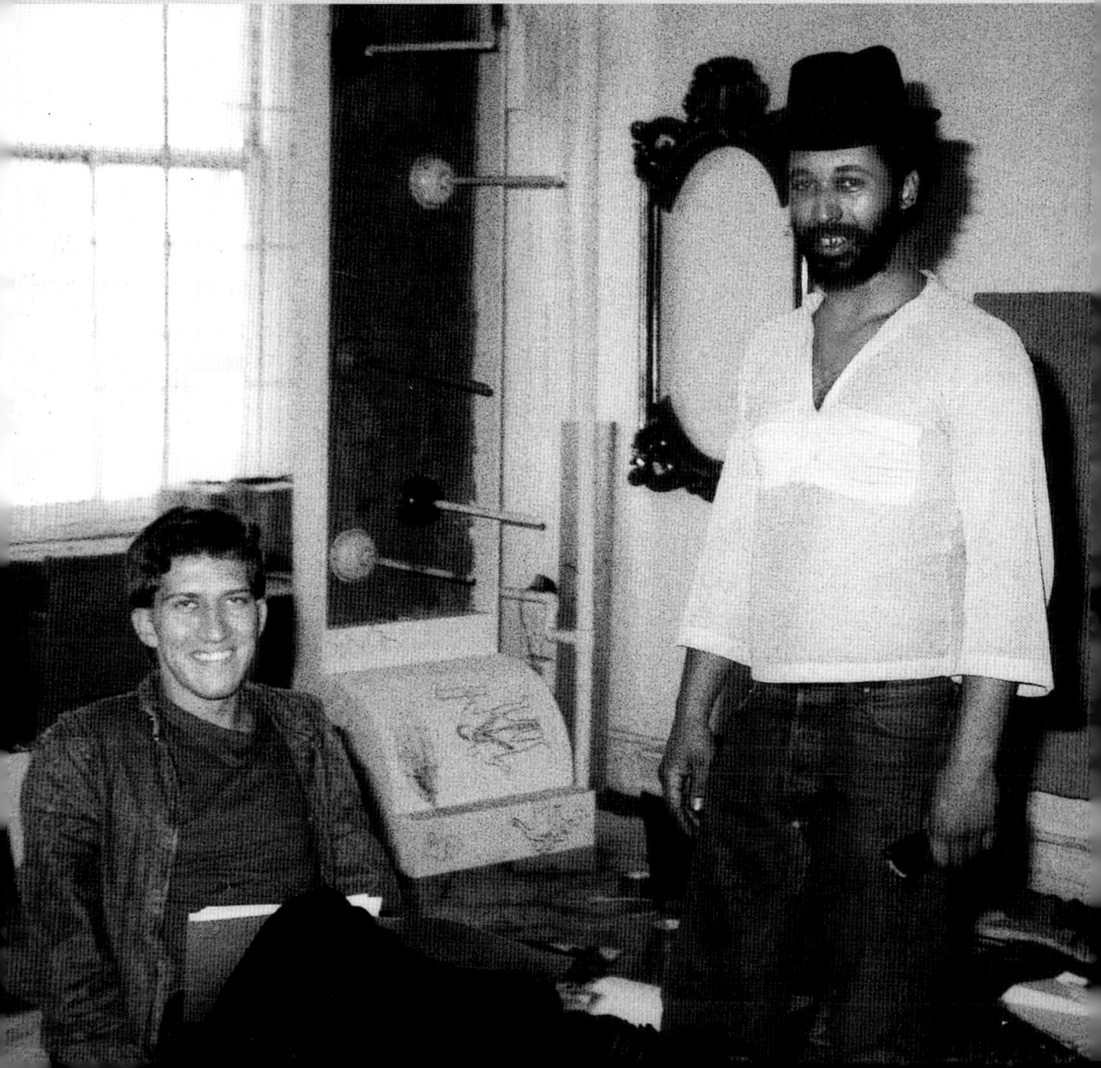

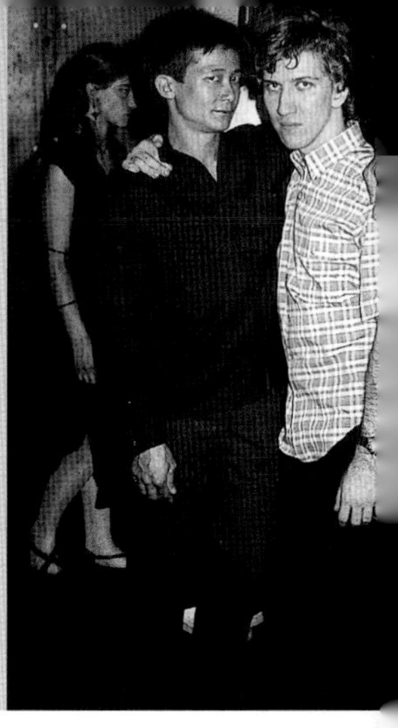

Andy Warhol assistant Benjamin Liu.

program ended dismally when the director of the museum resigned after he confessed to the police that he had tried to burn the museum down in an ill-advised attempt to play hero in the middle of a packed exhibition reception. The local Paterson artists became so demoralized they stopped showing up anywhere after that imbroglio.

Other new arrivals had been EV originals who had left for faraway climes and then heard the siren call and scampered back. Brian Goodfellow had been in Paris when he heard about all the moolah pouring into the figurative expressionist hands. At the end of the scene in 1987, Goodfellow was part of the group that wanted to start an East Village museum. He argued that even if there was a complete backlash against

It was this dinosaur painting, *Enasaurs*, that caught the eye of the Ron Feldman's assistant, Sean Elwood, which led to Mark's joining the Feldman Gallery in 1985. Later Sean Elwood published an early book of Kostabi line drawings, *Office Suite*, with an introduction by sculptor George Segal. Eventually Elwood opened his own gallery in Seattle.

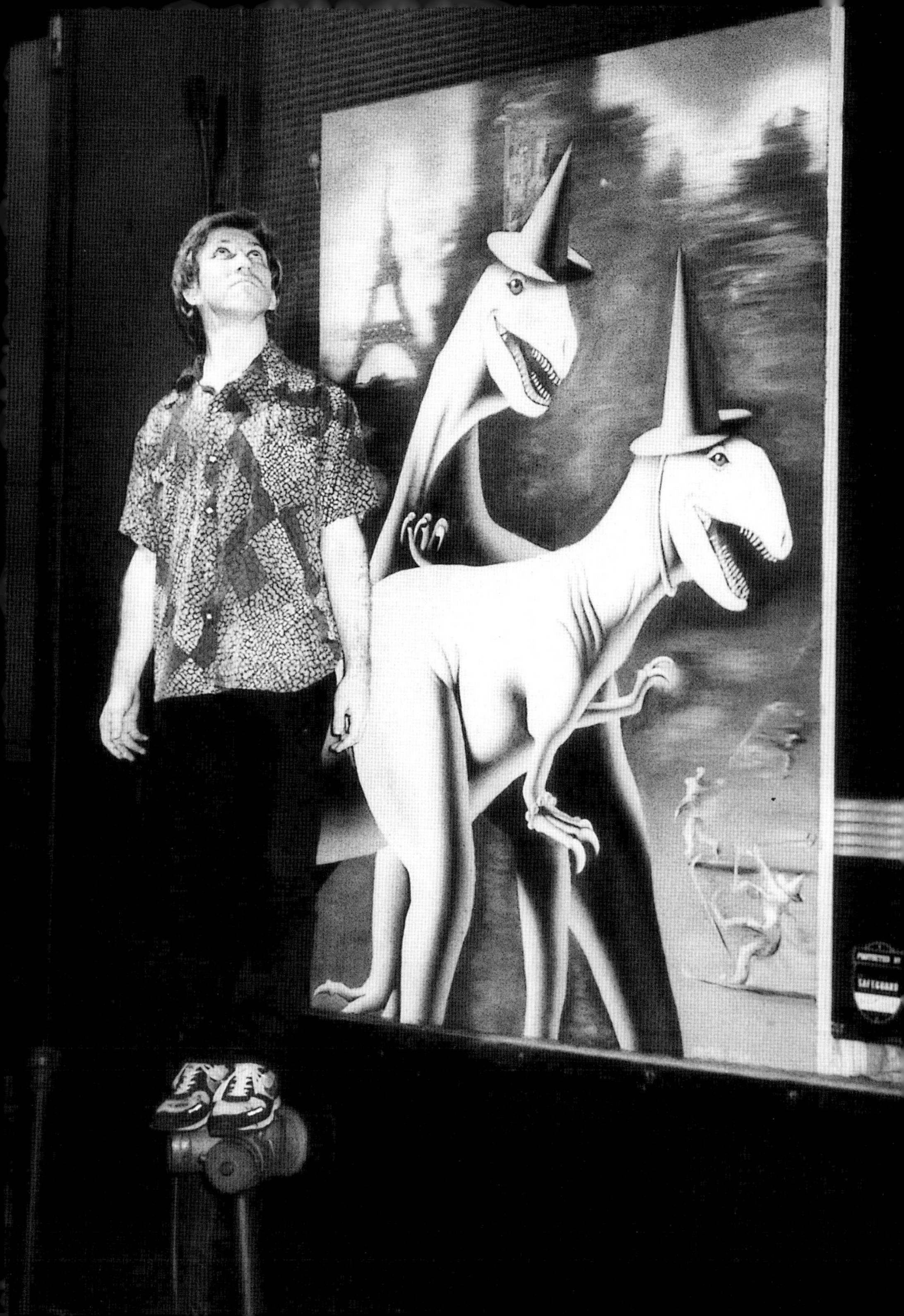

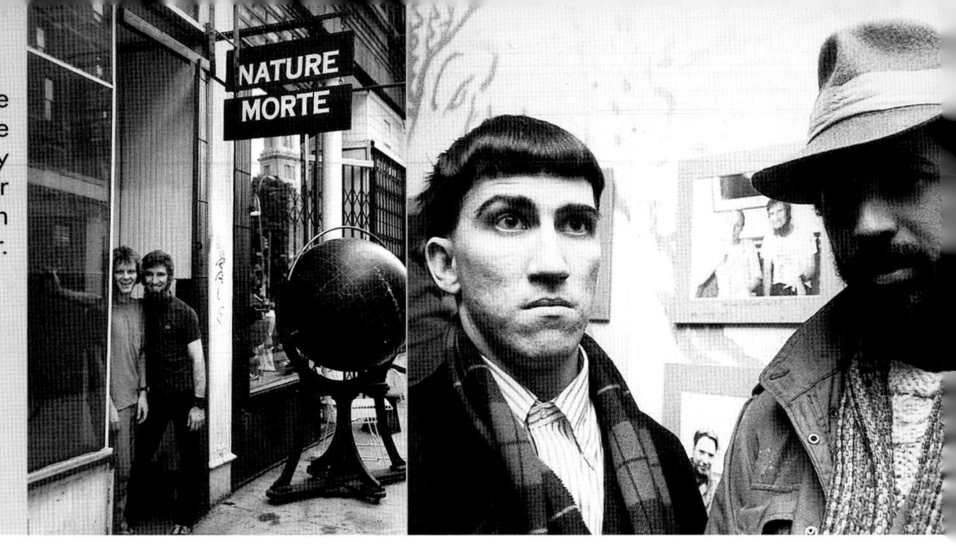

Nature
Morte
Gallery
co-owner
Alan
Belcher.

Joe Lewis at the Kosthappening
at Terror Street Gallery.

graffiti and East Village earnest political painting, there had been so much ink spilled on the Alphabetland explosion of the mid-80s that the movement had to be of some historical significance. His in-vain attempts to found a Museum of East Village Art were paralleled by the frustrations suffered by the group who tried to establish a Museum of American

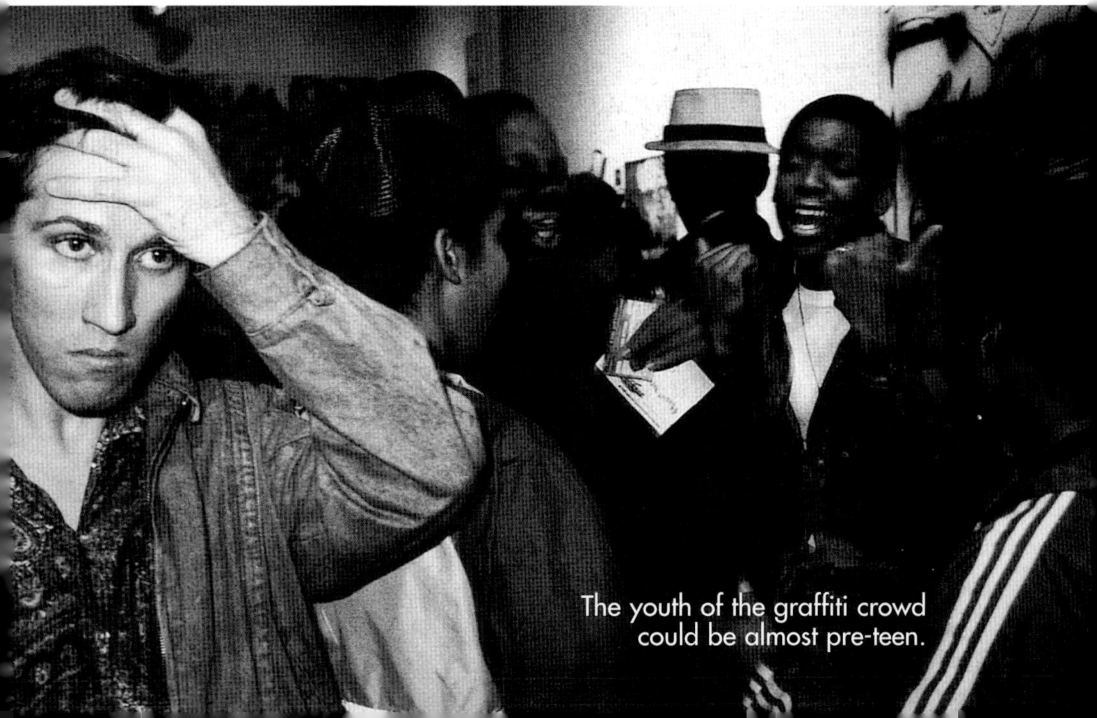

The youth of the graffiti crowd
could be almost pre-teen.

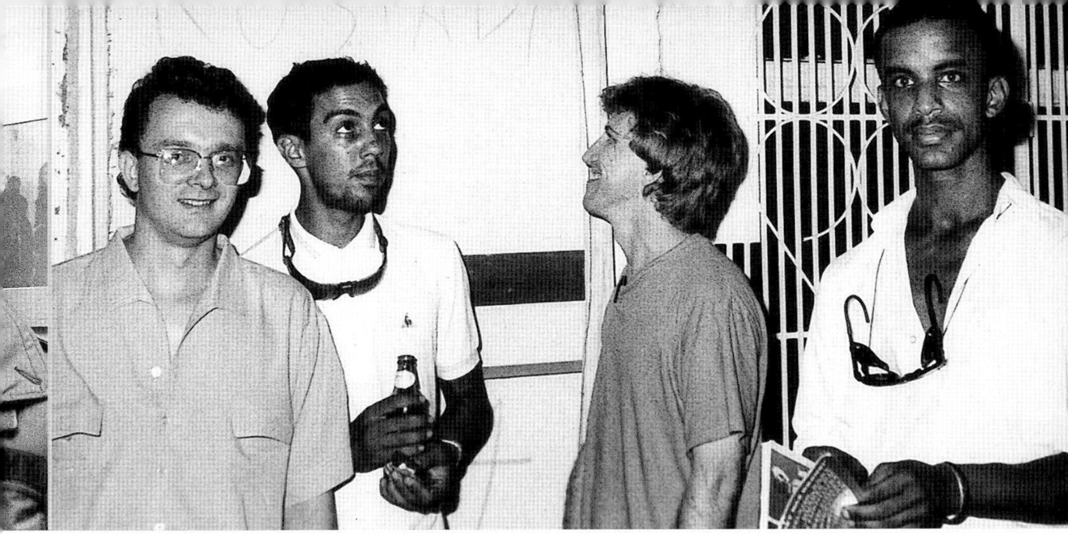

M-13 Gallery owner Bruno Meziere, famed graffiti writer Futura 2000 and Fred Critchfield, who died in his twenties, which was not rare among graffiti writers.

Graffiti. Just about no one was interested because it costs money to properly store art even when it is acquired for free. Brian is now all but forgotten but for his handsome photo taken by portraitist Timothy Greenfield-Sanders. Yet Goodfellow, Edward Brezinski and Robert Hawkins were the three artists who were first called "East Village painters" in an essay by Ted Castle in 1980. Hawkins didn't became a major star although the uptown collector Hedy Klineman bought a bunch of his canvases in the early 80s. The seminal critic Rene Ricard once claimed Hawkins was the only artist Jean-Michel Basquiat ever collected. Hawkins now lives in London where he is known for his eye-catching gold fangs.

The painter Ed Brezinski ran the Magic gallery on East 3rd Street in 1984 which is where I first met Mark Kostabi in July, 1984. I noticed Mark right off because virtually every person is the room was fawning all over him. Even the local critics flattered Mark constantly. For instance, in an interview in New York Beat magazine in May, 1984, Carlo McCormick announced that he was writing a biography of Mark Kostabi which ultimately turned out to be a five page feature but that is a pretty heavy imprimatur for a leading critic in the scene to be boosting around town.

I bought 20 Ed Brezinski canvases for thirty dollars apiece in 1985. I lugged them over to Mark's house before one of Mark's gigantic

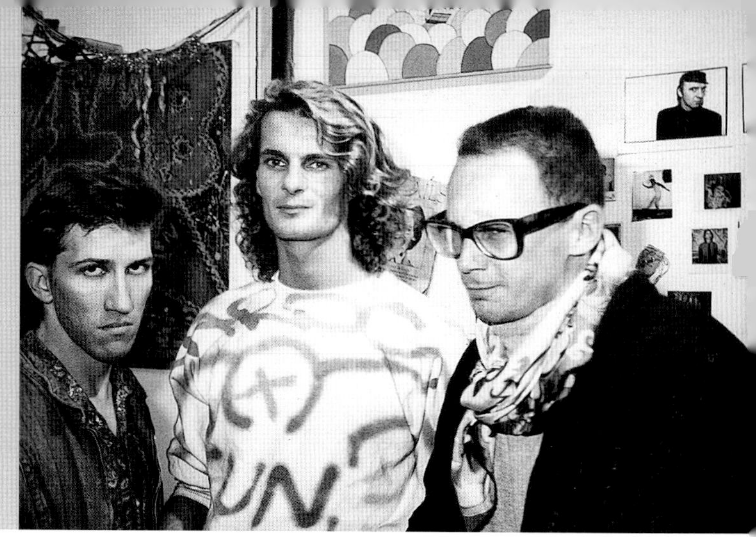

Designer Bill McGrattan and Arch Connelly who was one of the main artists at the Fun Gallery and then later died of AIDS.

house warming parties. The critic Steven Kaplan came over to me and chided me for buying so many. He said it wasn't good for any artist to have so many works just shut away from the public like that since I couldn't exhibit them all regularly. But Brezinksi painted so quickly he had done that many more within a month. I wasn't happy with the paintings so I soon gave them all away to random friends. I heard that after a few years they had all pealed and become worthless. Brian Goodfellow also demonstrated this speed painting tendency. In fact, it is one of the definitions of the East Village style and one which Mark Kostabi certainly exemplifies: unbelievable speed of execution. Goodfellow completed his canvas in under five minutes per work, less if he painted with the canvas flat on the floor. Not all East Village painters had such rapid fire approaches. Joel Handorff told me that he spent a full year on only one canvas. Handorff was exceptional because among other things he suffered a serious stroke and had lost the use of his main painting arm.

Rushed completion was integral to the East Village movement. In the early 80s, ghetto graffiti was impacting on the white art student community in Manhattan, primarily at the School of Visual Arts which Haring, Kenny Scharf and Rodney Alan Greenblat all attended and where Jean-Michel Basquiat hung out. It is the outlaw context of graffiti writing which forces the rapid getaway. The police are moving in. The tag has to be spray painted before the police bust occurs. Another gang may

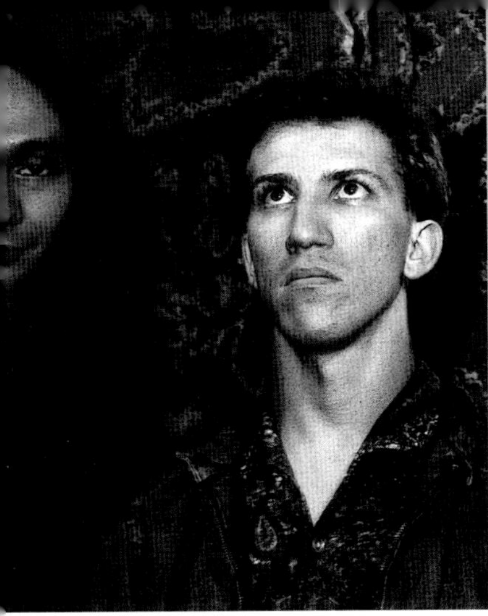

Fun Gallery co-owner Bill Stelling. After the East Village bust, Stelling went on to own a gallery on the Greene Street in SoHo.

be coming soon to paint over the image or attack the solitary writer. Art critics wrote breathlessly of running with the graffiti crew. Some believe a main reason that Haring and Basquiat's prices have remained high is that they died too young for their excessive work rates to have had sufficient time to glut their markets. Similarly the youthfulness of the East Village art culture is a parallel to graffiti culture because at age 21 the graffiti writer ceases to be treated as a juvenile criminal but as an adult offender so the penalties became much more strict. Graffiti writers tend to be under 21 for this reason. As the white culture aped the ghetto tradition it also picked up its youthfulness. Just as the graffitists did, the youthful East Village artists churned out centered, small scale, faux-radical paintings with little

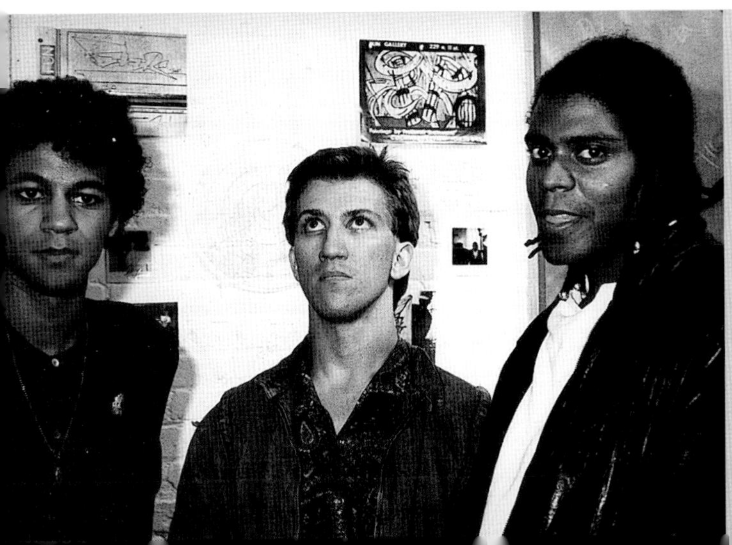

Daze and Vulcan in late 1985 right before Mark left for Australia. When Mark returned he quit the East Village for the Ronald Feldman Gallery.

Art critic Robert Pincus-Witten, gallery owner Pat Hearn and artist Thierry Chevalier. Pincus-Witten wrote a popular diaristic column for Arts Magazine about his encounters with the contemporary art world. It was at once astute art criticsm and an intricately detailed, high-brow gossip column which many art world insiders vied to be included in. His amusing descriptions of an artist's lifestyle, studio furniture or assistants were riveting. He was a regular in the East Village scene. Later he worked for Gagosian Gallery where he organized acclaimed historical shows, as he now does for C&M Arts, uptown. One day in 1986, while visiting Mark's Tribeca studio, Pincus-Witten titled approximately 10 Kostabi paintings, making him an early participant in Mark's "collaborative" creative process.

art historical or complex conceptual basis and with a take-it-to-the-people and "let's party" attitude. There was always an outlaw undercurrent to the East Village art scene fed by the surrounding lawlessness of Alphabetland. I saw a gallery-goer pickpocketed at an art opening and shout for help. Not one person at the packed reception lifted a finger to help him. Mark told me, "One of Basquiat's first assistants told me that even after Basquiat was rich, the assistant and Basquiat would still shoplift huge amounts of art supplies. He bragged about how they would load up their coats with the

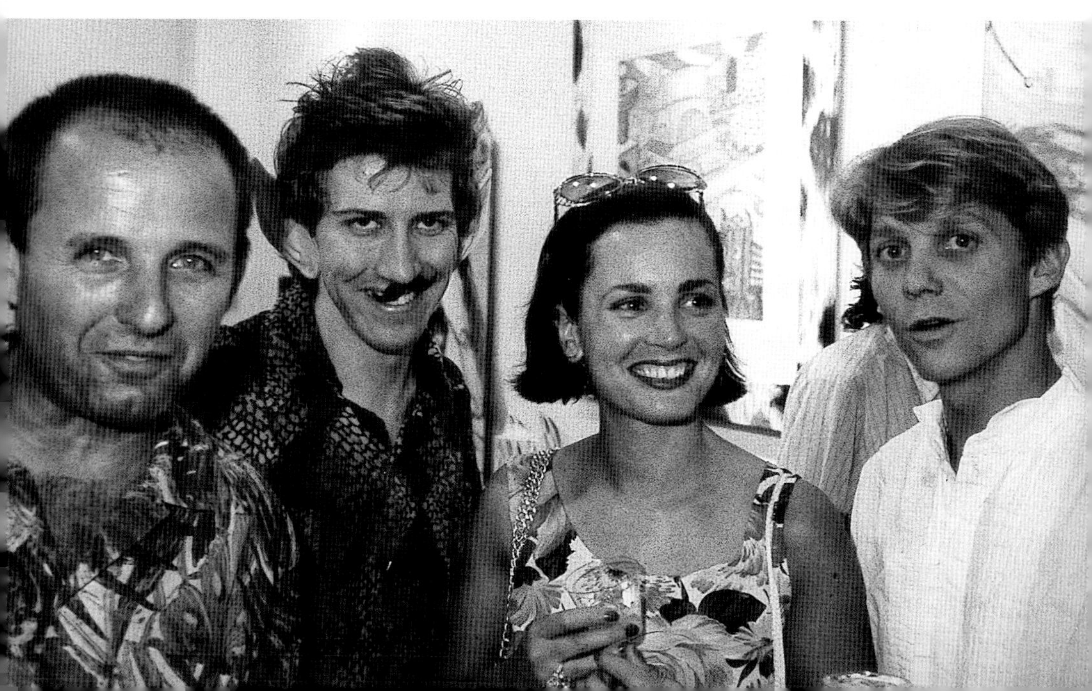

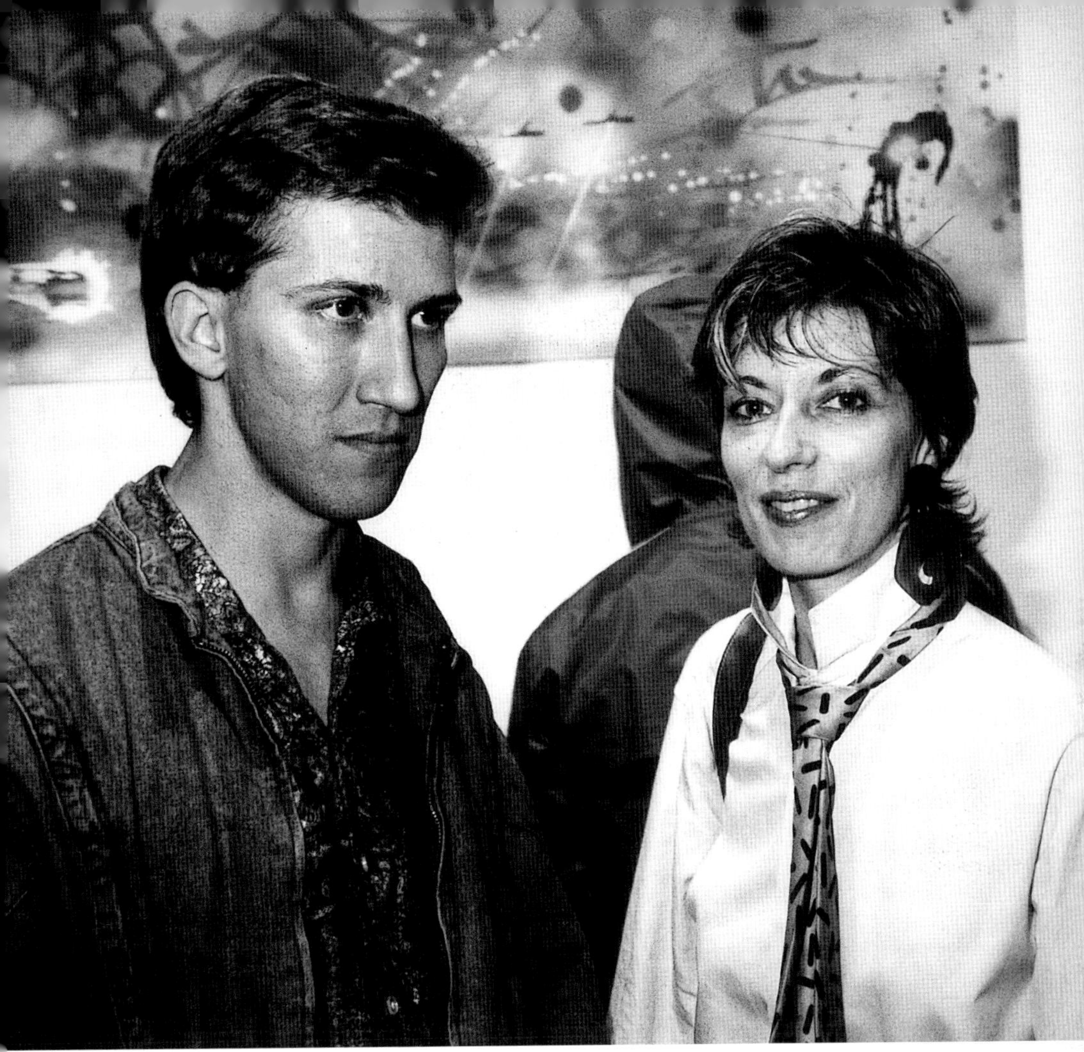

best quality paint markers. They did it just for the thrill."

The history of graffiti in New York can be divided into four phases. In the early 60s street graffiti exploded after the introduction of inexpensive, disposable magic markers. After *Westside Story* the gang marking turf-identifiers "Sharks" and "Jets" seemed to spring up everywhere done in magic marker script. A similar graffiti boom took place, this time on subways, with the arrival of aerosol spray can paints in the 70s. However it was the last two phases in the history of New York graffiti which clumped together in the early 80s that were decisive to East Village art. The transit system introduced a new kind of subway car that could be easily cleansed in 1980. Within a few years this new car had replaced a quarter of the trains in use and would ultimately replace them all. Previously a hosed down subway train would darken a graffiti writer's "piece" (for masterpiece), but the all important "tag" could shine through sufficiently so that the name of the artist was still seen. Anticipating a cleaning became part of a skilled graffiti writer's job. Artwork was designed that would be able to best withstand a muting-down cleaning. With the new cars, the hosing down completely removed any trace of graffiti within minutes. In the early 80s, graffiti writers began for the first time to seriously consider switching over to working on

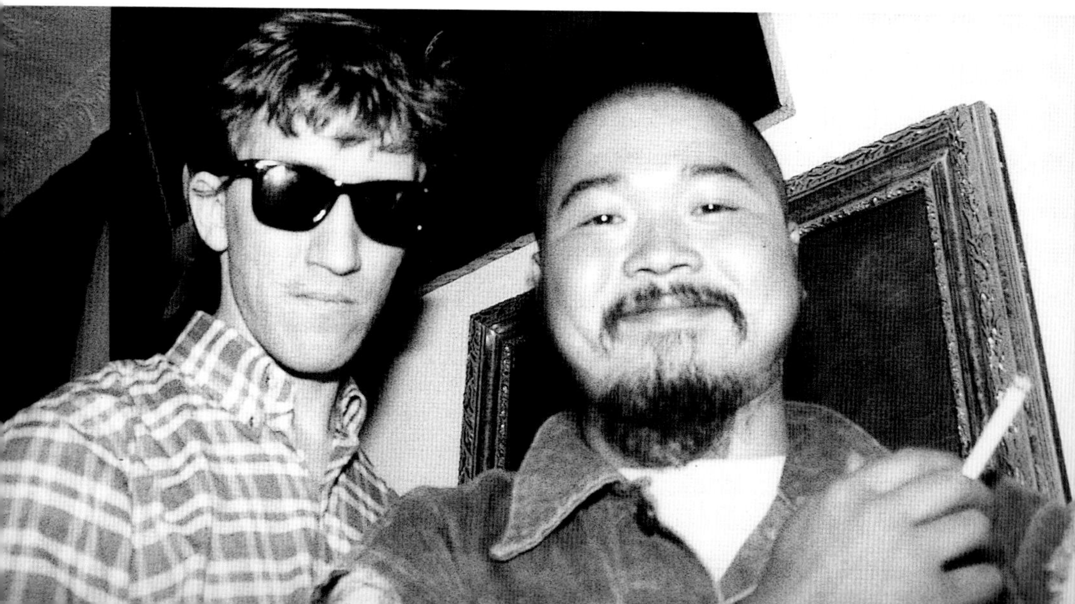

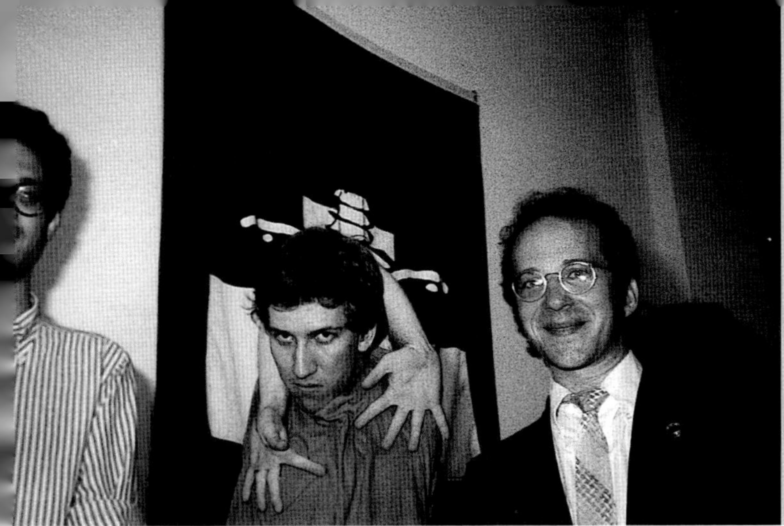

canvas as the only medium left to them after years of disparaging canvas work as selling out. Graffiti culture became more accessible to white dealers and white artists as it moved away from the subways.

The other incident which marked a new phase in graffiti culture occurred on September 15, 1983 when the 25-year-old black artist Michael Stewart was killed by the transit police while spontaneously scrawling graffiti in a subway station late one night on his way home from a party. He had been hogtied and suffocated after struggling during the arrest procedure. Adding to the suspense, Stewart lay in a coma for 13 days. There were accusations of a cover-up when it was discovered that Stewart's eyeballs had been removed during the autopsy, allegedly to hide evidence

Sculptor
Ken Hiratsuka.

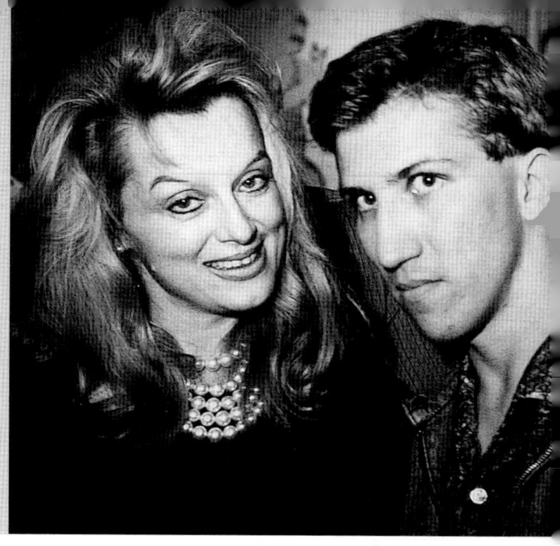

Gallery owner Barbara Braathen.

of suffocation. His family was ultimately awarded $1.7 million dollars in damages in a settlement of their suit against the transit police. The outrage felt in the artist community over this police brutality fed the growing momentum of graffiti as a happening aesthetic. It was at this time that suddenly-a-superstar Keith Haring was photographed smiling as he was arrested for doing his chalk figures in subway stations. Many East Village painters who had previously ignored graffiti began to incorporate graffiti themes into their work. When the Bronx Museum organized their well-received *Hip Hop* exhibit in 2002, the painting they included by Jean-Michel Basquiat was his portrait of Michael Stewart. After September 15,1983, for a few years, fed by the constant headlines as the Michael

Little Mike Anderson, who suffers from brittle bone syndrome, at the Area nightclub. Anderson was at the center of a national controversy when he permitted himself to be bowled at downtown nightclub parties despite his disease. He suffered no injury except perhaps to his dignity.

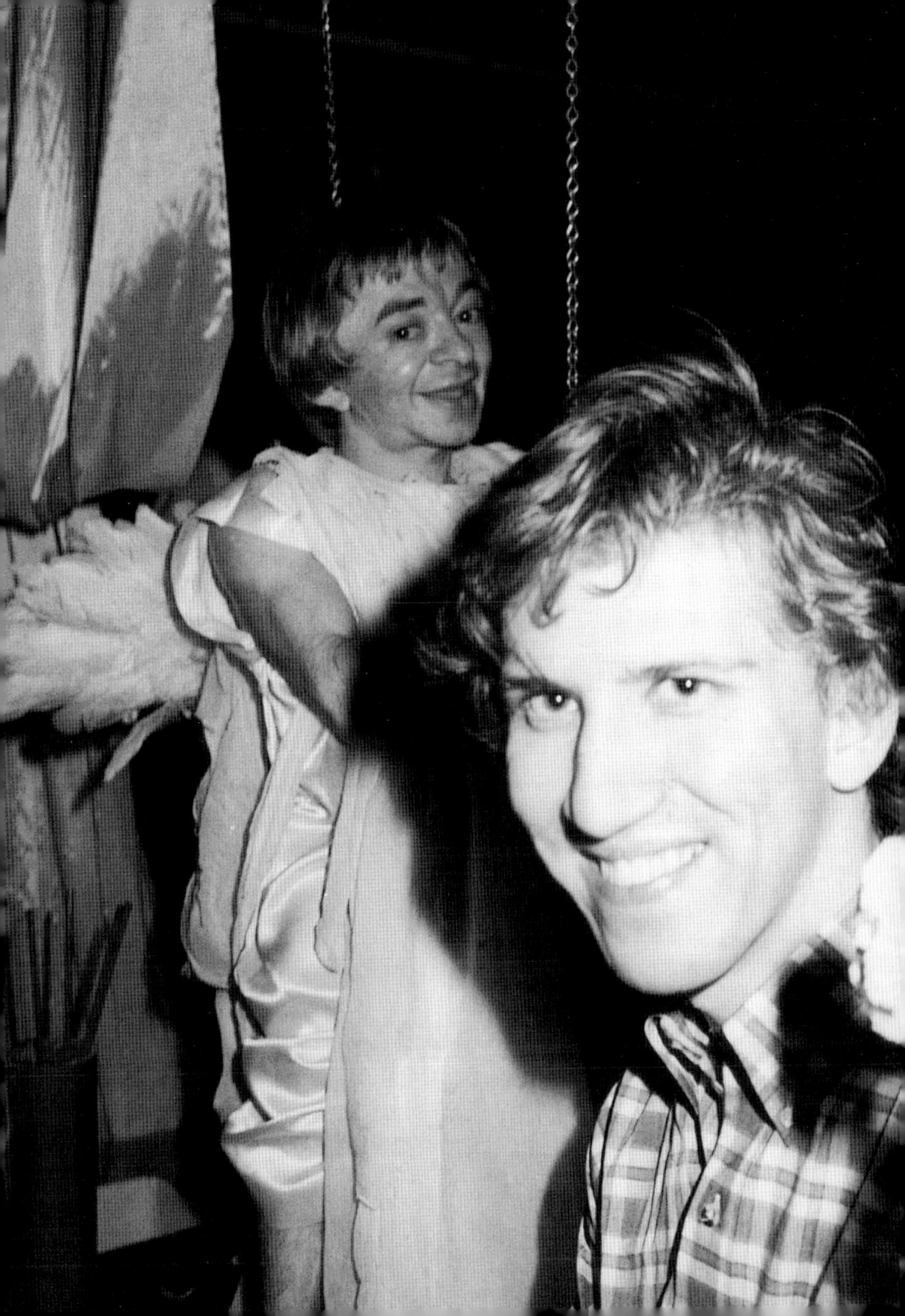

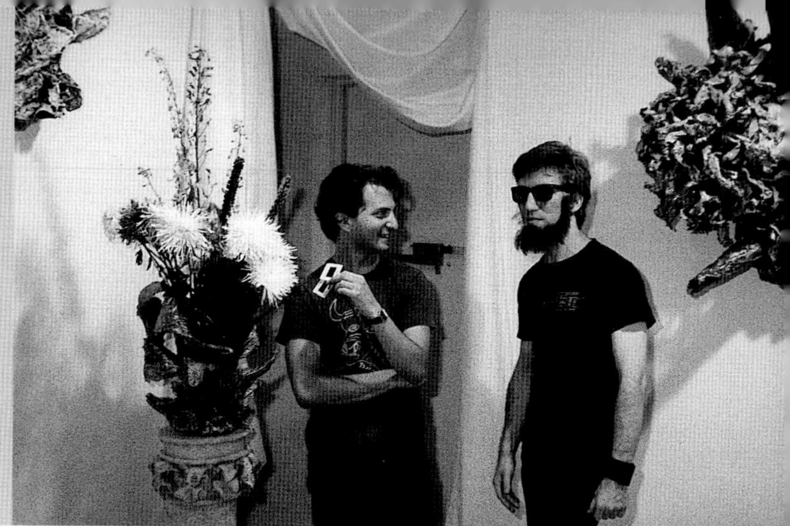

Stewart case went through grand jury after grand jury, any East Village artist who scrawled a statement on a wall could identify with Michael Stewart and feel like an outlaw taking a risk.

There was another East Village movement which grew up in a second more austere phase, "Neo Geo." But the Neo Geo clique was really lured in by standard art world enticements such as safer streets and cheap, available art showing spaces. In many ways the refined Neo Geo mood was the antithesis of "taking it to the people," which they snootily characterized as "backlash trash." Yet oddly the Neo Geo group continued the youthfulness of the East Village stereotype because even in the 1987 denouement of the Alphabetland gallery scene, the streets weren't really that safe and youthful legs ran the fastest from muggers. On the other hand, there were always a few older iconoclasts like performance legend Vito Acconci and painter David Diao who had somehow ended up among the East Village cadre, which right from the start never made any sense to anyone. They certainly were not drawn in by the reverse chic factor that had led many established SoHo artists like Francesco Clemente in 1983, and then Leon Golub, Sherry Levine and Ross Bleckner to guest show at the East Village galleries. The momentum that these big names provided the Alphabetland galleries at that time was inestimable. But by 1985, the East Village didn't need anyone's help. Things were zooming.

So there were all the opportunistic new arrivals flooding in,

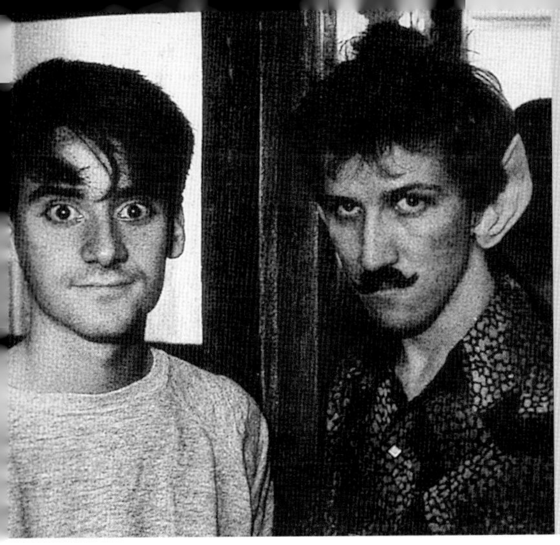

Artist Rodney Alan Greenblat at Gracie Mansion Gallery.
Despite an enormous reputation in his mid-20s as an East Village artist, entry in the Whitney Biennial, and inclusion in the permanent collections of most of the top contemporary museums in the world, Greenblat now no longer makes collectible art.
He currently lives in Pennsylvania and reportedly makes video games for children.

including me with my camera shooting away with its motor drive. The motor drive was my gimmick. I used a cheap motor drive that seemed to burn out every three weeks but it was worth it. If I took one picture, I always took four. The artists had never experienced consecutive pop-pop-pop shots like that. I caught them all breaking out of their pose and not really knowing what was going on as my flashes kept coming nonstop. Some of the artists would then go into a new pose, while others just froze but everybody pretty much had a great time. I managed to drive out all the competing paparazzi who could only take one photo at a time which just didn't give the same thrill. Being the only paparazzo on the beat was essential to my game.

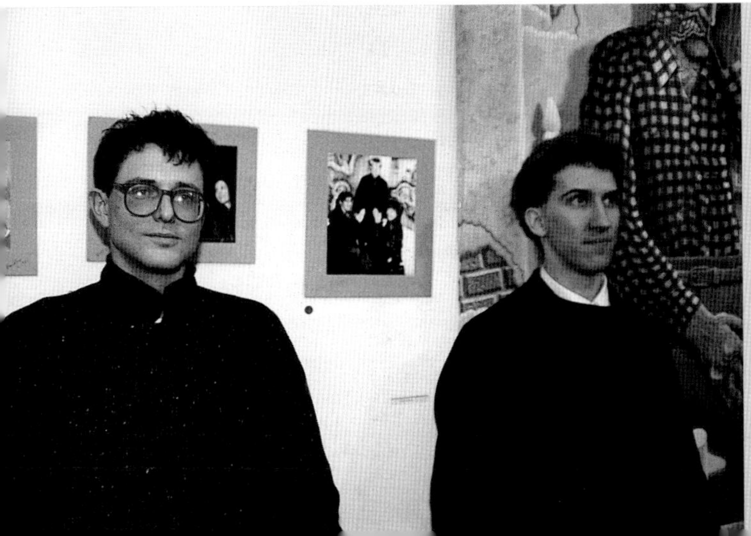

Artist Fred Tomaselli, who went to art school with Mark, was unknown during the East Village heyday. In the 1990s he became an art star, selling work to the Museum of Modern Art and the Whitney and appearing on the cover of Art In America.

Film-maker Tessa
Hughes-Freeland.
Painter David Sandlin
in the background.

I bribed the gossip columnist at the East Village Eye, Tony Heiberg (A/K/A "Tony Love") $75 to use my photographs with his monthly column. Otherwise all he got from the East Village Eye was a couple of free meals. I got a photographer's byline which was worth the

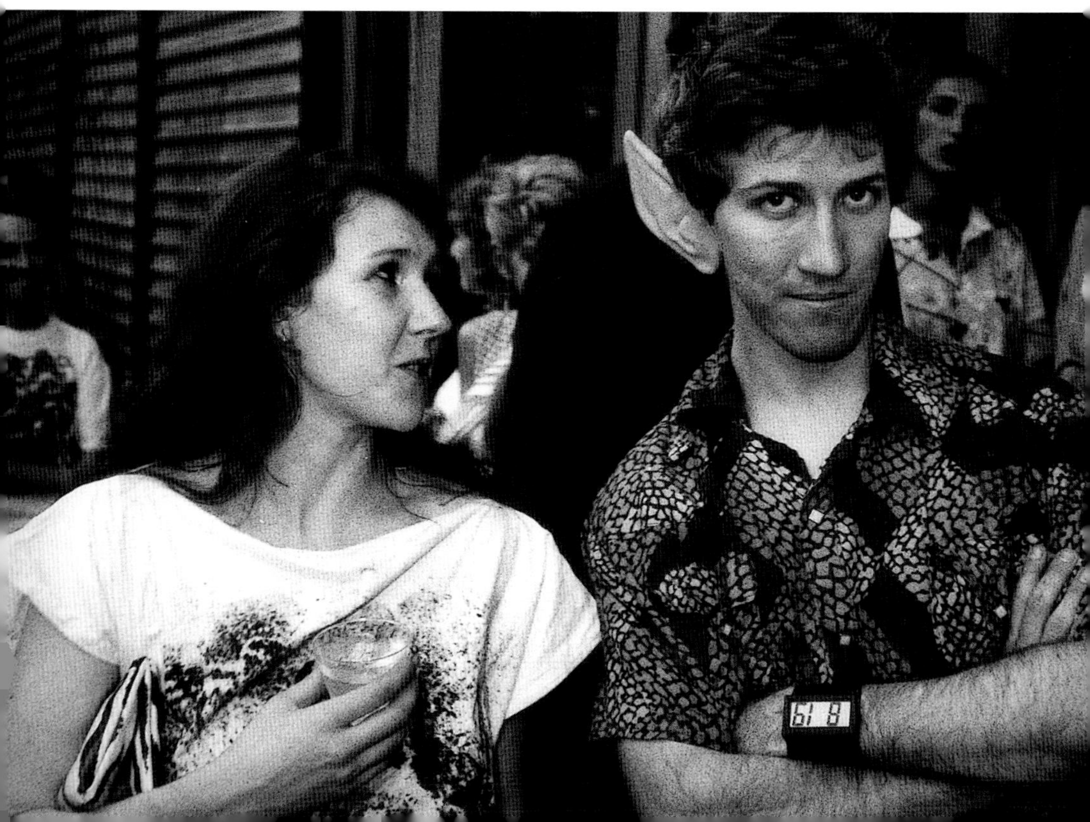

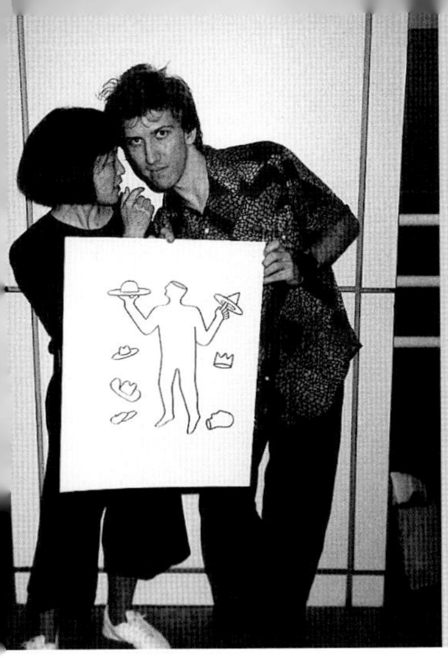

Hiroko Tanaka at Private Eyes nightclub where the doorman that night was Dolph Lundgren before he became an actor. Hiroko was a photographer and writer who frequently brought news of the East Village scene to the Japanese public. She and Mark introduced Timothy Greenfield-Sanders to Comme de Garcons who then hired him to photograph several famous artists in their clothes for a glamorous art-meets-fashion ad campaign.

bribe money right there in publicity to me. But much more importantly it meant that when I shot someone in a gallery they had a chance of being in the Eye that month. Since the artists were already going to the galleries to network and make career moves, being photographed and getting in the Eye just added another dimension to their gallery networking. At many of the openings I think I was the only person who was not an artist, because there were so few collectors showing up. I was also the only yuppie on the scene, which I was ashamed of, and the critic Steven Kaplan railed against me in a letter to the Eye, "So you've all been co-opted by Baird Jones' camera — beware! The misuse you experience will not be your own." Once I had the Eye as a regular gig, I was able to place my photos in some of the other downtown publications like the give-away rag The New Common Good. I even started getting some of my shots in the Learning Annex Magazine. By mid-1986, I started getting my pictures in Cover Magazine and its rival, Downtown Magazine. By then the East Village Eye had folded. Without that "star-making" motor drive pop-pop-pop it would not have been so overwhelming, especially since so many of the artists were drunk at the late night openings, which really multiplied the effect of the flash. At one of Mark's packed loft parties the translator Joachim Neugroschel actually tried to break my camera, out of rivalry I suppose. Over three years I spent $25,000 on film and development, but gifts of canvases from Mark helped defray the cost. I also traded photos of the artists for their

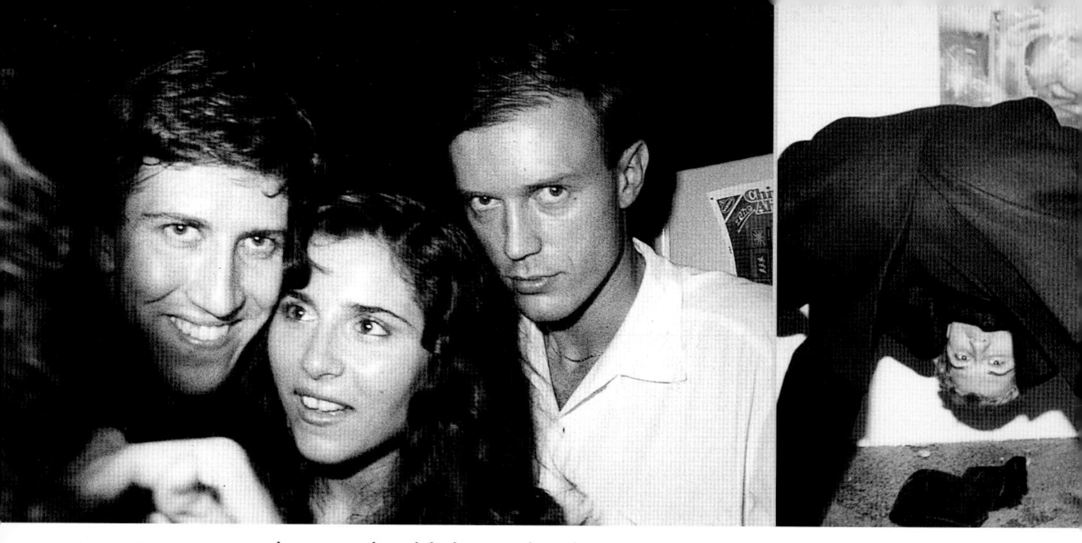

Artist Serena Bocchino and publisher Roland Hagenberg.

paintings, most of which ultimately turned out to be worthless but at the time were helpful in fleshing out the group shows I was curating.

Mark was a great mentor. I was always amazed at how tolerant he was to anonymous gallery-goers or alcoholic painters who approached him just to chat. Mark went out of his way to guide artists whom he encouraged and befriended. In many cases it ended with Mark feeling betrayed. The painter Martin Wong was an egregious example of such a friendship gone sour. Mark told me: "I met Martin Wong around 1982 while shopping for art supplies at Pearl Paint where he was a clerk. Martin would perch on the store's high storage balconies, like a strange enthusiastic clown, as he spoke to customers. He loved the graffiti artists who frequented Pearl Paint to buy or steal art supplies. Martin liked my work too, despite the fact that I was white and went to art school which he thought was uncool. He said my work was 'new wave,' like Keith Haring. At the time Martin was painting dragons and Chinatown imagery in an eccentric, hippy folk art style. He was showing his work in restaurants like Dojo's and funky bookstores. I encouraged him to pursue a more sophisticated contemporary look — focusing on buildings and bricks alone and to drop his prejudice against the white East Village art scene. He only liked young black and Hispanic graffiti artists and collected their art feverishly. He was repulsed by everything about the white East Village

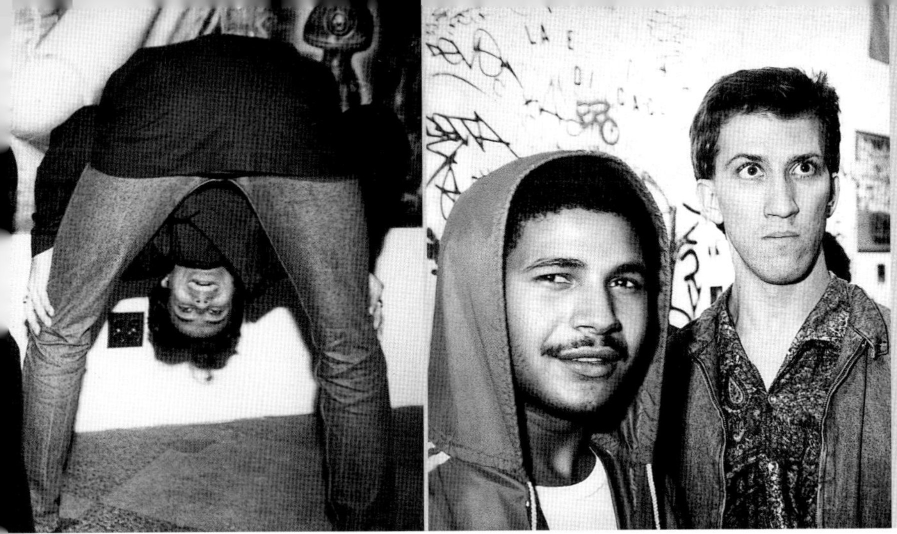

Daryl Trivieri moons in front of his artwork at the Chronocide Gallery.

Graffiti artist and Keith Haring collaborator LA II.

art scene. I told him if he wanted to be famous he should get on the East Village bandwagon. Martin did and started calling me his 'coach.' In fact he no longer addressed me as 'Mark' but as 'Coach.' We spoke for 3 hours every day while painting, he from his Clinton Street studio and me from my Rivington Street studio where Richard Hambleton was my landlord.

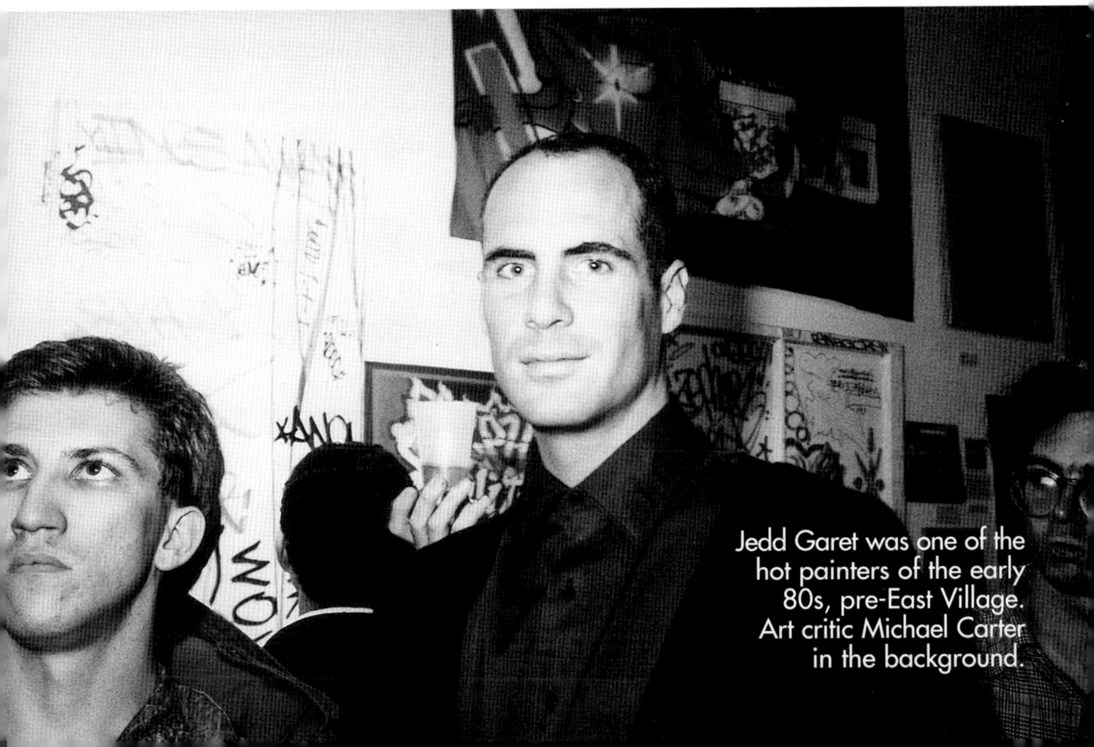

Jedd Garet was one of the hot painters of the early 80s, pre-East Village. Art critic Michael Carter in the background.

Arts Magazine (RIP) writer
Mark Frisk, India Northrop,
Gail Bach and D.D. Chapin.

I got him into about a dozen group shows and got him his dealer, Semaphore Gallery in SoHo. I also got him into a show at the Bess Cutler Gallery in SoHo which led the Metropoltan Museum to acquire one of his paintings. After a while I started noticing that he never returned the favors so one time when I could have got him into a specific group show, I didn't.

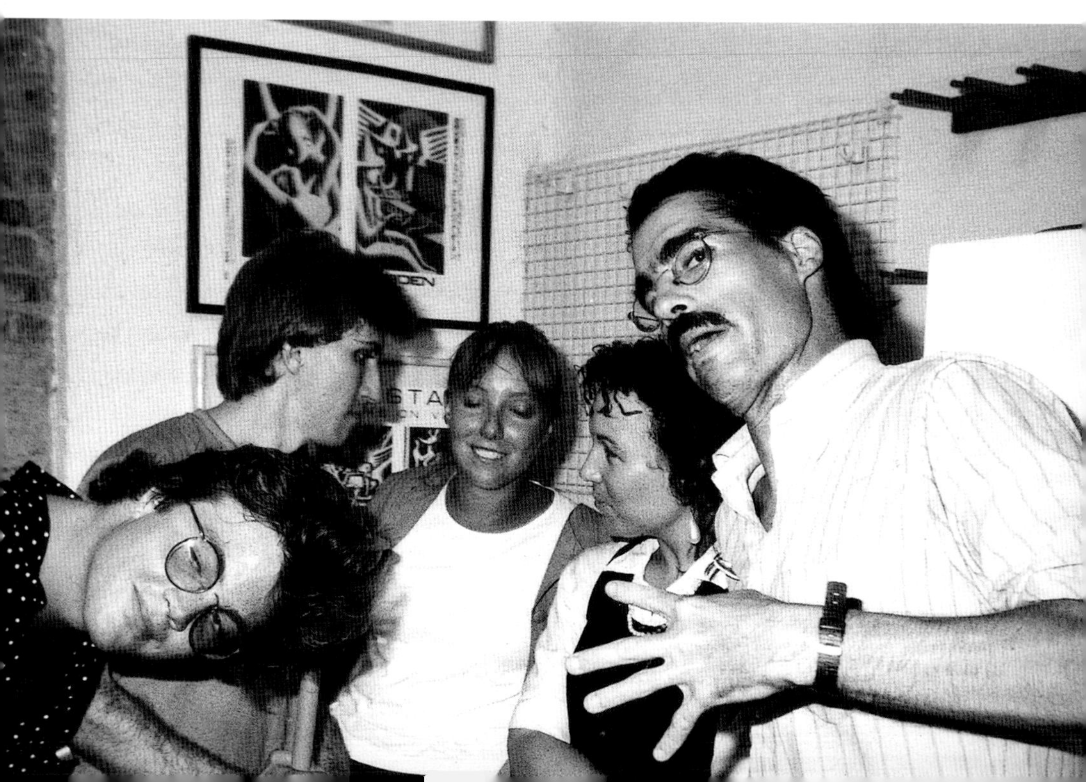

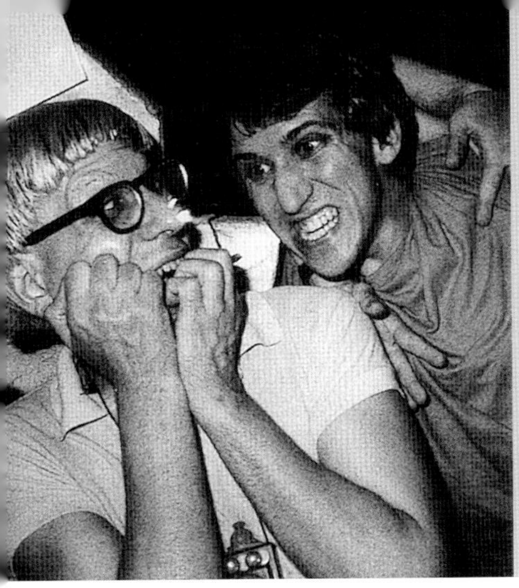

Performance artist Hapi Phace takes mock fright at ABC No Rio.

Martin got mad and asked me why. I explained and we had a falling out. Years later he encountered my brother Paul in an East Village restaurant and spat in his face, saying, 'This is for your brother.'"

Wong, who ultimately died of AIDS, confirmed Mark's view to me, admitting in 1985, "In the summer of 1983 I was working at Pearl's Paint selling paint. These graffiti artists used to come in with wads of one hundred dollar bills. I'd say, 'Where did you get that, guys?' and they'd laugh and say, 'From painting.' So I decided to become a painter. Kostabi pretty much pushed me into it. He convinced me to be an artist. I never really considered myself an artist but Mark kept insisting. He was trying to build up my confidence. He convinced me that the East Village was going to be something. Kostabi would call me up and tell me about a gallery show and then we would crash it. We'd just show up on the hanging date and put our paintings in the prominent places. We crashed a show by Gracie Mansion at Kamikaze in December, 1983. We just showed up. We didn't even bother to show up at the show itself as long as our paintings were up, it was just another show to crash. Then I think Gracie expected us to ask to join her gallery, but we never did. We also crashed shows at Danceteria, lots of one night shows at the Underground, the *Terminal* show at the Brooklyn Academy and nobody realized that we had just crashed the space. We just forced our way in, although I think Mark was actually invited most of the time and I was the one who was crashing.

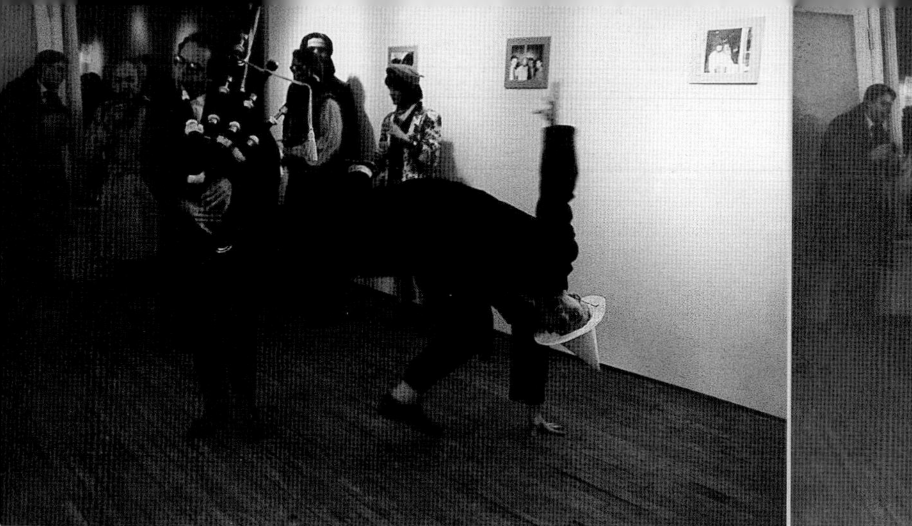
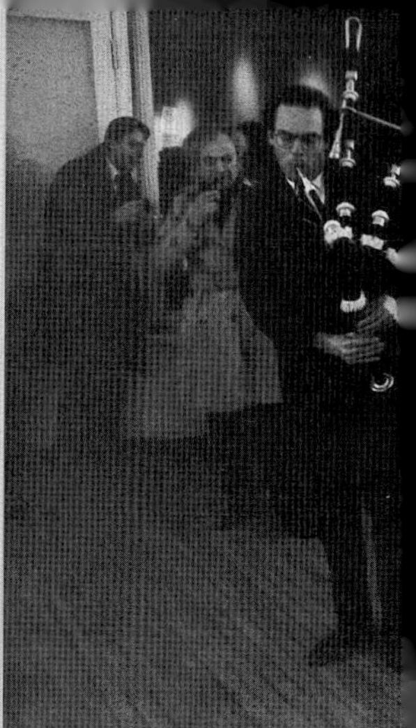

Michael Parkinson on the bagpipes at the 1986 *In Memory of Joseph Beuys* Kosthappening.

He was generous enough to bring me along into the shows."

When I was photographing, being a complete novice, I often screwed up the shot. Mark, instead of chastising me, would just say that one of his Kostabisms was that "Flaws are opportunities." There was always a sense that Mark could reverse weaknesses and in a surprise turnaround make them into strengths. Oddly, I felt that Mark could make his nerdiness, even an odd ugliness to his features, into a decisive strength as a photographer's model. In 1985 many of the people I interviewed commented on Mark's physical unattractiveness. His nerdy assistant at the time Stephen Klein, no Beau Brummel himself, said, "There is a flattening of Kostabi's features, his head reads like a Brancusi sculpture-head, almost like an abstraction of a face. His head also seems too big for his body, the nose, the ears and the eyes read as if they were just stuck on to the flat surface, just like Mr. Potato Head." The downtown film-maker Tessa Hughes Freeland told me in 1985, "When I first met Kostabi I thought, what an odd looking person, with this huge moon face, he could hardly speak to anyone, barely say hello. He lacked confidence. He doesn't like women very much." Yet Mark took this oddball look and spun it into a double-jointed, bizarre rubber man circus act while I photographed away in the summer of 1985. Similarly critic Walter Robinson told me in 1985, "Mark is an immigrant. That's why he comes off as weird – as a creepy kind of mutant. This

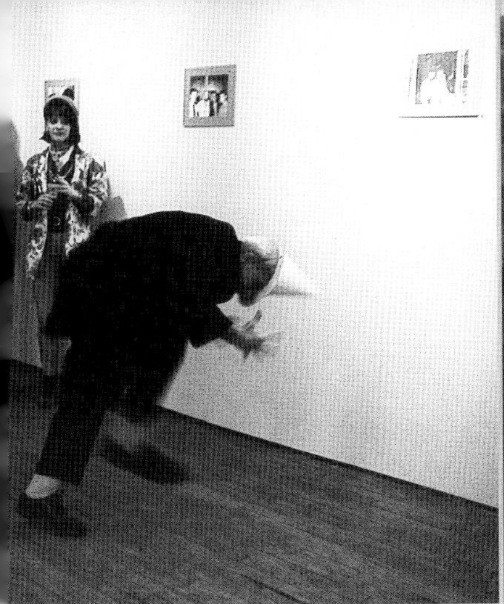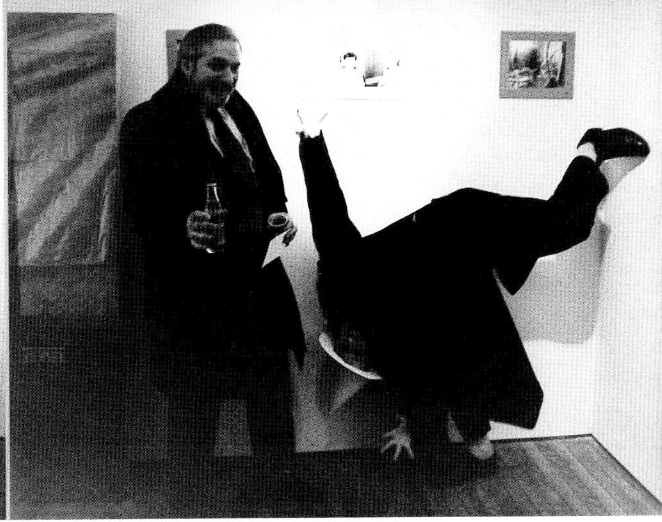

Gallerist Bill Simon at a Kosthappening.

strange mutant creature." Mark's real first name is Kalev in the same way that Paul was known to all in the East Village period as Ena, and as late as 1991 when I curated Paul's artwork at the New England Museum of Contemporary Art he wanted to formally show as Indrek Kostabi, all Estonian names. Mark told me he was always very conscious of his Estonian roots growing up in sunny California: "Even though we were living in an upper-middle class neighborhood in Whittier, California, and had a nice house on a hill with beautiful gardens and a great view which included the ocean and Catalina Island, for several years while I was in elementary school we had no car or TV. I was under the impression that we were poor and I felt ashamed of it to the point that I would lie to my friends in school that we did in fact have a car. Then I had to make up more lies to explain why no one ever saw it. Apparently my parents ran into financial difficulties sometime after buying the nice house in the nice neighborhood. My mother had to walk great distances regularly, carrying heavy bags of groceries. Some fellow students in school would continually make exaggerated imitations of my parents' strong Estonian accents. These cruel bullies would yell out things like 'Oola goola goola' in a high pitched voice which was supposed to represent my 'foreign' mother. They would also taunt me with reminders like 'you're poor, you're poor.' This early outsider status contributed enormously to my extreme ambition. I've always

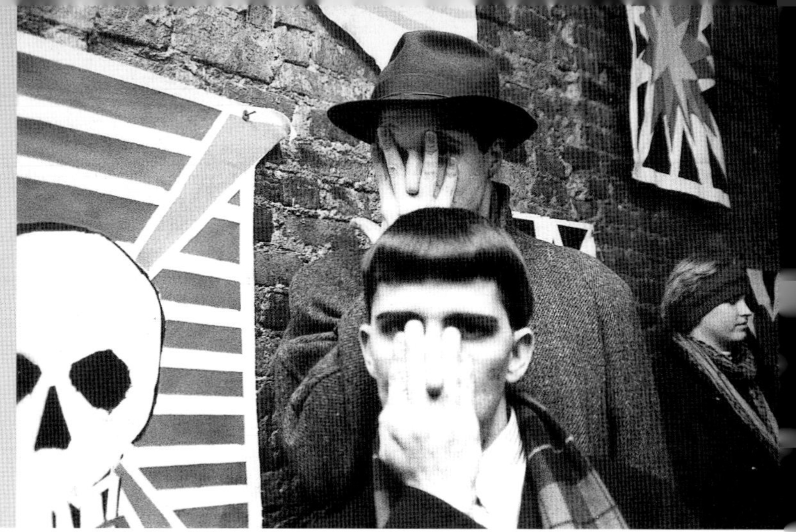

Chris Walker of the Paris Review. The Paris Review was well known for publishing drawings by artists the moment they became hot in the New York scene.

been motivated by an 'I'll Show Them' attitude." Even today Mark includes as the first sentence in his bio that his parents were immigrants.

But the East Village crowd was tolerant of unusual types which was a good thing since even downtown's most secure success stories seemed to bomb out unexpectedly. Right from the start in the East Village scene there were disconcerting flameouts. Civilian Warfare was a fantastic gallery on Avenue B which showed David Wojnarowicz, Greer Lankton and Richard Hambleton. Civilian Warfare was one of the true East Village pioneering spaces, opening on the same day in March, 1982 as another legendary East Village gallery, Nature Morte. The owner of Civilian Warfare was Alan Barrows who was urbane and charismatic. But one day the gallery was just shuttered and all the artists were dejectedly walking around saying that Alan had just fled in the middle of the night owing them money and the rent was way past due. I never saw Barrows again. His partner, Dean Savard, who was such a nice guy and who apparently had financed most of the gallery's expenses by selling heroin, died of AIDS shortly after that.

The gallery which took over the Civilian Warfare space was Chronocide. They represented Joe Coleman, a painter and performance artist who made his reputation by strapping explosives to his chest under his raincoat and then detonating them in the middle of his performances, which was a shocking and masterful presentation. His detailed and

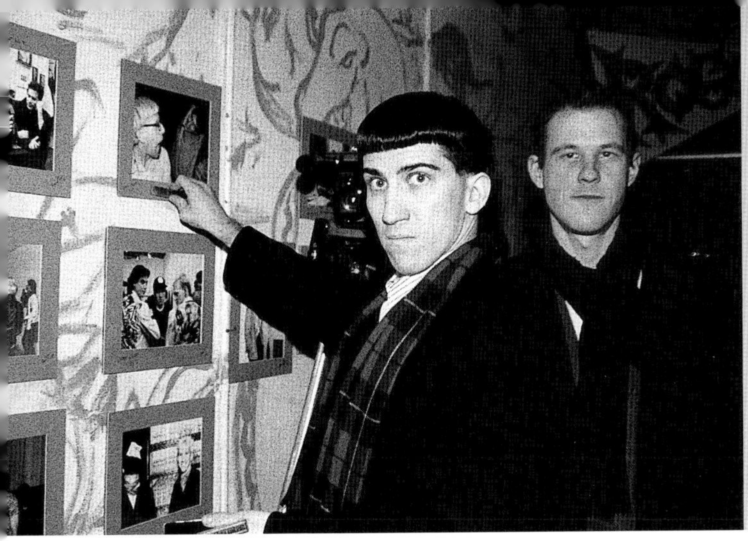

Painter Edward Brezinski at the Kosthappening at the Terror Street Gallery. Brezinski left for Berlin for several years after the East Village movement collapsed.

ghoulish paintings still command a cult following. Chronocide Gallery seemed to have struck gold with the painter Daryl Trivieri who became a close friend of Mark Kostabi. Trivieri looked like he might become, if not the next Haring, perhaps the next Kostabi. But then it was discovered that Trivieri had sold to Kostabi pal Joachim Neugroschel 103 drawings for $50 each when Mark was getting $500 a drawing — so it was just too much of a bargain. The discovery casually came up in a conversation between Mark and Joachim. Oddly, the drawings were awful fakes, almost as if Trivieri wanted to get caught. Neugroschel went to the police and Trivieri disappeared immediately. So Joachim lost over $5000. It turned out that Trivieri was an out-of-control heroin addict. Mark said,

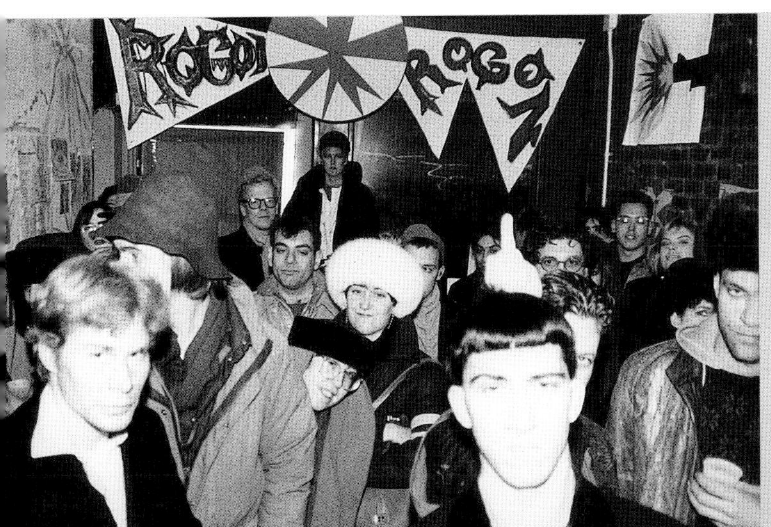

The Kosthappening at Terror Street Gallery: On the left is Logan Evans whose family was co-owner of the Yankees before George Steinbrenner. In the background is gallerist Jon Gerstad of Nolo Contendere Gallery. To the right is FA-Q.

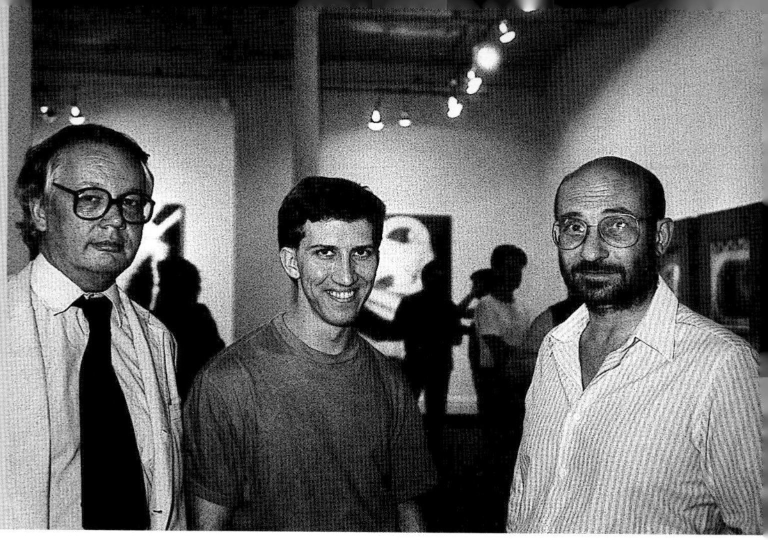

"Joachim would buy three drawings a week. Daryl told Joachim that I had traded drawings for Daryl's canvases. Joachim believed him but then he got suspicious and finally told me." The case dragged on for a while after that because, as Mark told me, Joachim strangely and persistently wanted the forged drawings back from the police, which the cops refused to go along with. No one ever saw Daryl Trivieri again although Mark heard he tried to do the same thing with forging other artists' work later on.

AIDS ultimately swept through the East Village artists taking an horrendous toll: Keith Haring, David Wojnarowicz, the portrait photographer Peter Hujar, Tim Greathouse, Luis Frangella, Arch Connelly, the curator Nicholas Moufourrage (who was very active in the South Bronx), Red Spot, much later Martin Wong, nightclubbers Haoui Montaug, Madonna's best friend Martin of the Lucky Strike Bar, John Sex, writers Cookie Mueller and Paul Taylor and many others. Since so many of the East Village artists were junkies who shared needles, AIDS spread via contaminated needles as well as through gay sex. When I showed the photographer Jimmy DeSana at the Nassau County Museum of Fine Art in 1987 in a show I guest curated there, DeSana was already suffering from AIDS. He wanted to show the self-portrait, *Rope*, in the group show. *Rope* (which was also in the collection of William Burroughs and had shown at one of the earliest Colab shows in Washington D.C.) showed DeSana hanging from a noosed rope, naked with a hard-on. The Long

Island pooh-bahs ruled that the erection should be covered with a red sticker, which brought such outcries of censorship that DeSana went on a local radio station in protest and hundreds of AIDS activists showed up to picket the museum. The museum was forced to never use that annex

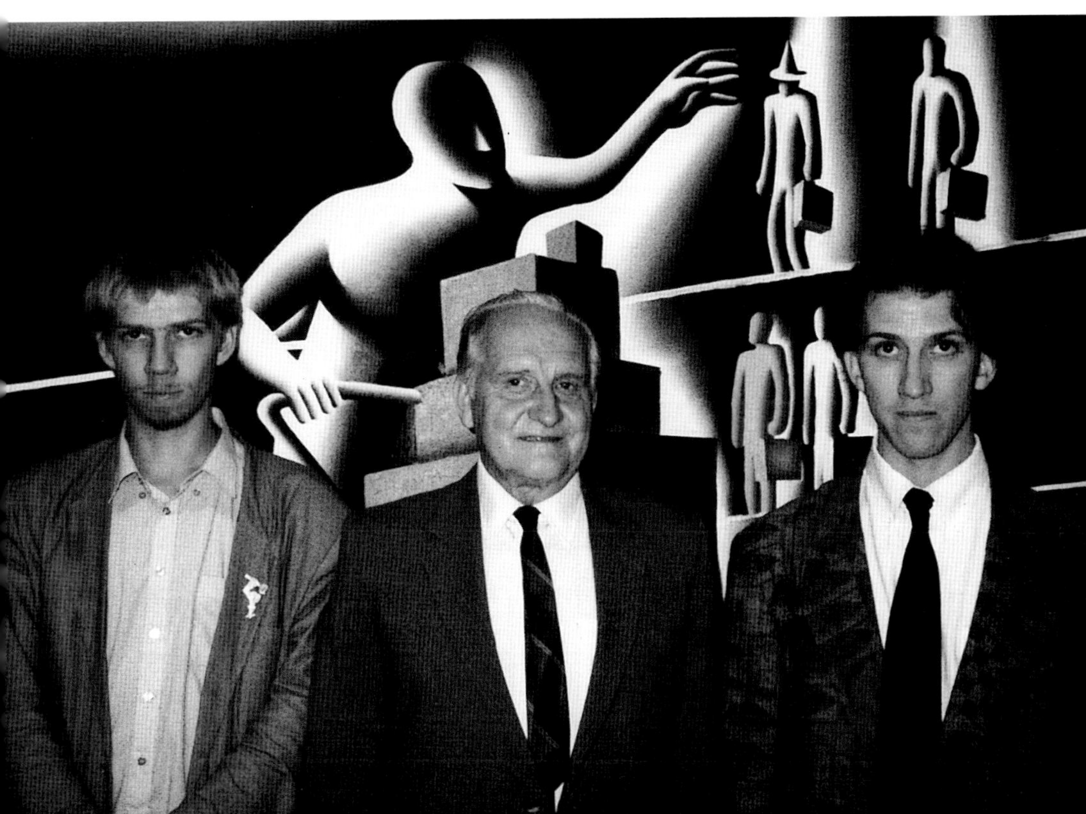

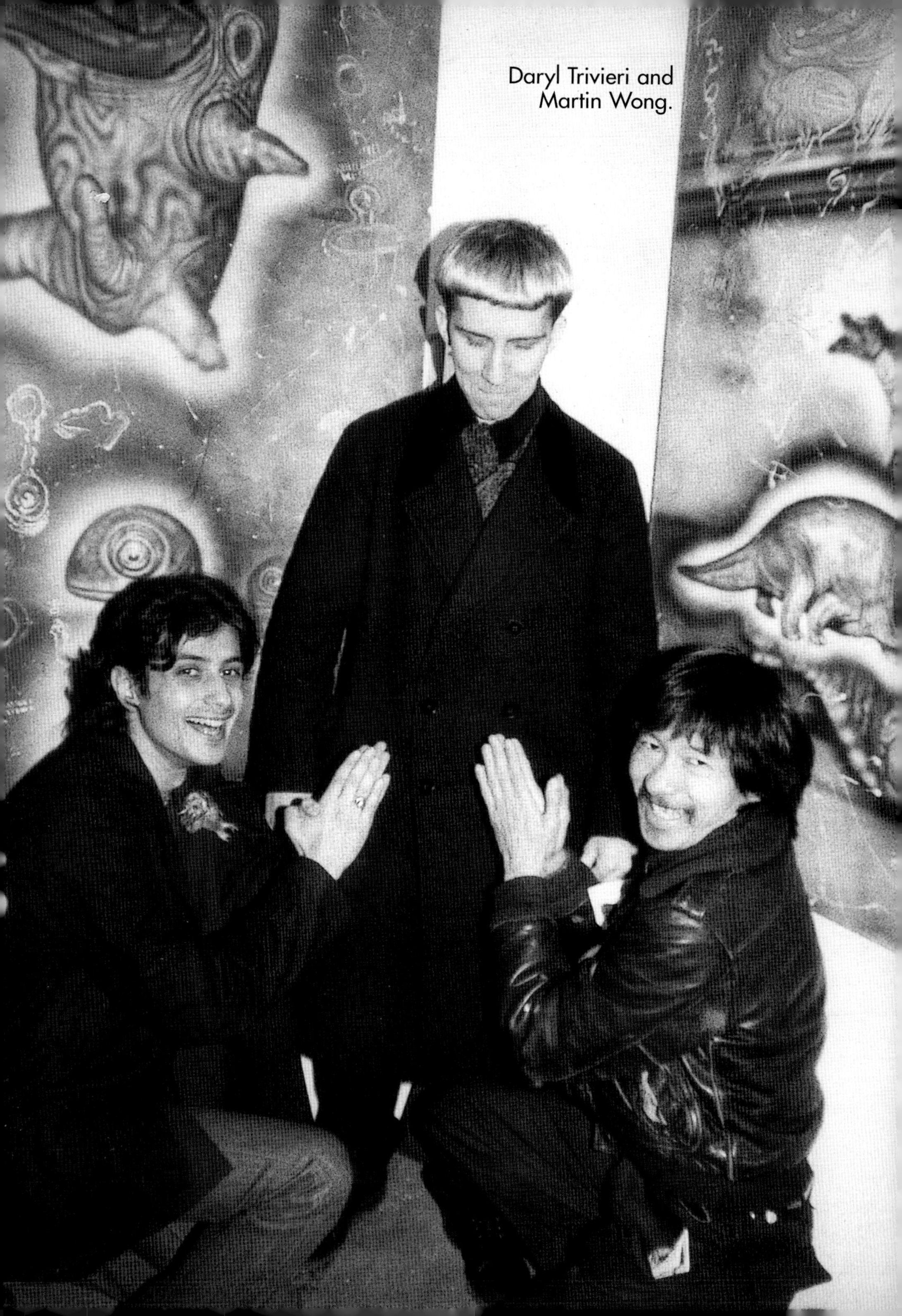

Daryl Trivieri and
Martin Wong.

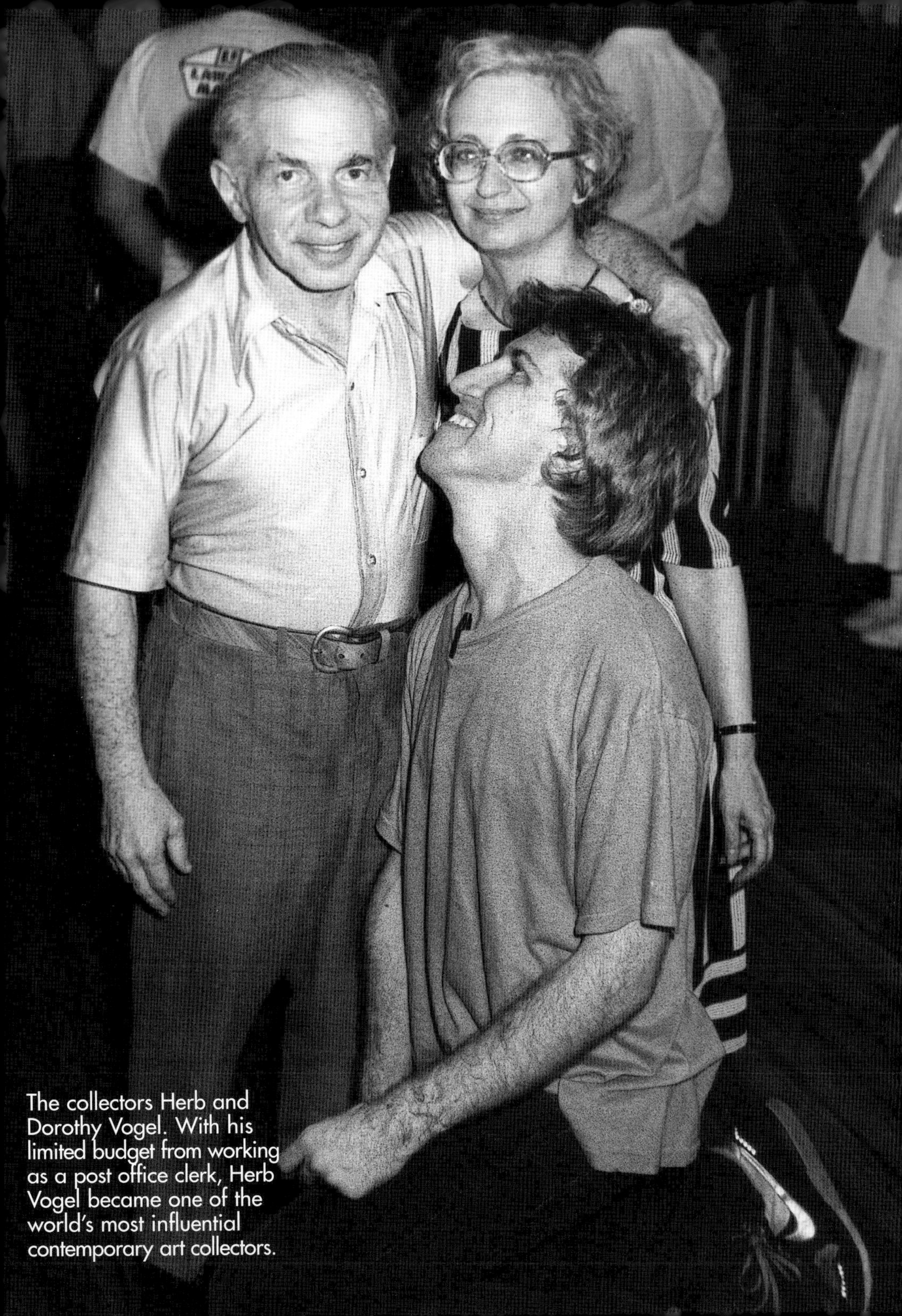

The collectors Herb and Dorothy Vogel. With his limited budget from working as a post office clerk, Herb Vogel became one of the world's most influential contemporary art collectors.

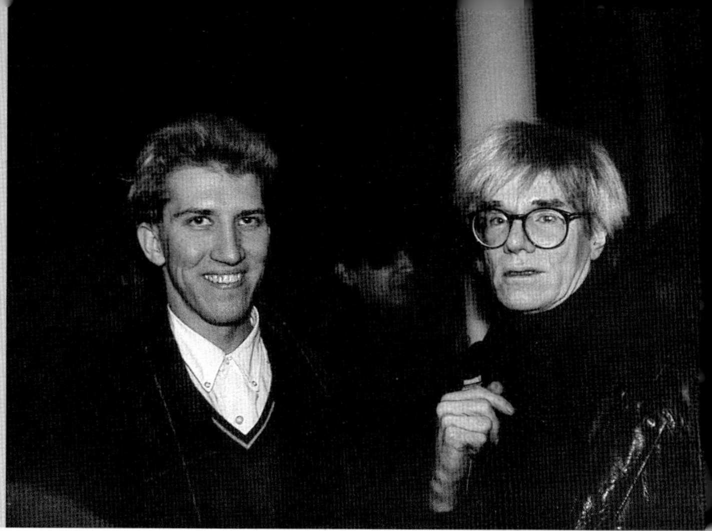

Andy.

building again for exhibits. The museum officials never spoke to me again, but DeSana was grateful to me until his death two years later. We had a ceremonial unveiling of that photograph at the Tunnel where club director Rudolf peeled off the sticker. Everyone made jokes about how small DeSana's genitals were but there were few jokes about what AIDS did to the downtown artworld.

Many felt that Keith Haring was incapable of expressing sorrow with his art (his memorial to the concentration camps is considered by most his least effective artwork). The same could be said of Rodney Alan Greenblat's monotonously upbeat cartoon visions. The happy face mood of graffiti-inspired East Village expressionism just didn't click with grief.

Mark had begun changing his hairstyles constantly at this point, Terror Street Gallery.

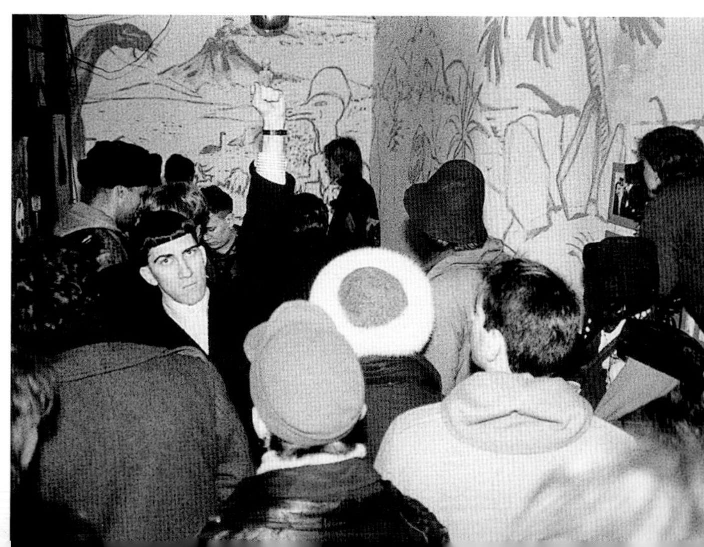

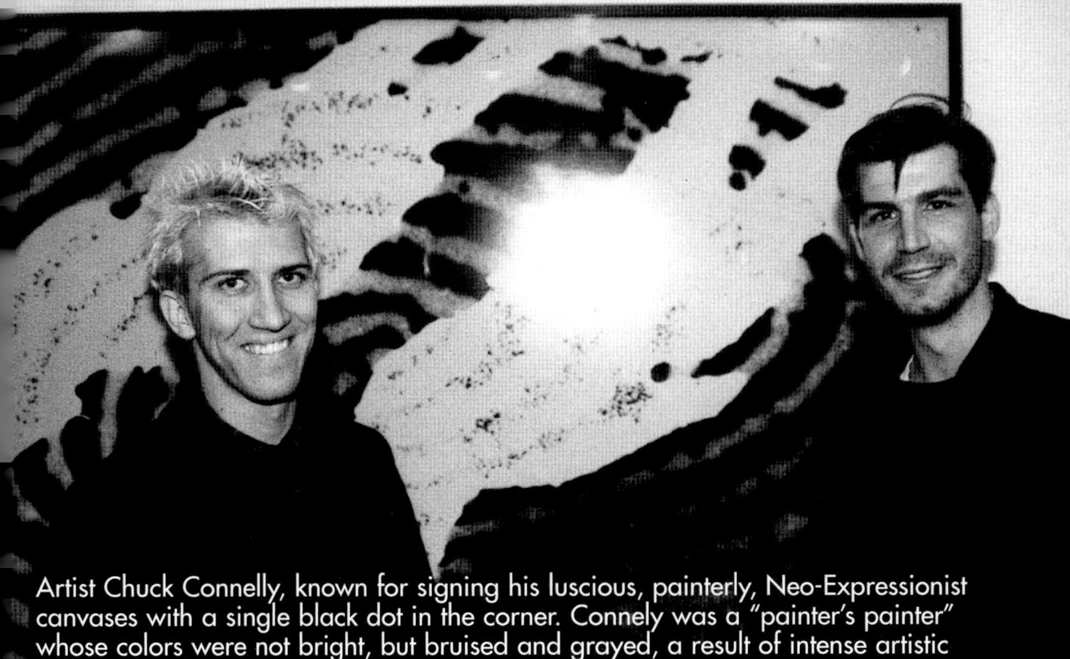

Artist Chuck Connelly, known for signing his luscious, painterly, Neo-Expressionist canvases with a single black dot in the corner. Connely was a "painter's painter" whose colors were not bright, but bruised and grayed, a result of intense artistic battle and multiple reworking of the canvas.

The Kostabisms "Sadness is When the Video Store is Closed," or "'Do you feel pain at other people's misfortune?' Answer: 'Only when I laugh.'" comes the closest of any 1984 East Village inspiration to dealing with melancholy through its pure shallowness. Kostabi's work deals with emptiness, negating both joy and sorrow, ultimately placing him in the best position to deal with the "party's over" defeatism of the end of the East Village movement in 1987.

Perhaps no artist illustrates the unexpected "decline of the East Village in 1987" phase better than Judy Rifka. Rifka had cut her teeth during the all important Colab days in the early 1980s. Judy Rifka played all the right political games, and her early association with Colab got her, along with word artist Jenny Holzer, into two Whitney Biennials. Showing at Brooke Alexander Gallery in SoHo, she had just the right mix of East Village sass and SoHo stability that her canvases were in the ten to fifteen thousand dollar range and her SoHo shows typically sold out. Her stretched canvases over bumpy frames had become a signature style and her distinctive jumpy drawing line was all her own as well. I gave a Rifka

Tama Janowitz's *Slaves of New York* was cast as a movie by Merchant and Ivory during the heyday of the East Village scene. I ended up with a very small part in it.

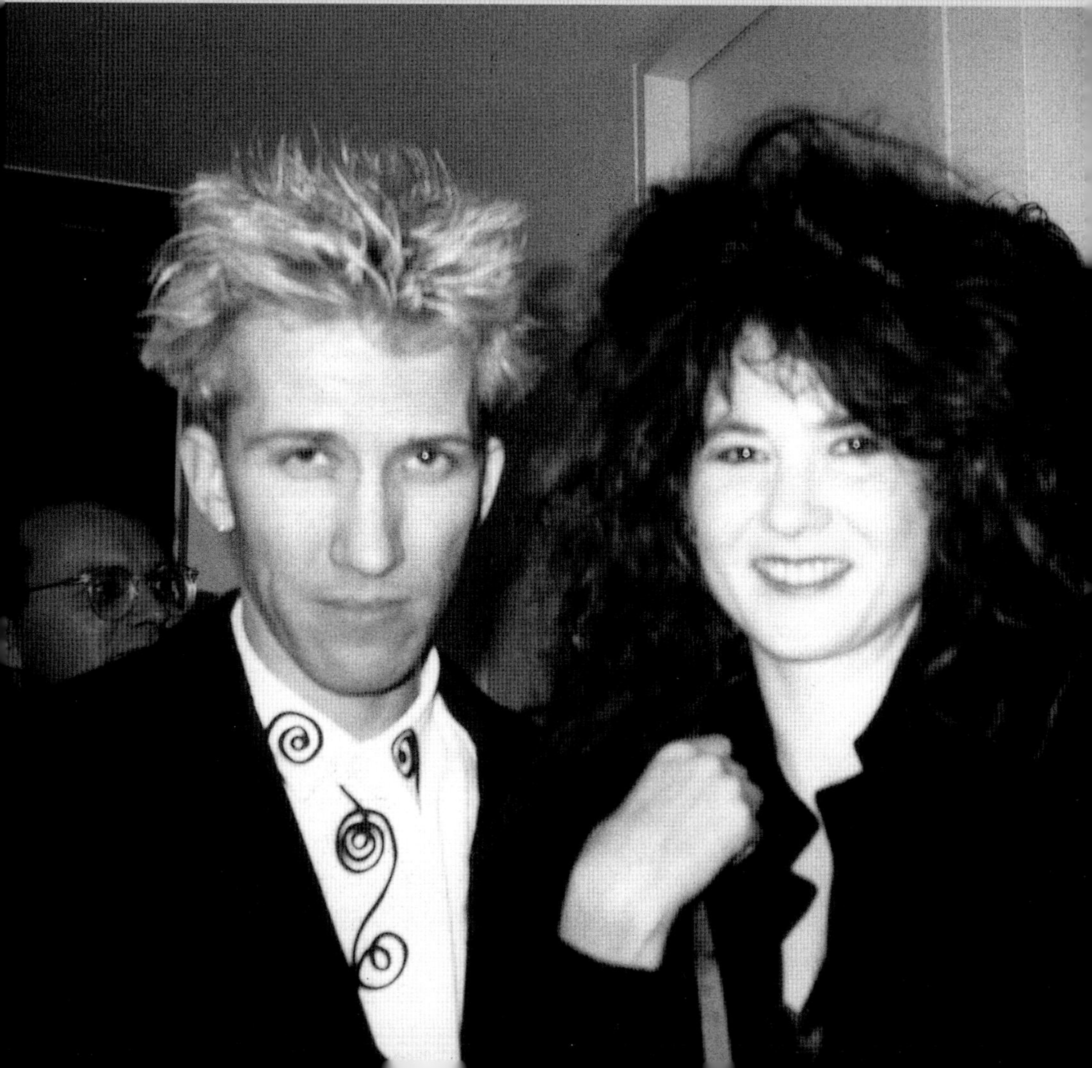

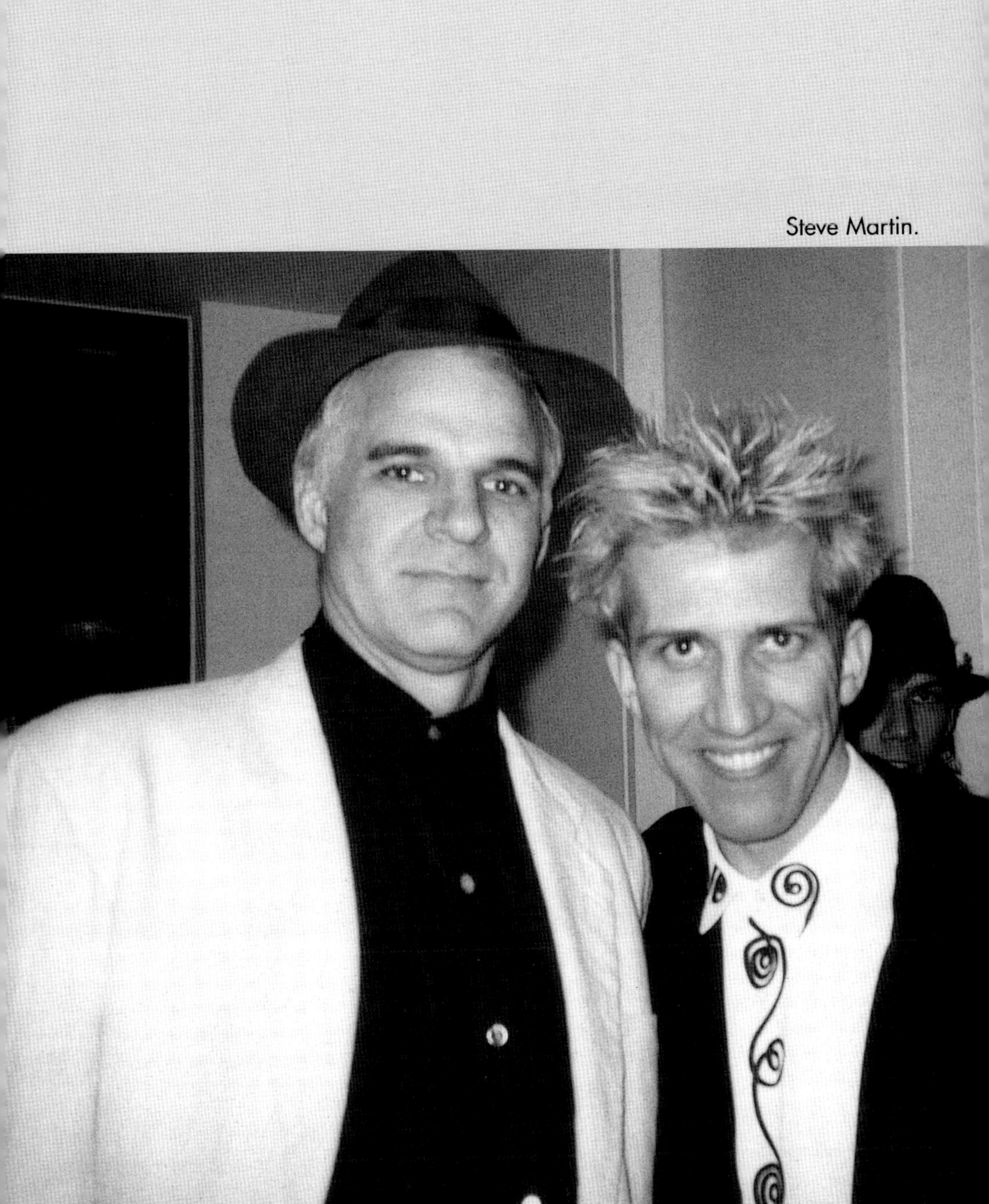

Steve Martin.

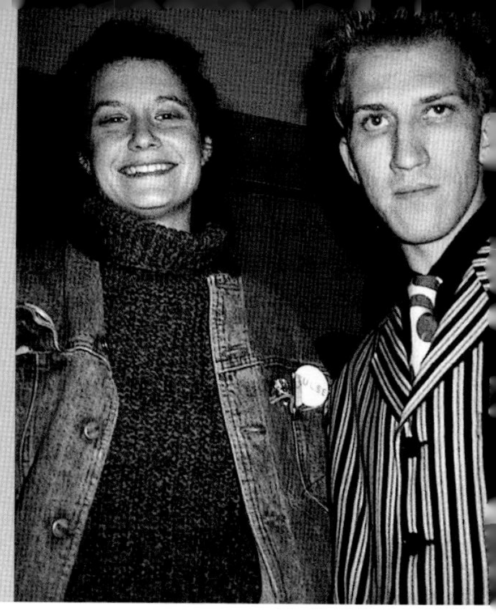

Karen Finley's outrageous performances made it logical for her to follow in Andres Serrano's footsteps as the avant-garde's next censorship superstar but her moment of glory never seemed to arrive. The downtown scene just dimmed out too quickly in the late 80s and early 90s to support any new stars.

print to the Metropolitan Museum in 1986 after she was on the cover of Art in America with a rave write-up for her *Acropolis Series*. But when the East Village movement faded in 1987 it reached out and dragged her right down with it. She never got into another Whitney Biennial. Rifka's relationship with Brooke Alexander ended in acrimony and threats of litigation as the gallery closed. She appears to have had scant gallery representation in NYC for the last fifteen years. Judy is now seldom seen in person in New York galleries although she lives in the city. Her art is even less visible. Even among radical political artists such a precipitous decline is rare. Yet Rifka was only an East Village artist by association. One would have thought she could have sidestepped the negative momentum.

In July 1987 I wrote a story for Downtown Magazine, *Are Mark Kostabi and the East Village One and the Same?* Downtown Magazine had given me a regular two page photo spread but I had gotten an additional one page feature assignment tacked on which that week I devoted to Mark. In a fluke that story proved a significant launching pad because it caught the eye of New York Magazine which then gelled into the People Magazine story on Mark (perhaps helped along by the fact that my father, Cranston Jones, was the Senior Editor at People). Mark told me, "The way I remember it was that it directly caught the eye of Matthew Rose, who then wrote a one page article on me for New York Magazine, which led to CNN and many other mass media pieces about 'Mark Kostabi — the artist who doesn't paint his own paintings.' One of my big goals was always to be in People Magazine. After researching and learning that their art writer was Michael Small, I called him about 10 times, for about a year, to pitch him my story. The fact that Cranston Jones was a Senior Editor of People might have helped but I'm not sure. Baird definitely deserves credit for breaking the 'Mark Kostabi who doesn't paint his own paintings' story, which in general made me extremely famous."

My Downtown Magazine feature on Mark listed out the usual flattery litany which Mark adored like the fact that he had been the youngest living artist ever collected by the Museum of Modern Art. I had to phrase it like that because there were a bunch of young dead European

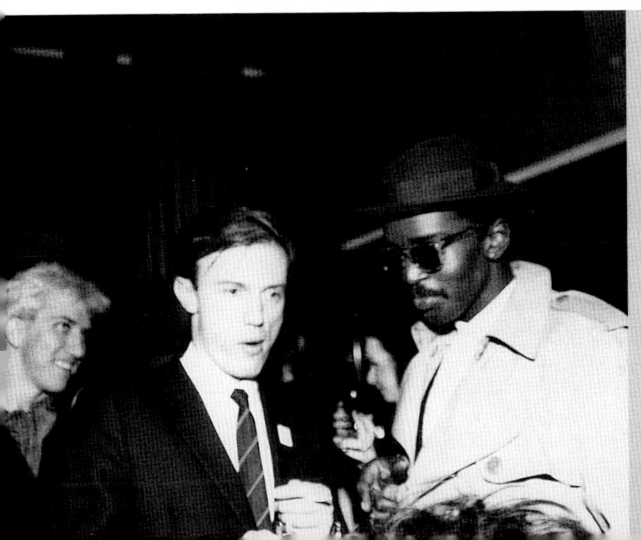

Publisher Roland Hagenberg and Freddie Brathwaite ("Fab Five Freddie"). At one point rap and graffiti were at an equal level, but rap quickly out-distanced its painting partner. Brathwaite is now known mainly for his musical appearances on MTV but at one time he was also a prominent graffiti writer.

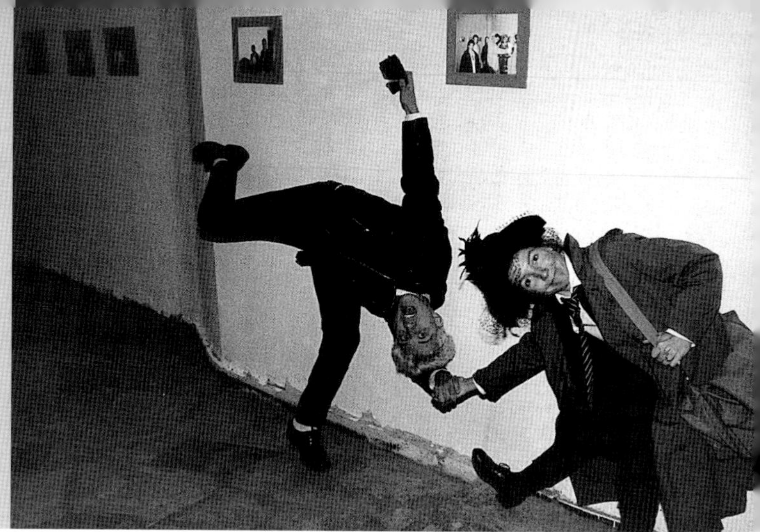

Lady McCrady
dances at the
Kosthappening
at Ground Zero.

sculptors whom MoMA had acquired who had died during WWI so we were never sure it was completely true about Mark actually being "the youngest living." Apparently the youngest posthumously acquired artist was Gaudier Brezka who died at 19 in WWI. Mark had been only 24 when MoMA picked up the Fashion Moda print portfolio in 1985. The other artists included in that portfolio were Rick Prol, Fashion Moda co-director James Poppitz, Crash, Leon Golub, Ronnie Cutrone and Daze, all of whom were older than Mark.

Then there was Mark's astonishing claim that in 1985 he had been in 450 group and solo shows. I was showing Mark every chance I got, at least once a week. Once on a rainy Sunday afternoon we went

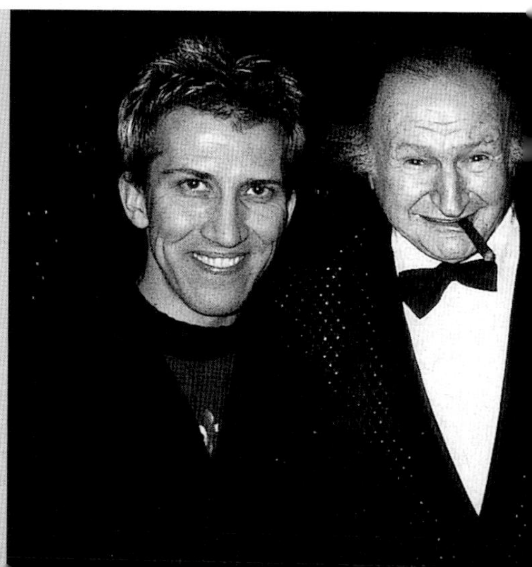

Grandpa Munster
and *Car 54,
Where Are You?*
actor Al Lewis.

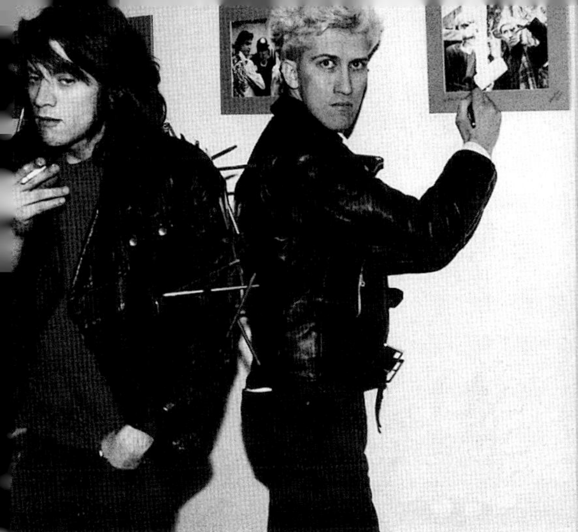

Ground Zero Gallery owner James Romberger at the Kosthappening at his gallery.

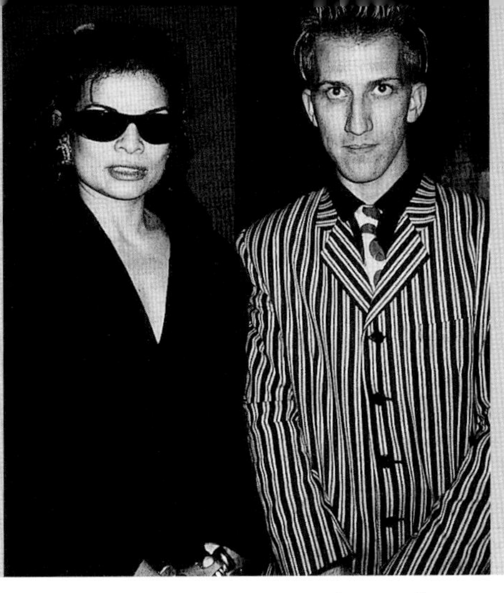

Bianca Jagger was a regular at the gallery receptions, often escorted by painter Ross Bleckner.

down to ABC No Rio where I had put together a group show with the striking title *East Village Greatest*, featuring Brian Goodfellow, Kim Keever, Fashion Moda founder Stefan Eins and a few other East Village painters. I often put these high fallutin' titles on the shows because I thought they looked great on the artists' resumes. There was an unexpected poetry reading going on in the main room at ABC No Rio, so we had to put the show in a side hall. Then they would not let us put nails in the walls so we ended up just putting the artwork on the floor, leaning against the wall. The cramped place was soon mobbed with people going down on one knee to look at the art. The show was really just for the reception. We took the art back after two hours, a real guerrilla show. Few of the artworks were for sale since I owned almost everything except for one painting Stefan Eins was unsuccessfully trying to sell for thirty bucks. It was common at the East Village shows in the mid-80s for down-and-out artists to show up and try to hawk their painting for next to nothing. When the laws changed and psychiatric hospitals starting disgorging patients onto the streets in the late 80s and the homeless ranks swelled enormously, the whole storefront/street gallery reception experience was changed. Homeless people were drawn to the scene. Real beggars started invading for the wine and the company, and in the winter for the warmth. But during the

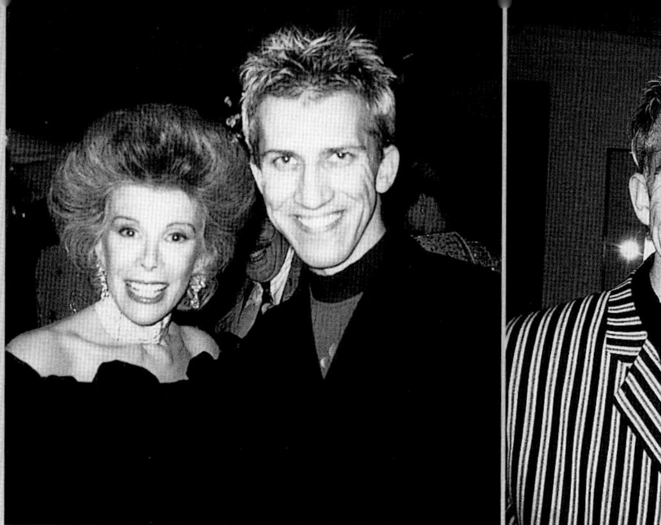

William Wegman,
1970s Video Art

East Village heyday only the painters were panhandling and the begging had no stigma to it. But the artists hardly ever sold their paintings even with a big discount. For instance, I managed to buy two Jean-Michael Basquiat artworks at Jennifer Ex Bowen's Pyramid Club auction in 1986 for ten dollars apiece because I was the only person present that had any cash available for the purchase. I later sold them both uptown for $500 each. They were the color xeroxes that Basquiat had hawked for a dollar apiece in front of the Museum of Modern Art in 1980 and which David Bowie as Andy Warhol is seen buying with Dennis Hopper at the beginning of Julian Schnabel's movie *Basquiat.*

Jean-Michel Basquiat seems to be the East Village artist whose reputation has best survived the decline of the Loisaida aesthetic. Yet the reasons for his sustained momentum seem obscure. Many parvenues copied his mannerisms but could not duplicate his success. Basquiat's last assistant, Rick Prol, so aped his signature style that it became almost embarrassing. Prol rapidly disappeared as a legit player in the art market despite several positive reviews in the prestigious Art in America. The art critics Peter Frank and Michael McKenzie coauthored the book *New, Used and Improved,* which featured many of Basquiat's images, yet their views on Basquiat could not be more divergent. McKenzie told me, "Basquiat's work is simply fake naive art that was sponsored by greed and pathetic guilty white

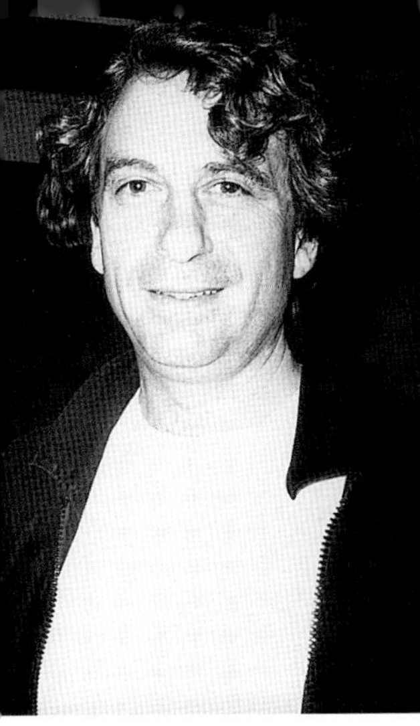

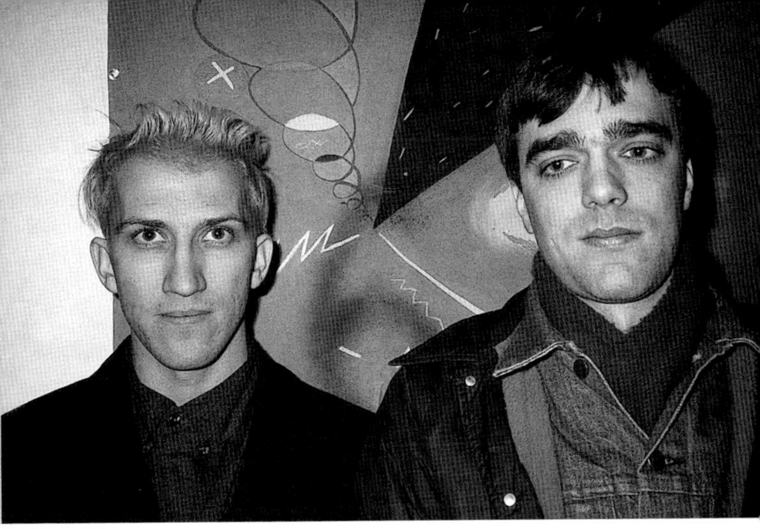

pioneer, although best known
for his dog photographs.

Painter Rich Collichio who was
the director of the 51X Gallery.

liberalism. Basquiat's biggest talent was convincing guilty white liberals that they didn't understand him because he was a poor black man, which, of course, he wasn't but rather a middle class con man. Basquiat was just a no-talent drug abusing con man who had enough money to pretend and enough con man in his blood to violin guilty white liberals. Maybe the white art world wants a black art hero who is a drug addict. Basquiat registered with me as a disgusting no-talent hustler." While Peter Frank countered, "Basquiat was a success partly because he moved the graffiti aesthetic into the fine art realm without reducing and taming graffiti itself, which he was able to by not really doing graffiti in the first place but by

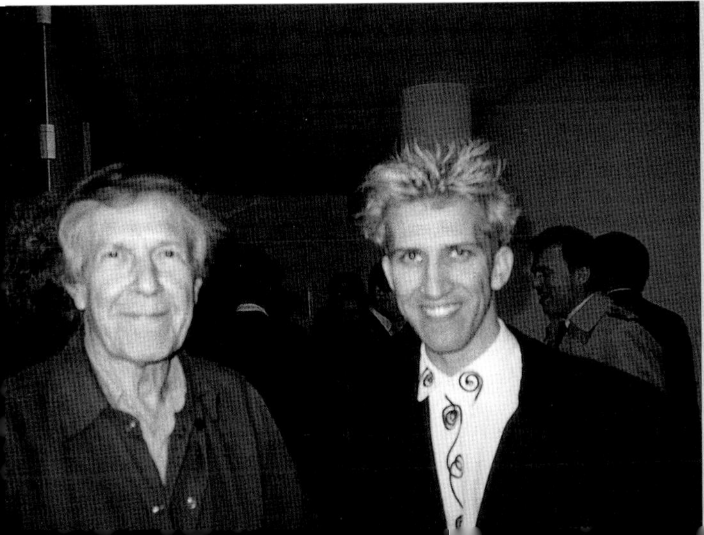

Avant-garde
composer John Cage.

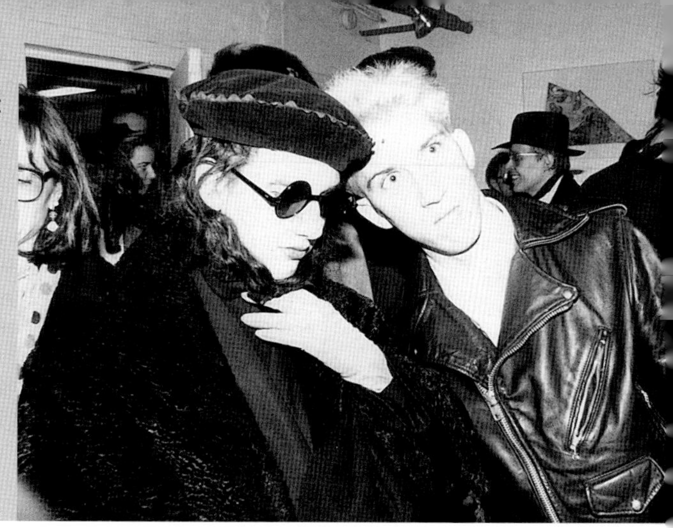

Sex tips writer Anka Radakovich, sister of East Village painter Jim Radakovich. To the left is painter Anne Shostrom. In the background is the ubiquitous Bernd Naber.

doing graffiti-influenced art. He was both a brilliant, committed artist in command of powerful native talent, insatiable curiosity and a supple social cleverness." Although Basquiat inspired the East Village artists aesthetically, and although he hung out constantly in the scene, he had climbed quite a different career ladder. Novelist Tama Janowitz recalled going to several receptions in 1983 that Jean-Michel's then-girlfriend Interview Magazine's advertising director Paige Powell organized for him in her spacious West 79th Street apartment. The path to JMB's ultimate collaboration with Andy Warhol was begun then with Powell's prim invitations printed on Tiffany stationary. That kind of career trajectory is not an Avenue A networking route, but one based on connections and greased with uptown money.

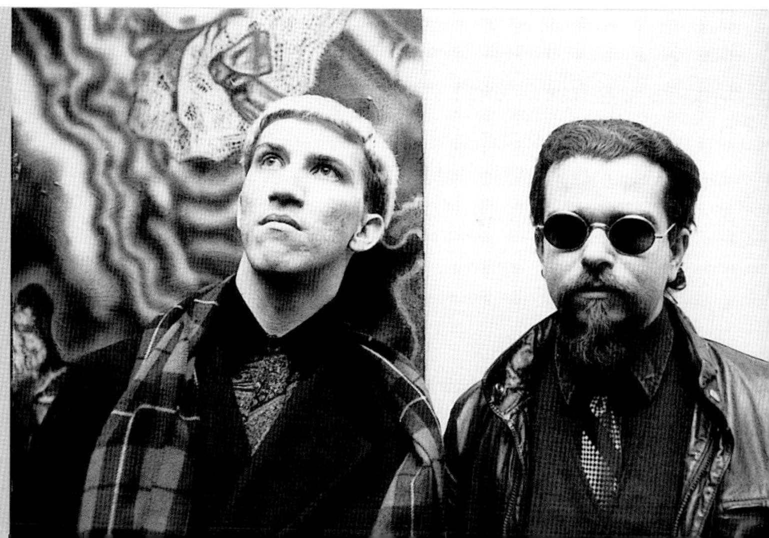

Artist Joe Coleman, known for his imaginative, visionary paintings and for his shocking performances where he sometimes bit off the heads of live rats.

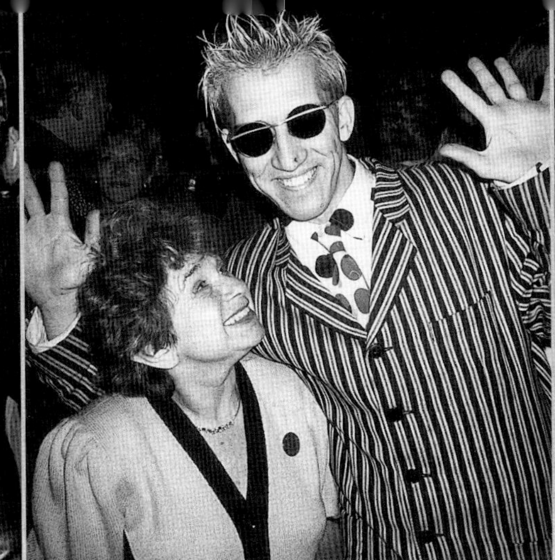

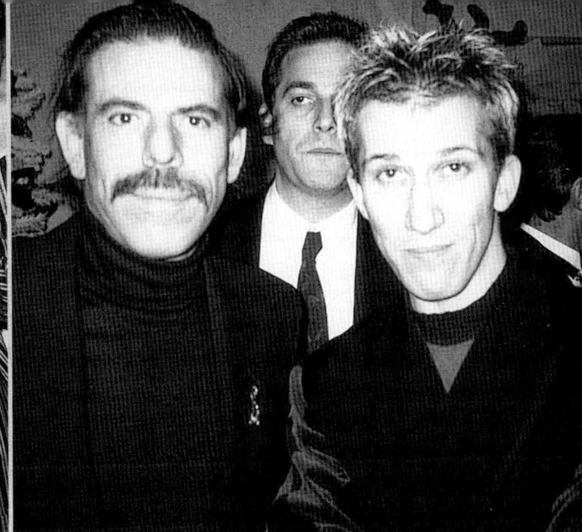

Ruth Westheimer seems to notice that Mark's clothing and sunglasses are becoming increasingly bizarre.

Peter Max.

In 1985, Mark was giving me art constantly. Even though he was totally generous about it all, I still used to get him to sign contracts. Technically I always gave him at least fifteen dollars for each painting. Once I bought a large painting, *Amateurs Imitate - Professionals Steal*, for fifteen dollars. I got Mark to sign a contract and that way I figured it would be tougher for Mark to later renege on the deal if he changed his mind and wanted the painting back. Just as we finished the contract, James Danziger, who would later own a top photography gallery, came in and bought a comparable canvas for fifteen thousand dollars while I just sat there choking on my guffaws. By the time I was through the summer of 1985, Mark had given me eight canvases (and one huge painting by Daze) and I was showing them around the clock, although Mark had a knack for naming the gifts in an insulting manner, one of them he even called *Piss Poor*. I tried to convince one hick critic that this title only meant Mark was dead broke when he painted it but that line wasn't convincing. Ultimately I curated Mark Kostabi solo shows with those gift paintings at the Paterson Museum (NJ), at the New England Museum of Contemporary Art (Brooklyn, Ct), Stamford Museum (CT) and in group shows at the Nassau County Museum of Fine Art and at the Museum of Cartoon Art at Ryebrook, NY. So in 1985 of the 450 shows Mark was claiming, I was probably responsible for seventy of them.

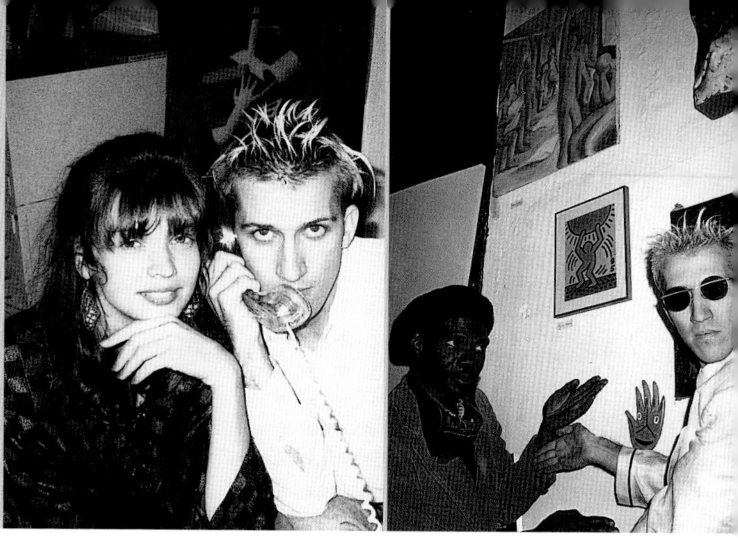

Thom Corn at Fashion Moda in the South Bronx. In the background is Mark's painting, *Piss Poor* above a Keith Haring and Rodney Alan Greenblat's *Hand*.

Mark joined the Ronald Feldman Gallery in Soho in the fall of 1985. Ronald Feldman told me that he was attracted to Mark because "I felt that Mark was an artist who took chances." When Mark pulled out of the East Village scene he took his name off the exhibit roster where it was usually the top name. But he was also great at showing up at the receptions, typically in outrageous garb and many times with an entourage or with a critic or a big player like Molly Barnes, perhaps followed by me and my motordrive camera. In a small world, like the "Global East Village," an eight person group show might feature Mark as the big name, four painters from the gallery stable, maybe a big name like Keith Haring that was actually not for sale but was from the gallery owner's personal collection and then a few new names that were on tryout and if they sold they had a chance to join the gallery. Mark's departure first to the Ronald Feldman Gallery and then to Kostabi World ended his need to do the group show circuit and contributed to the ultimate bubble burst of the East Village scene in 1987.

Although the East Village was still zooming in 1986, the South Bronx outpost Fashion Moda had fallen off drastically when Stefan Eins, after running the place for ten years, turned over the directorship to James Poppitz. Mark had never been a fan of Fashion Moda. He told me, "I was never interested in Fashion Moda. It seemed like such a chore to

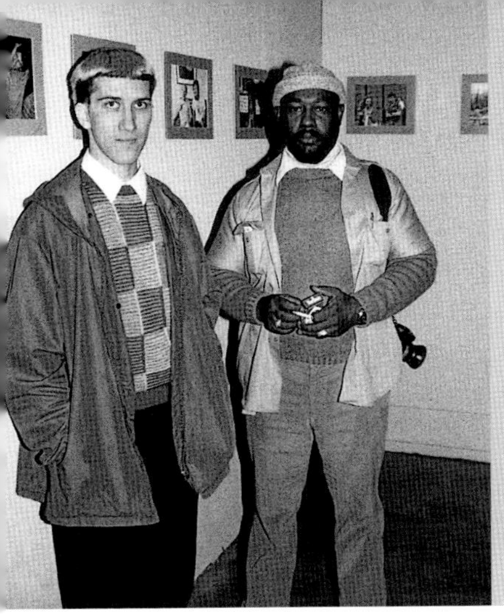

Fashion Moda co-director Juma Santos at the Kosthappening in the South Bronx.

go all the way up there by subway just to be in this dilapidated-looking alternative space where people seemed content to keep things that way. I moved to New York to move up in the world. I wanted to see my art in the Museum of Modern Art and large pristine galleries where art was treated with respect, not as funky decoration for a trashy, drunken, drugged-out party. The East Village was rough-and-ready also, but few people actually wanted to stay that way. Pat Hearn was always upgrading the architecture of her gallery. Most of the artists really wanted to show in SoHo and did so at every opportunity." I curated dozens of shows at the declining Fashion

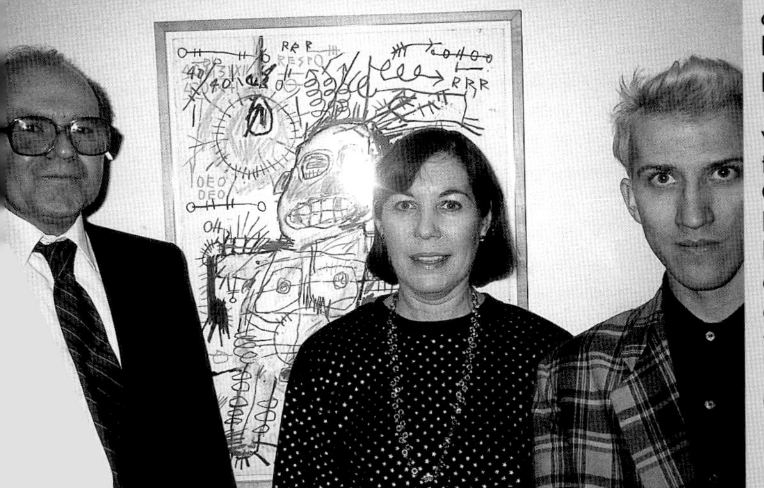

Collector Norman Dubrow with curator Diane Waldman in front of a drawing by Jean-Michel Basquiat that Dubrow had just given to the Guggenheim Museum. Dubrow was one of Mark's first collectors, buying his drawings from Semaphore Gallery in 1984. In the early 1990's he was a regular creative consultant at Kostabi World. He designed many Kostabi paintings, including *The World According to Mark*, which he then arranged to be acquired by the Groninger Museum in Holland.

Dubrow continues to be a very active, influentual collector to this day. He is founder of the Dubrow Biennial, an acclaimed alternative to the Whitney Biennial.

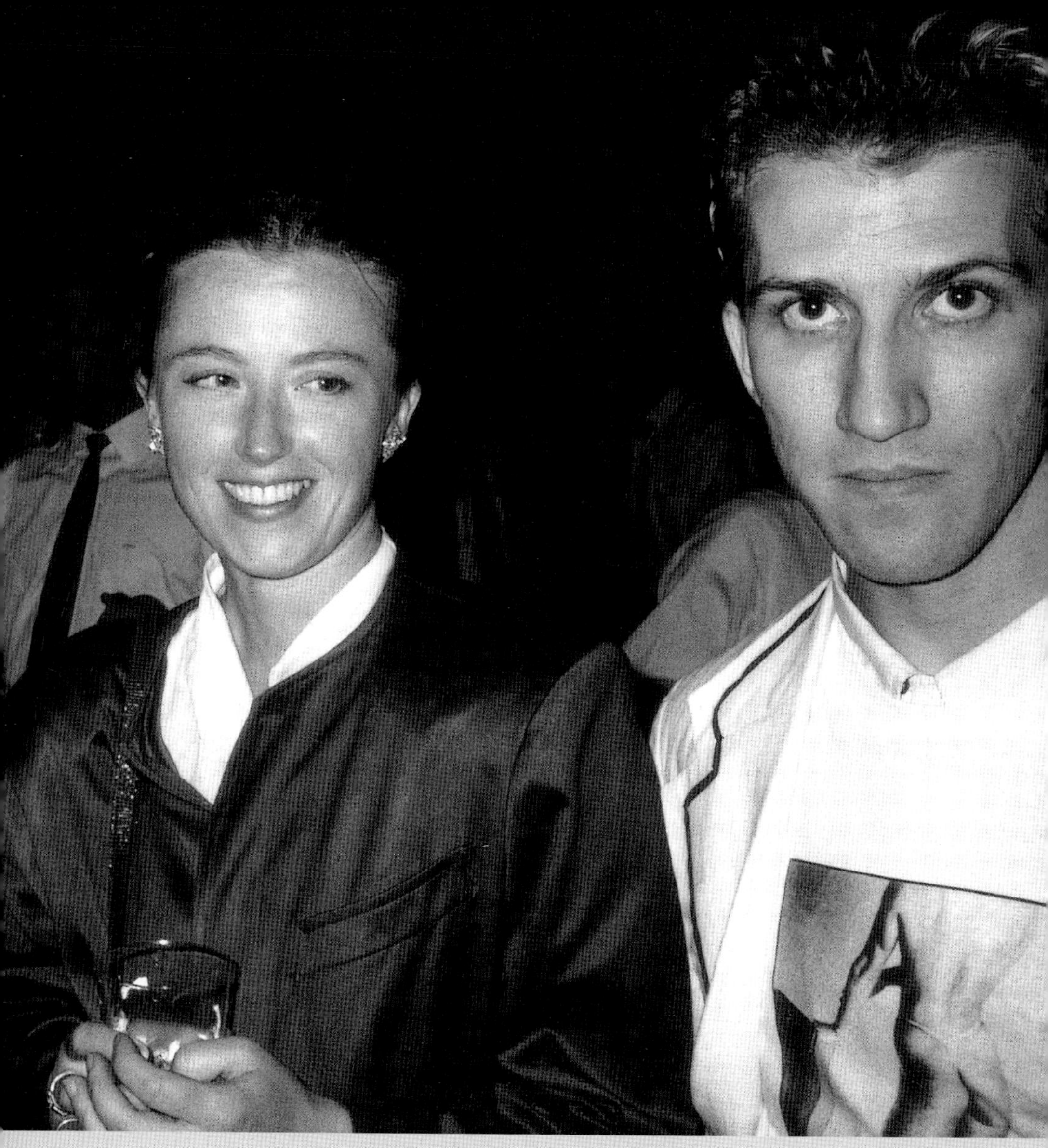

Photographer
Cindy Sherman.

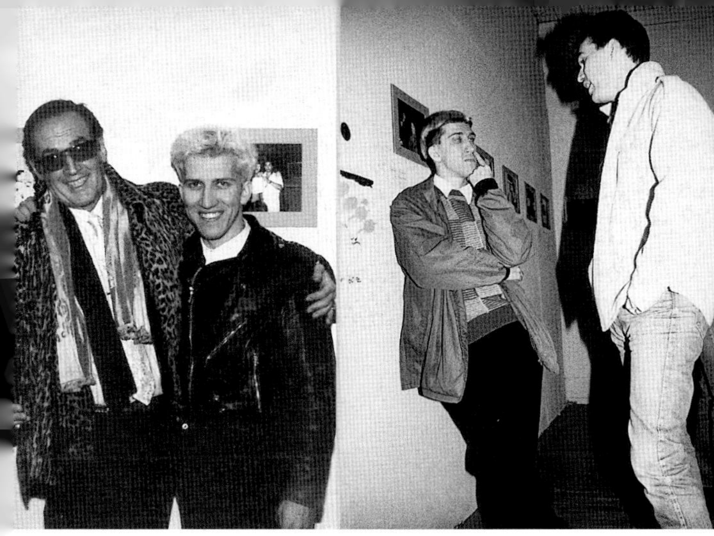

Performer Craig Vandenberg at the
Kosthappening at Ground Zero Gallery.

Moda during the reign of James Poppitz. The media devoured the South Bronx hype I fed them. I mounted artwork by Caroline Kennedy's husband Ed Schlossberg and called the show *South Bronx Neo Geo*. We had a dozen paparazzi from the tabloids show up. Every time the door opened everyone's head jerked, expecting to see Caroline Kennedy walk in the door. Of course she never showed up. Plenty of preppies came to my afternoon receptions because they mistook the affairs for being in Riverdale, which was the only Bronx they knew. I kept putting "South Bronx" in the titles of the exhibits so much that my compatriots at Fashion Moda started to complain I was exploiting the area's poverty. Stefan Eins came back on the scene more and more as James Poppitz seemed to lose his stomach for the venture. The other co-director was Juma Santos who dubiously claimed to be Malcolm X's grandson via Betty Shabazz. The average attendance at the Moda openings was around a dozen people, all of whom felt like elite members of some secret society. As Mark accurately observed, everyone got pretty trashed. There really was no great security threat, provided we evacuated the premises by nightfall. I remember wearing a bulletproof vest when I went out to the gallery by myself. The local community looked at us with curiosity or, at worst, estrangement. We left expensive exhibits of art by Keith Haring up on the walls for weeks and there was never any theft.

Eins insisted on calling Fashion Moda a museum. He was jubilant

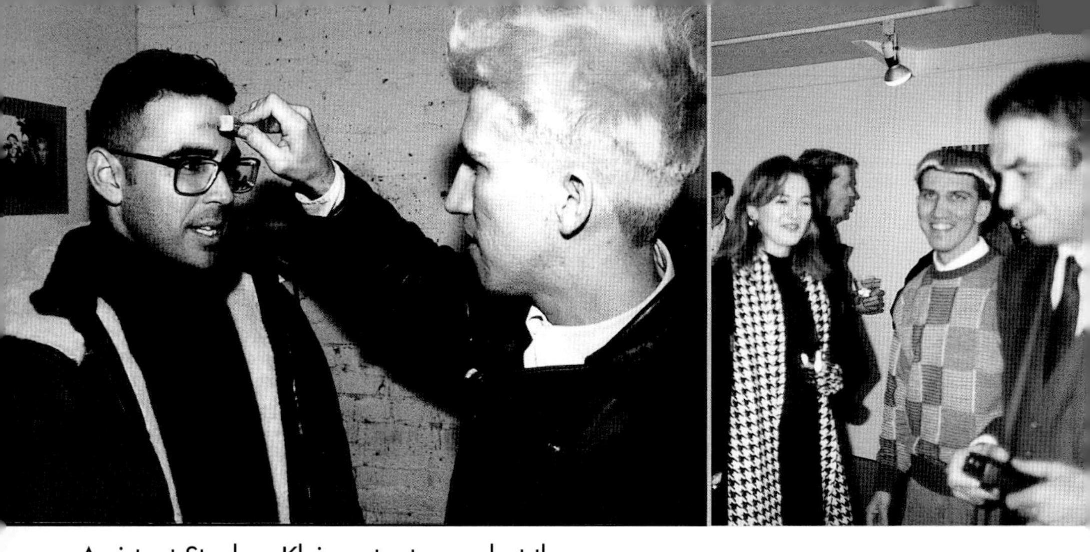

Assistant Stephen Klein gets stamped at the
Kosthappening at Ground Zero Gallery.

then when Art in America listed the place in their museum guide. No doubt
Fashion Moda had cachet in the art world. I always tried to travel my
museum curations there to take advantage of that "resume kill" factor.
I traded the desperation the directors felt for attendance into my getting
myself named as a co-director in 1988 shortly before they closed down
the space for good. There was a last ditch effort to relocate Fashion Moda
a few blocks away in a building that had a huge hole in the roof where
the Israeli artist Tsvi Ben Aretz had a dirt installation. But it came to nothing.
The roof never got fixed up and Ben Aretz's installation was the only art
activity that ever took place there.

There was always a sense that the South Bronx was the proper
home for graffiti because that was where the subway trains were parked
at night. There was also the mythos that poor ghetto denizens were somehow more authentic as graffiti writers. In many ways the whole East Village
inspiration was based on graffiti. Many of the best East Village painters,
such as David Wojnarowicz, would put rudimentary stencils up on the
street walls, their version of graffiti, and even Jenny Holzer's stickers can
be seen as her form of tagging. West Coast gallerist Molly Barnes claims,
"Graffiti is now a viable art movement in L.A. where people are still outraged
by the desecration of their white, neat neighborhoods." But as graffiti
became an international movement it lost its luster in New York City.

Master painter Alex Katz was asked if he was surprised at how quickly the East Village movement ended in the fall of 1986. He said he was not, because he had seen a similar bubble bursting when The Happenings came to a sudden stop in the early 60s. Katz has an early connection to Mark Kostabi because they were both involved in the Dec. 18, 1984 scandal when during the show *In the Public Eye* at the George Washington Bridge Bus Station, Mark's painting was stolen while Katz's was left untouched. This was considered especially noteworthy because Katz' work, *Lawn Party*, a portrait of people of several races, was valued at $50,000 while Mark's was self-appraised at only $5,555.55 (owned by Larry Gagosian). According to the show's curator, Gary Welz, it was

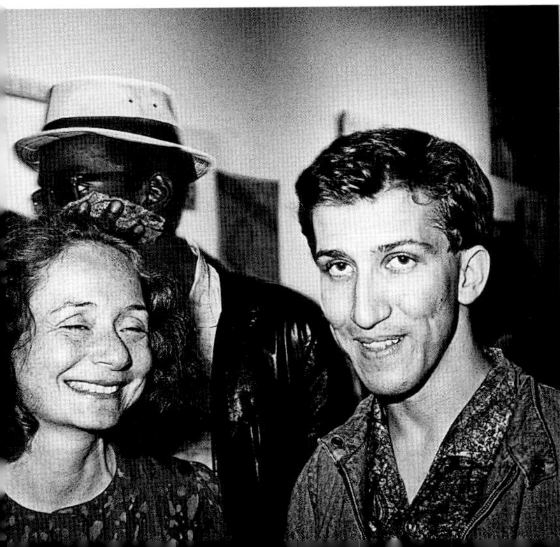

Collector Dolores
Neuman and artist
Fred Brathwaite in
the background.

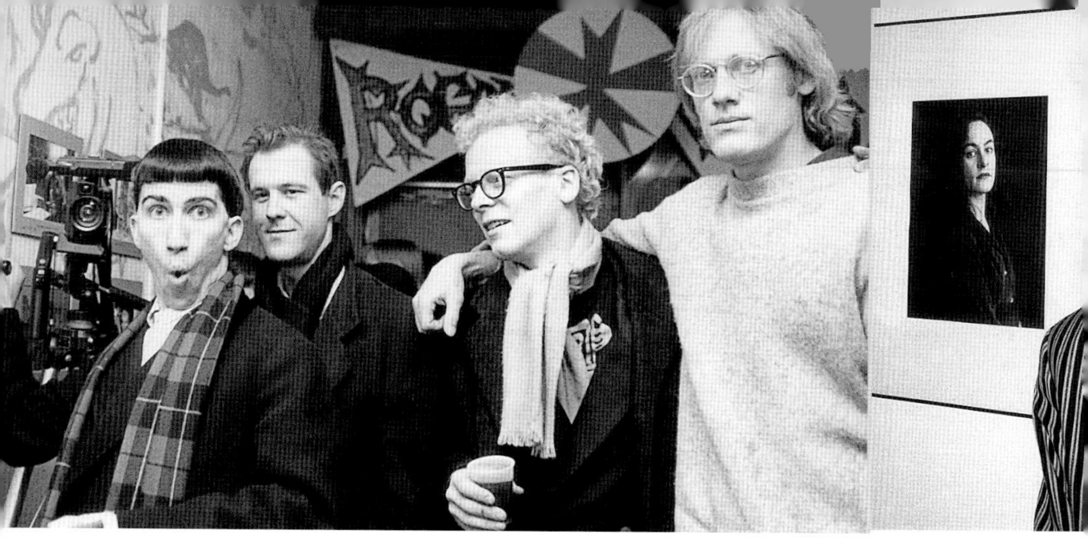

Painter Edward Brezinski, gallerist Jon Gerstad and painter Dab.

not the aesthetic triumph over Alex Katz Mark claimed, but more simply that Mark's large painting was within easy reach while Katz's smaller work was higher up and thus out of reach. All the paintings were hung from the bus station ceiling. The theft was widely reported in the New York papers at the time and Mark's work was never recovered. It is an example however, of how many times Mark's work has been stolen. Additionally Mark claims he has lost close to a million dollars to dishonest gallery owners, collectors, and assistants. His house has also been robbed several times.

It is also interesting that Alex Katz used The Happening analogy for the end of the East Village because Mark called his series of

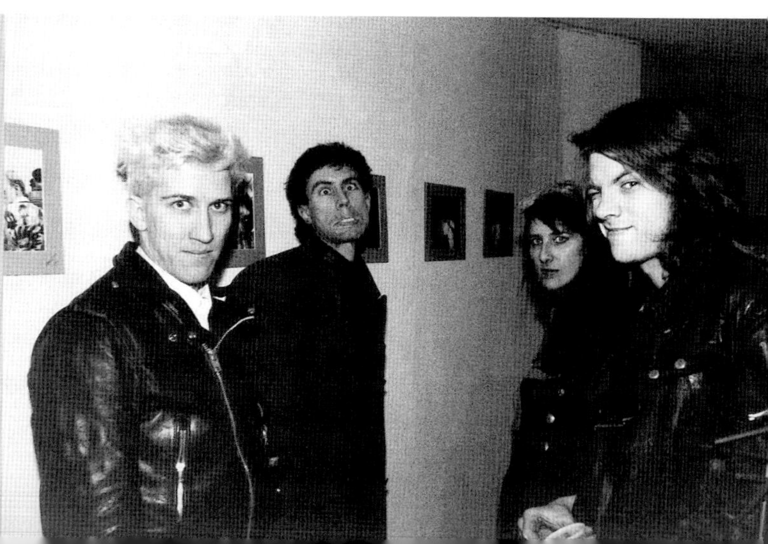

Painter Ford Crull makes faces while gallery owners Marguerite Van Cook and James Romberger look on at the Kosthappening at Ground Zero Gallery.

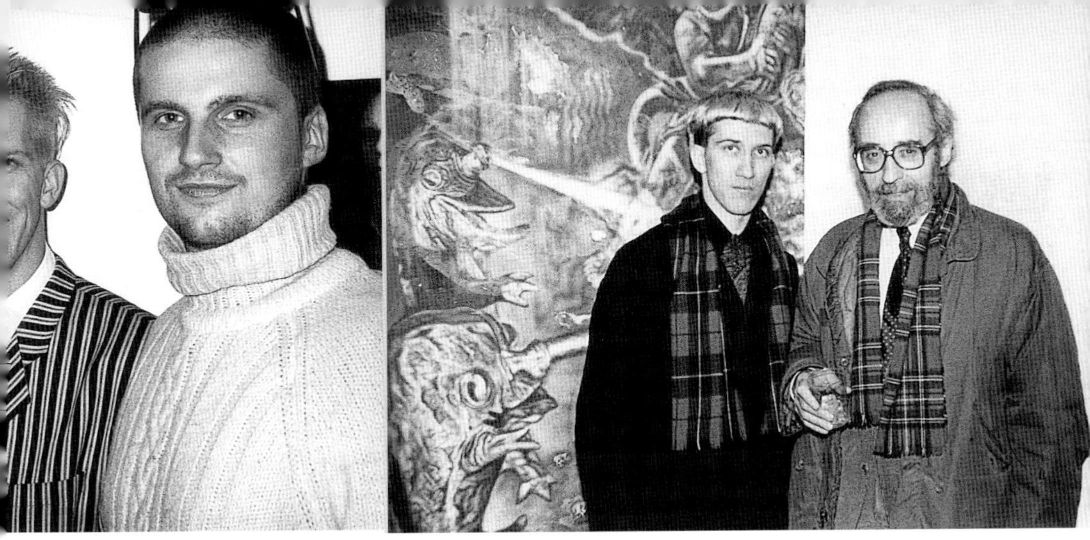

British painter Paul Benny. Timothy Greenfield-Sanders' portrait of Annette Lemieux in the background.

Mark's first lawyer, Jerry Ordover, who also represented Leo Castelli, Roy Lichtenstein and many other prominent art world figures.

events in 1985-86, which I curated with Mark, the Kosthappenings. The Kosthappenings were exhibits of photographs that I had taken as Mark's personal photographer, primarily during the summer of 1985. The blown-up photographs (mainly black and white) were signed on the matting by both Mark and me. Mark also often doodled on the photo or printed his cynical slogans which he called "Kostabisms." We had eight of these shows and sold the photographs for $25 apiece. Several of the shows sold out and all the shows were very well attended. Average attendance was around fifty people, typically half artists and half yuppies. The yuppies were my friends from the Upper East Side who were also mainly the ones who bought the photographs. The Kosthappenings were written up in the New York Daily News, NY Talk, and the East Village Eye. They pretty much occurred at the best East Village galleries, although we never had one at Gracie Mansion (although Gracie had agreed to do it). The photographs were put on the walls with double stick tape and the invites were just cheap card stock Xeroxes. For the last Kosthappening, *In Memory of Joseph Beuys, January 23, 1986*, we had gotten big enough that we had a bagpiper and extensive security. I paid for everything involved and also kept the money from all the sales. By the end of it, Mark had already become such a star that he was wary of the event not attracting

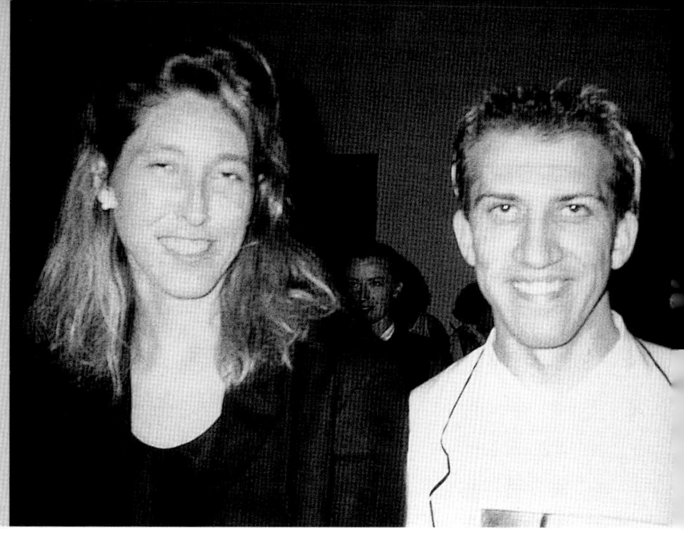

a good enough crowd to be an acceptable Kosthappening which is pretty much why we stopped doing them.

The number of galleries in the East Village continued to grow throughout 1985. Semaphore Gallery's Barry Blinderman who had been one of Mark's reps up until Mark's exclusively joining the Feldman Gallery in the fall of 1986 told me at the time, "I've calculated that a new gallery opens every two weeks. It's getting to the point where there will be a gallery for every artist." The influx of newly minted East Village galleries was turning the East Village into a heaven for collectors and artistic wannabes, but the quality of the product was thinning out disastrously. I remember David Wojnarowicz's sculpted head with maps on it passing from gallery to gallery for months in 1986, always front and center in each gallery, with its price declining slowly. I thought, "Something is going wrong here, the sculpture is just being shuttled around for its prestige value as an East Village trophy but nothing is selling." But the artists were being met with open arms everywhere they went. They were the new stars. Mark told me: "I have memory flashes of walking through the East Village in the 1980s on a sunny spring day, being much younger, naive, innocent and hopeful. I remember being happy and excited. It was like being in love. Success was so easily obtained." Molly Barnes remembers the last days of the East Village, "The galleries were small and crowded in 1985 and 1986 and we went to 6 or 7 receptions a night.

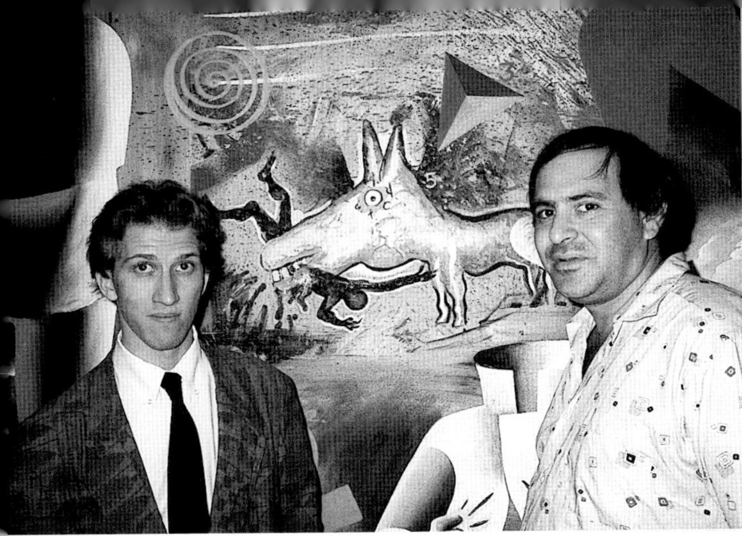

Curator and critic Paul Miller, who is credited as filming (with Paul Tschinkel) the only existing Basquiat interview.

Almost all the galleries were showing the same artists and the same few collectors were always there. You could recognize them by their fur coats. The critics were there and the groupies and the photographers. I was always getting my picture taken and I loved the whole scene. No one bought anything for over $200. There was always a fight, a sweaty window, a lot of beer and enormous enthusiasm among the artists as to what they were doing. They really thought they had discovered art, and maybe they had." At nightclubs, East Village artists would be met by doormen with a fistful of free drink tickets. What fashion designers had been to the 70s, painters had become to the 80s, as long as they were white.

Graffiti had failed dismally before the East Village got

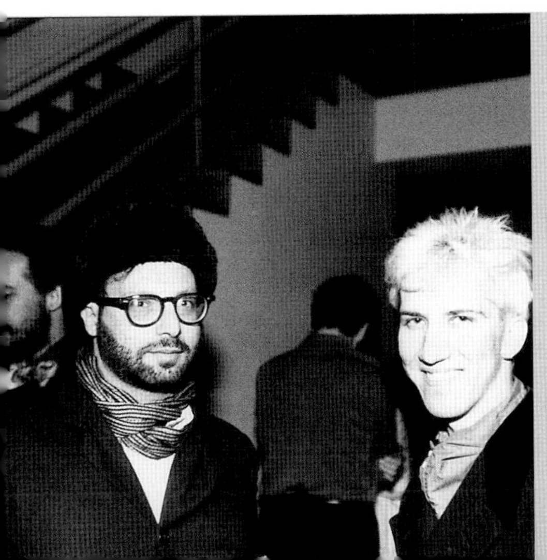

Painter Dan Asher at the Bayama restaurant for the 1986 East Village Guide party. Joe Lewis in the background. Before emerging as a painter, Dan Asher was an acclaimed photographer known for documenting the Punk Rock world at its beginnings. During the East Village heyday he was a friend of Basquiat and a fixture at the Red Bar, the most important East Village after-opening hang out. He was known for his unpredictible, explosive, "anti-establishment" personality and for selling his primitive, oilstick paintings for as little as $5 each. He sometimes resembled a homeless person but always had a paperback copy of some literary classic in his back pocket. Eventually he evolved into a Conceptual artist who now shows at the prestigious Paula Cooper Gallery in Chelsea.

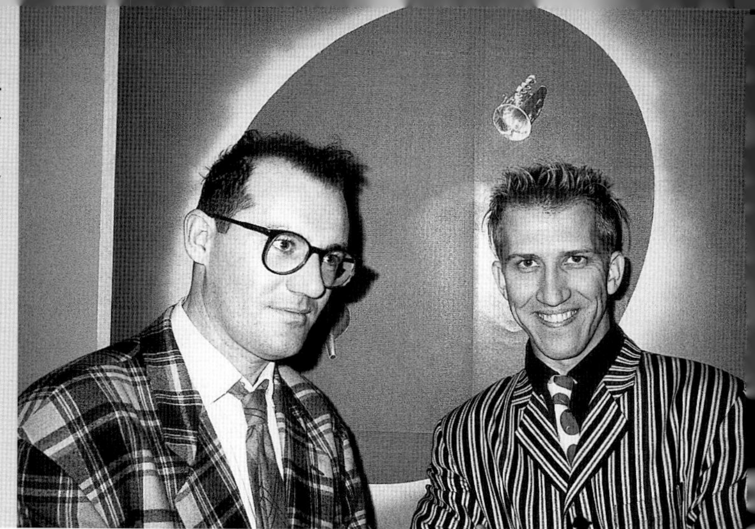

Art critic Paul Taylor at the New Museum for the Malcolm McClaren show which Taylor curated shortly before he died of AIDS.

sucked down. I remember the graffiti writers were getting agitated about not being called the "G word" while the East Village was still thriving. Then around six months later the Lower East Side painting market started to tank. Critics and collectors lamented that the transition from subway train to canvas tended to overly center the graffiti writers' composition. Peter Frank said of this chronic problem, "The formal centering in the gallery-oriented work of the graffitists was part of their larger tendency to let the canvas format intimidate them. It was inevitable: the kids were thinking in pictorial, not in painterly, terms, and when faced with the near-square shape of the canvas, either treated it like a frame in a comic strip or as their understanding of a Painting Hanging In

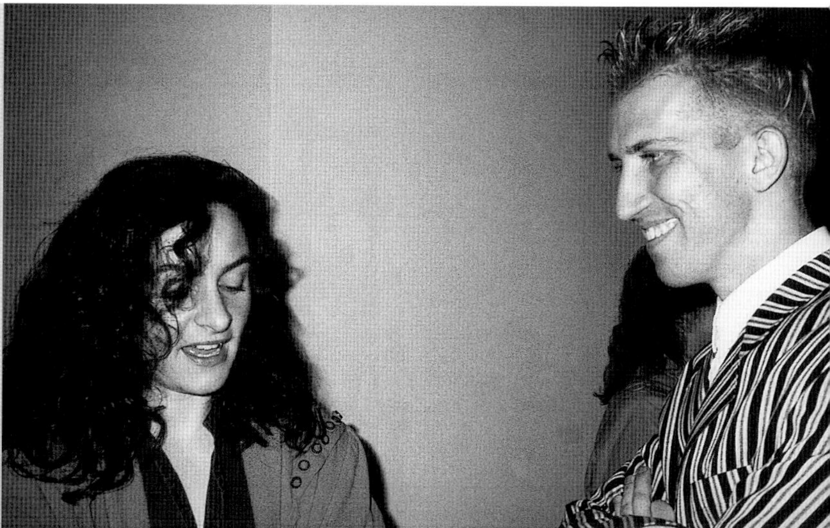

Photographer Annette Lemieux.

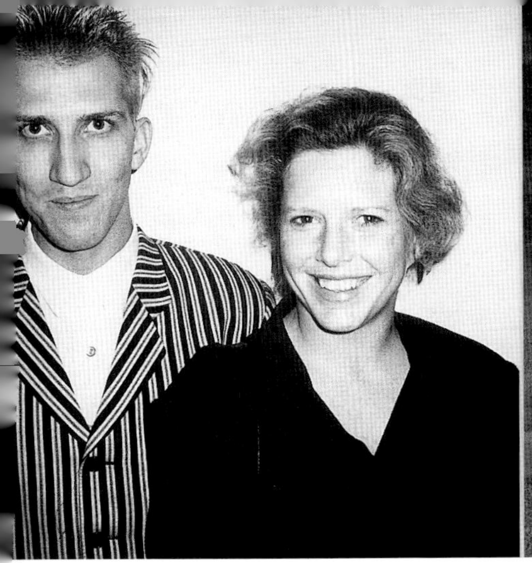

Journalist Lucy Danziger. Lucy's husband James Danziger owned one of the top photography galleries in SoHo for many years.

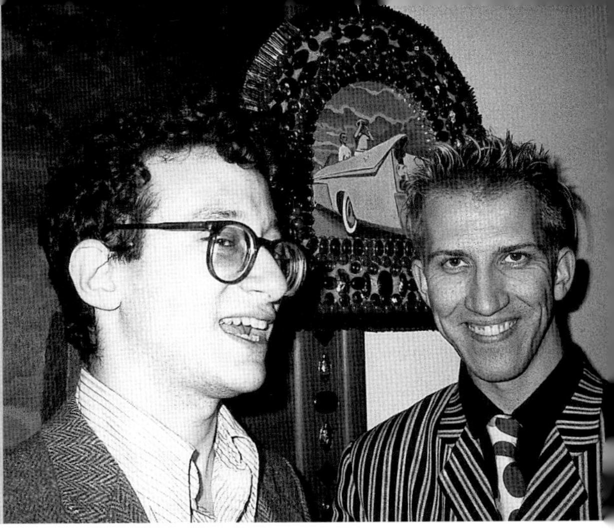

Gallery owner Paul Deitsch in front of a kitsch sculpture by Rhonda Zwillinger. Zwillinger had to move out west when her body reacted negatively to the glue she had been using in her artwork.

A Museum. Or both which resulted in the worst and the best of the lot. It was a step down from the frieze format of the subway train and wall, the running horizontal which fit, even enforced, the calligraphic, the written character of 'true graffiti.' I was sure that graffiti would influence graphic design more overtly than it has, and its most overt impact has been through meta-graffitists who were doing something else as well, such as Haring and even Kostabi whom I consider the two great cartoon-painters of the 80s. The one aspect of contemporary design for which graffiti has been directly responsible until now has been the dense, eye-straining, deliberately unwieldy page design of computer-related publications such as Wired." Collectors also rebelled at the salon-unfriendly appearance of many of the rough-edged taggers. One Park Avenue matron was said to have ruefully commented, "I don't care how good a painter A-1 is, I don't want him in my living room."

The East Village bubble burst suddenly in the fall of 1986 when the new art season brought a shift of most of the top gallery spaces over to SoHo, where they promptly failed en masse, both critically and commercially. Mark says: "I did not expect the East Village art scene to collapse so quickly. But now I understand that the

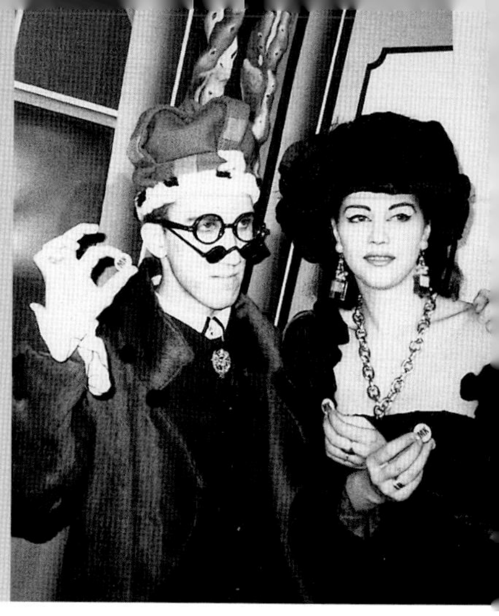

East Village art scene collapsed so quickly because leases were up, rents went way up, and the media was ready for the next thing." Critic Alan Moore saw it more as an issue of quality: "East Village art was linked to Neo-Expressionism, the painting movement championed mainly by Italian and German artists. In fact this was wrong; it was more like a wholesale return to traditional modes of making art among younger artists, and not devotion to a particular style. But, also what brought the scene down was the quality issue - too much of the art was simply not very good. It was local product, mixed up with graffiti and cartooning, and not capable of sustaining the leading American position. It was the upsurge of this exciting and dangerous cultural district which attracted people, more than the work. The East Village was paralleled by increasingly visible artists' districts around the world. For a scene so linked to fashion, well 'live by the season, die by the season.' Once the world art community had gotten their taste of the East Village phenomenon it was time for something different."

The conventional wisdom was that rents tripled driving out the galleries. NYU moved in from the west, Chinatown encroached from the south, and yuppies swarmed in from everywhere during the late 80s. The only cheap gallery spaces left were over on Avenue C and Avenue D and beyond. These blocks were also the least convenient and the most dangerous. In fact the only gallerist left standing representing

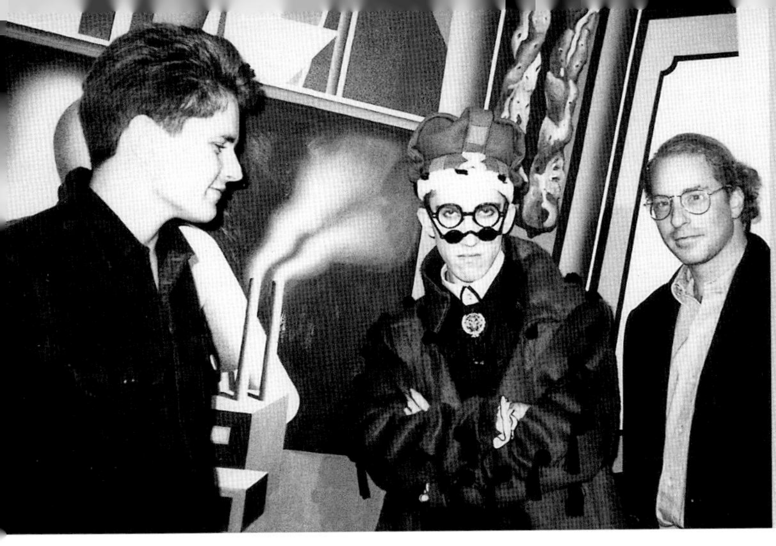

Fashion designer and artist Stillman Rockefeller showed his art at Fashion Moda which caused ample controversy. Here he is on the left, next to Mark and writer Matthew Rose, who wrote an early article about Mark for New York Magazine which triggered a carnivalesque media blitz.

the East Village aesthetic in the 90s was DD Chapin who was an AMC auto heir whose wealth sheltered him from the financial battering the other spaces suffered and even he ultimately shuttered down after a few seasons.

Peter Frank says, "The East Village saw the bohemian-gentrification pattern played out at warp speed. Everyone took 5-6 year leases between 1980 and 1982, and when they cleaned and sexed up the neighborhood, they were rewarded with tripled rents when their leases were up for renewal. By 1987 the galleries had blown alphabet city for SoHo or private dealing or even L.A., the restaurants and cafes had closed and the artists had boogied across the river." But with such a glut of galleries at the time, certainly a pruning of even half the galleries

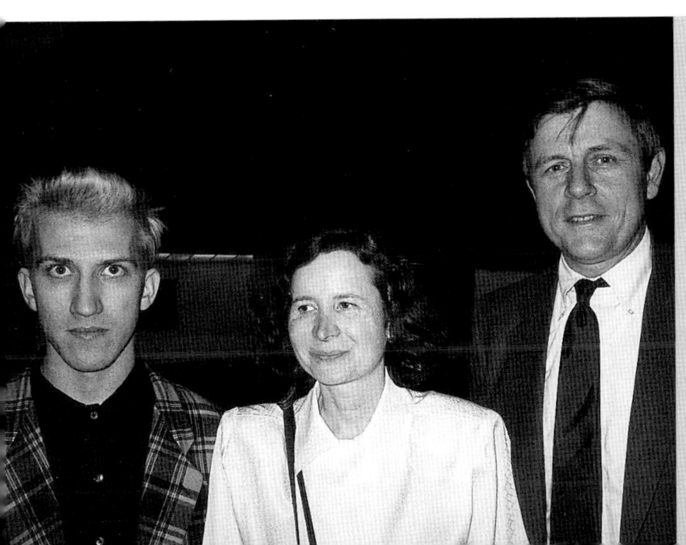

Collectors Lenore and Herb Schorr, who bought Mark's *Upheaval* canvas, which they then donated to the Neuberger Museum in upstate New York.

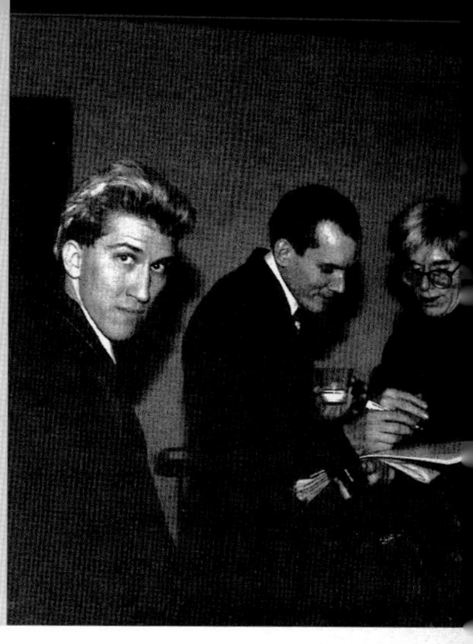

Painter Philip Taaffe signs an autograph for Andy Warhol. Andy charmingly surprised many young artists when he asked for *their* autograph.

would have been a healthy factor and some of the best Lower East Side galleries like Gracie Mansion actually stayed on well into 1989, but were just neglected for all their troubles.

The fact that Mark had made a significant amount of money compared to the other threadbare artists had allowed him enormous artistic freedom at this time. Many of his art projects succeeded partly because they were (or seemed) expensive, at least compared to the budgets of his impoverished Alphabetland peers. In 1985 Mark made a small local splash when he threw dollar bills at a wild throng at the Palladium Disco in a trick that essentially just cost him a hundred bucks. He recounted, "Around the time that my painting, *Climbing*, was on a Palladium wall, I was asked to participate in a performance above the dance floor. Scaffolding was erected and numerous East Village artists, myself included, were painting a collaborative mural while music blasted, and the crowd danced and watched us from below. Halfway through the live painting performance I turned away from the canvas and began throwing dollar bills, one-by-one, to the horde below and watched as all the hands grabbed and fought over each dollar bill. Eventually I threw the remaining stack of about 50 dollar bills and the people went wild. My goal was to upstage the other East Village artists. "

As Mark grew richer, his budget and his media impact also

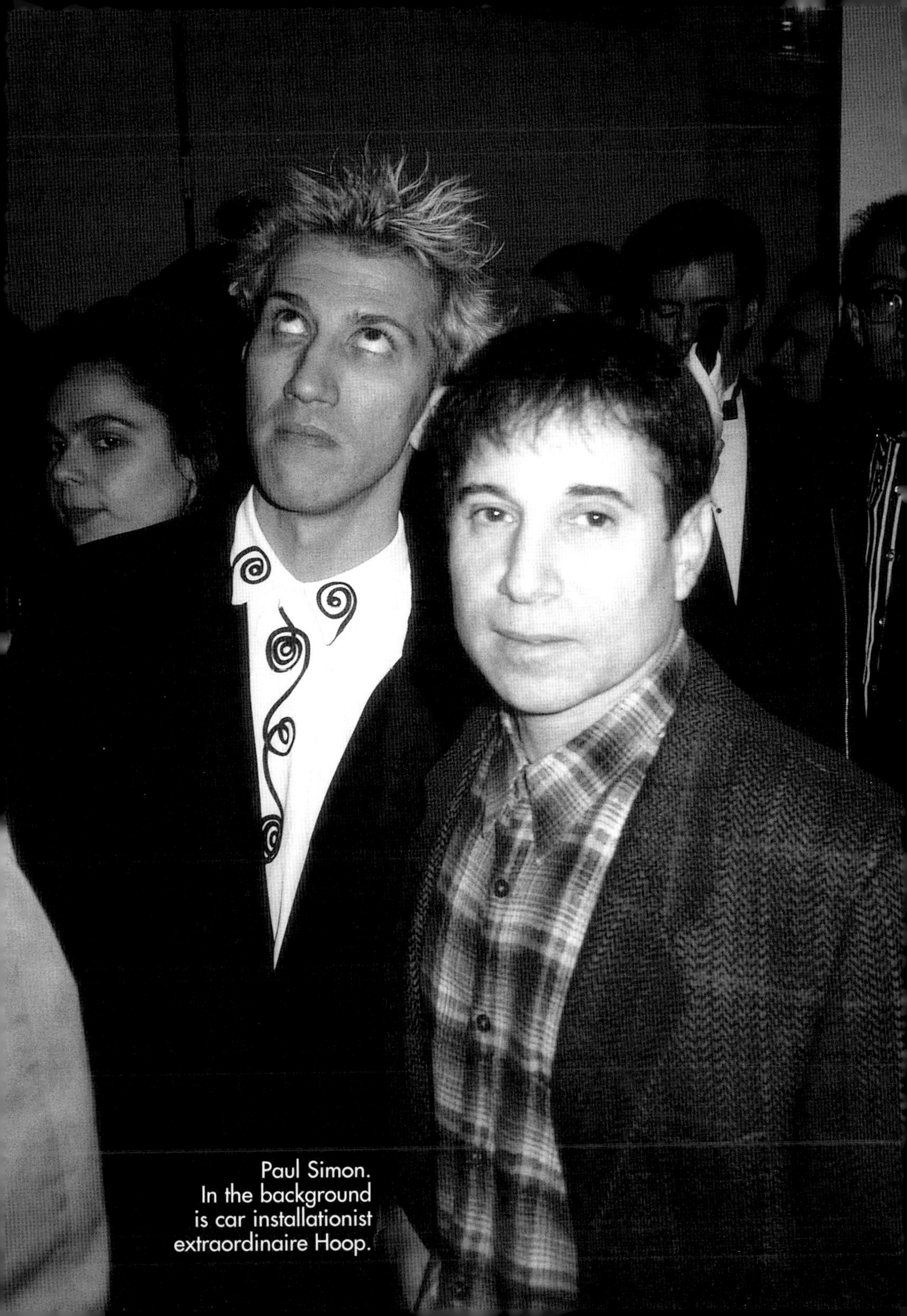

Paul Simon.
In the background
is car installationist
extraordinaire Hoop.

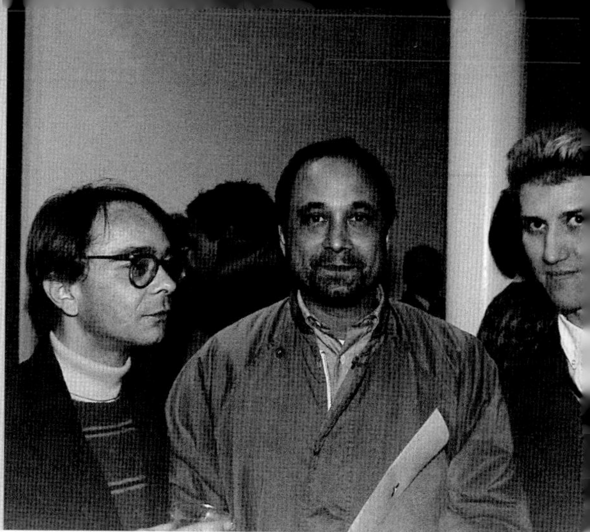

Art critic Gary Indiana and painter Ross Bleckner at the Moke Mokotoff Gallery on Avenue C. One option as rents were raised in the East Village in 1986 was to go much further east, where it was inconvenient and still dangerous. The Moke Mokotoff Gallery tried that approach, opening between Avenue C and Avenue D in a gigantic space, but had minimal sales and closed after a brief run.

grew. Another seemingly expensive project was Mark's hundred dollar bill jacket. Mark recalls, "My jacket was made from hundred dollar bills totaling $17,000. The money was taped onto a normal suit jacket and pants. It was my money. I used it for my People Magazine shoot. The shoot lasted over 4 hours on the windy Kostabi World rooftop. The cold wind started blowing the hundred dollar bills off me which created a panic with assistants running to grab the bills before any would fly over the roof's edge. I was freezing for my fame." It was hard to imagine Mark's East Village competitors like Richard Hambleton, who by then had gone homeless and was regularly being seen fishing around in garbage cans for food, being able to come up with $17,000 in cash. As Mark's career

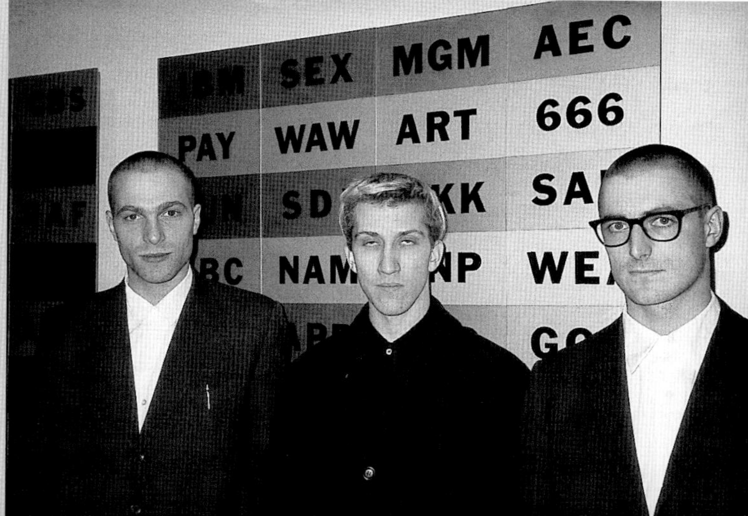

The Grey Organization. Arguably the first "Young British Artists", for a while these two guys were everywhere but they haven't surfaced in over a decade in New York.

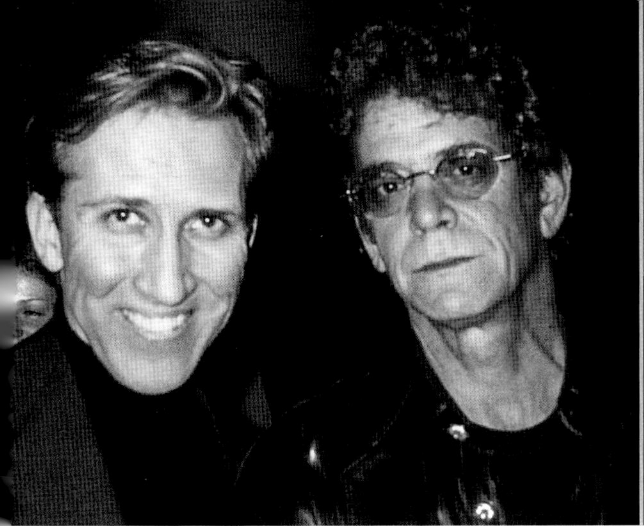

Lou Reed. In the background is painter
Isca Greenfield-Sanders.

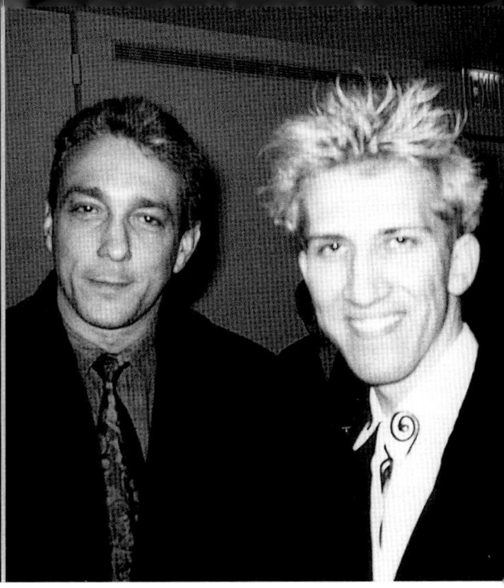

Popular Chase Bank art
buyer Manuel Gonzalez.

took off, it increasingly became a case of the rich getting richer.

Mark's disdain for a quick profit allowed him to defy Sly Stallone who was buying Mark's paintings, in the same way he had defied Absolut. Mark recounted, "I first insulted Stallone in People Magazine in 1986 where I said he only bought Kostabi's with tits & ass in them. Then, with the media goading me, I went further on television, on *A Current Affair* with Maury Povich. I told the story of how he couldn't make up his mind about which Kostabi to buy until he went to the bathroom at the Feldman Gallery. In the bathroom at the Feldman gallery there was a poster of my painting *Dealing With Mr. Know-It-All*. When Sly came out he asked, 'How about the one on the poster in the bathroom?' Sly bought a total of two paintings and one sculpture. I said on A Current Affair, 'Stallone made up his mind after he relieved himself.' I believe it was this comment which infuriated Stallone and caused him to ask his curator, Barbara Guggenheim, to return the paintings which I then agreed to buy back. The other painting, *Lovers*, was of two nude lesbians making love while listening to the same walkman. Both had sold for a total of $30,000. which I then refunded to Stallone. Then we began a series of verbal insults in the media which actually lasted for a few years until I finally realized that the media was responsible for continuing and amplifying the mean-spirited fight. At the height of our

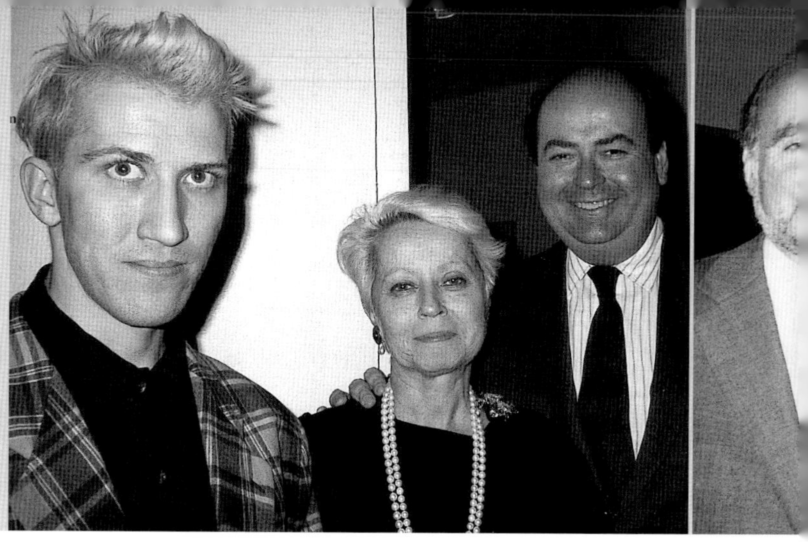

verbal war, despite his negative opinion of me personally, Stallone said he just liked his Kostabi sculpture, called *Venus*, so much that he couldn't return it. Eventually, I sent Stallone an apology letter. He didn't respond. Then, about a year later, after the critic Paul Taylor interviewed me, first repeating some terrible things that Stallone had just said about me, obviously trying to fire me up to get a retort, I responded by sending Stallone a second apology letter, explaining how I believed the media was manipulating us to fight. This time he accepted and the gossip columnist Cindy Adams graciously reported that we had called a truce, quoting from his letter to me. Stallone was a big collector in the 80s. He owned works by many major artists. Anselm Keifer was one. He is also a painter himself and we showed at the same gallery for a while in Beverly Hills, the Hanson Gallery, on Rodeo Drive. People surmised that his being a painter, and his respect for me as an artist, made it especially hurtful when I insulted him. I learned from the experience that I was being selfish and was unfairly exploiting a celebrity, just like many people were doing to me as I became more famous. I acted like a baby because when he bought my work I was really thrilled and wanted to meet him. He was too busy. I, like a selfish baby who couldn't get his way, responded by insulting him in the press, as a second attempt to exploit his patronage." One of the odd aspects of Mark's impulsive criticism of Sly Stallone was that one Kostabi canvas that Stallone bought, *Dealing with Mr.-Know-It-All,*

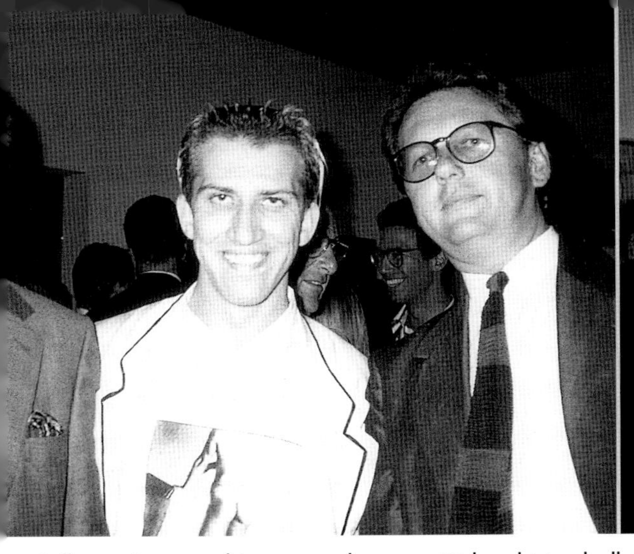
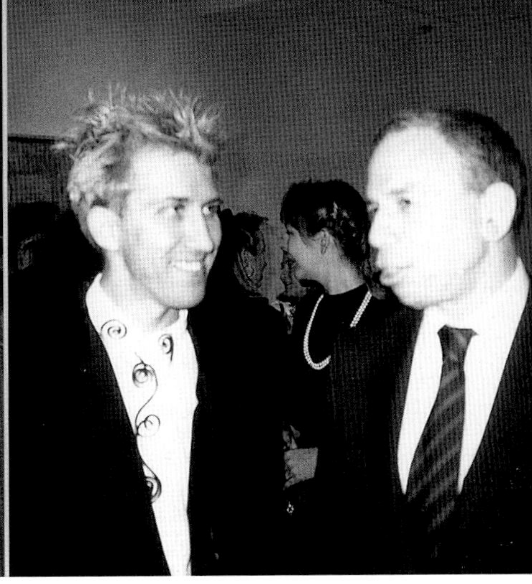

Collector Raymond Learsy and curator Richard Marshall.   Publishing tycoon Sy Newhouse.

is actually just a slight female figure with a large flashlight and has only minor "tits & ass" content. So Mark was really stretching to put Stallone down. But this element of Mark saying anything, in essence biting the hand that had fed him, was another example of his willingness to lose money perhaps because he had already made so much. This came at a time when the other East Village artists were panicking as their careers and grand expectations evaporated. Mark was willing to burn bridges because he was so confident that his winning streak would go on forever.

When Mark was booked on the Morton Downey Show, Mark managed to terminate the show after only five minutes. Ultimately nothing

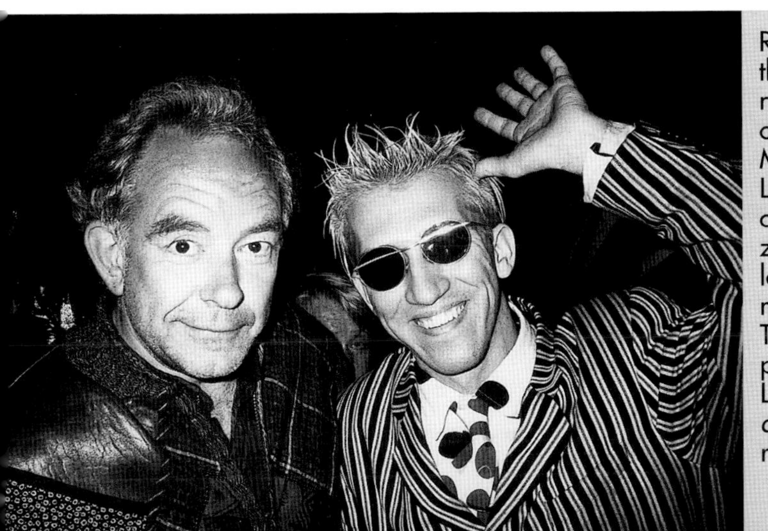

Robin Leach once told me that he single-handedly reported the first twenty cover stories for People Magazine in 1974. Leach made a fortune owning rock music magazines in the UK in the 60s, lost the money and then made it back with his hit TV shows in the 80s. Mark's popular appearance on Leach's *Lifestyles of the Rich and Famous* was rerun repeatedly for years.

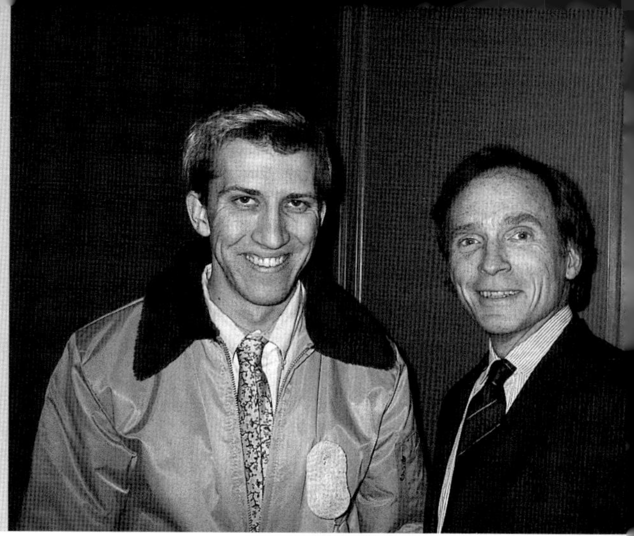

Dick Cavett told me that his talk show was all consuming in the 60s and that he became so depressed that when he was being shuttled to and from the studio and saw the green grass of Central Park he was so disoriented that he would wonder whether it was Fall or Spring.

was aired after Mark got into a wild brawl with the physically much bigger Downey, and in the bargain Kostabi lost a $20,000 canvas. Mark told me of the incident, "I was invited to be on the Morton Downey Jr. Show, at the peak of its notoriety. The show's theme was *Art or Garbage*. One of the other guests was the art team Cockrill/Hughes, known for the controversial political porn book, *The White Papers*. Cockrill/Hughes also showed at SoHo's Semaphore Gallery. I had three of my painters on the left side of the Downey set, who were to paint Kostabi paintings throughout the show while Downey and I debated at center stage. Before the taping began, Downey told me that I was a 'genius.' He compared me to Michelangelo, Rembrandt, Rubens, Raphael and other old masters who were known for

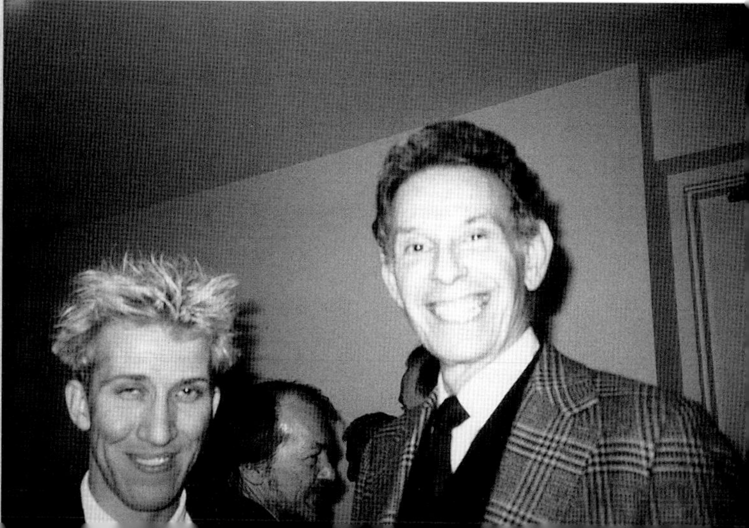

Collector Eugene Schwartz with painter Bob Dombrowski in the background.

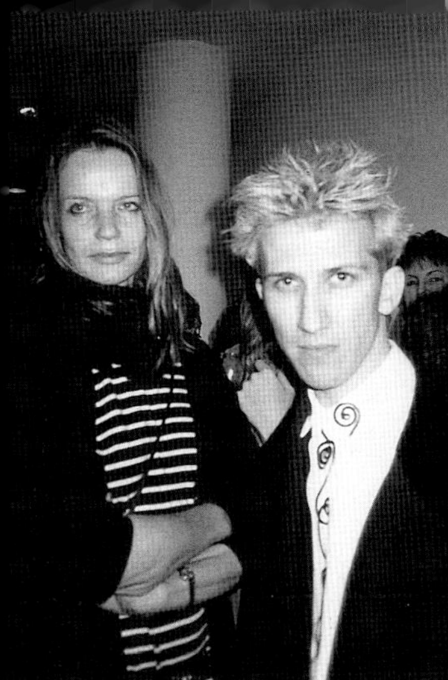
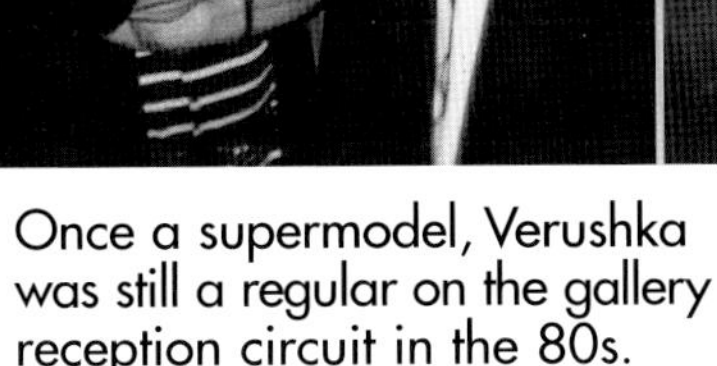
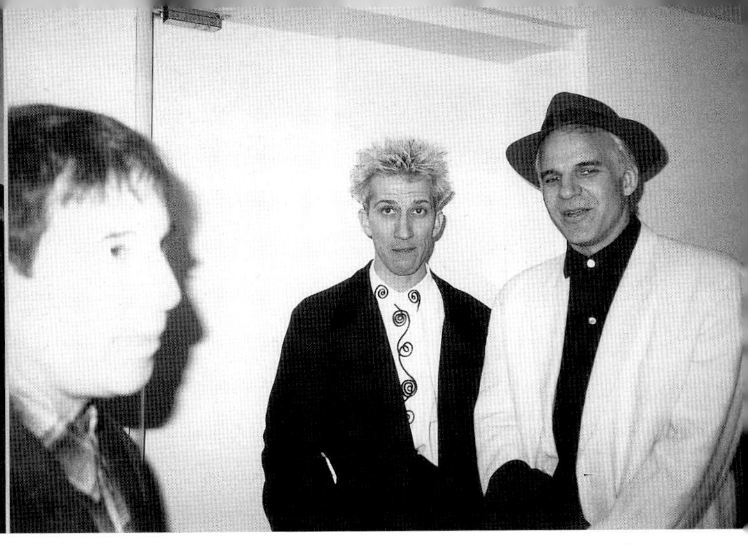

Once a supermodel, Verushka was still a regular on the gallery reception circuit in the 80s.

Paul Simon and Steve Martin. Famous as a comedian, actor and writer, Steve Martin had an art show, called *Invisible Art*, at the Molly Barnes Gallery in Los Angeles, shortly before Mark joined the same gallery at age 19.

using assistants. But then when the taping began he suddenly referred to me as an 'a--hole.' I felt tricked. He started a parody of performance art by wrapping himself with telephone cords. I decided to get in on the action. Unleashed from my microphone/chain I jumped onto Downey's huge back and began a fake fight, pretending to wrap the phone cords around him tighter. When we broke for commercial, Downey told me it was great. He said, 'Let's keep it up.' When the taping began again, I ran around the set in my bright red Yohji Yamamoto suit like a crazy ferret. When I came near Downey (who was known for chain-smoking) he blew smoke in my face. I responded by picking up his large ash tray and dumping the contents on his head. He went ballistic and hit me. He chased me. He grabbed and tackled me. He put me in a chokehold and yelled, 'YOU'RE DEAD, YOU RED-SUITED, LITTLE COCK-SUCKER!' He was physically a huge person. He jammed my chin into the concrete floor. I was bleeding. The camera man was hovering just a few feet away. With my free hand I grabbed a paper cup filled with bright chartreuse paint that I had originally planned to throw onto a large black, white, and red portrait of Downey which I brought on the show. But now I thought I was going to die and everyone else thought it was all show business. My only

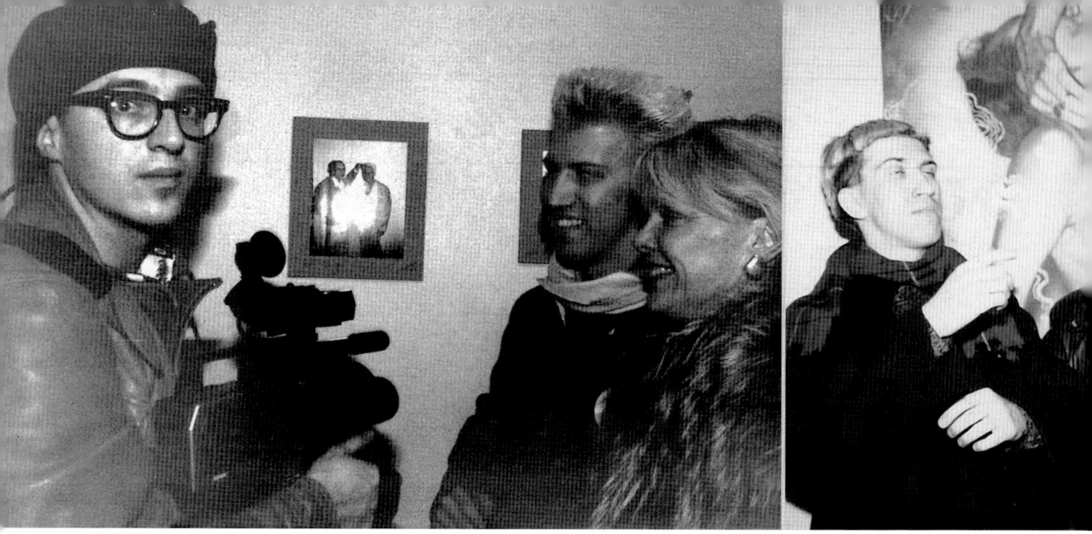

Nada Gallery owner Jim C, L.A. Gallery owner Molly Barnes (Mark's first dealer) at the Kosthappening at the Nolo Contendere Gallery.

chance was to throw the paint into the camera lens to let them know it was real. When I did, the show was clearly over. Two huge security guys pulled Downey off me. I heard police or ambulance sirens. Someone urged me to leave the studio immediately. I walked for more than an hour all the way from the New Jersey television studio to Manhattan, straight to the offices of the New York Daily News to report the story. The show never aired because our fight happened in the first five minutes and they never finished taping the rest. They released to the news only the part where I threw paint at the camera. I assume they chose not to release the rest of the footage because it was clear that Downey was the real physical aggressor. He went too far. The story immediately became national news, with extensive features in the National Enquirer and many other tabloids. I appeared in the tabloids wearing a neck brace and Downey had a thumb cast. Downey claimed I bit his thumb. He had me arrested and I had him arrested. Downey claimed that I had also destroyed a $10,000 camera lens with the paint I had thrown. Both our cases were thrown out of court. The judge said he didn't want to waste time giving two publicity hounds more press. Downey didn't return my $20,000 painting which I left on the set."

"After several months of trading public insults, I went to a party at the Chippendale's nightclub. When I discovered Downey was also there

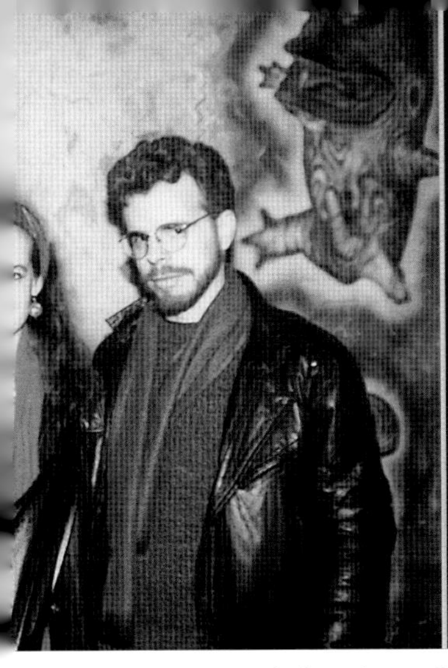

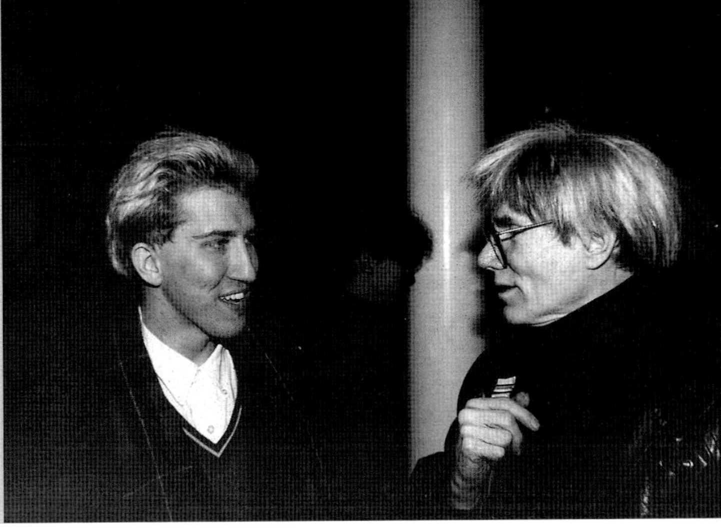

Painters Bruce and Rhonda Wall.   Andy Warhol at Moke Mokotoff Gallery.

I expected violence. But instead of attacking me, Downey unexpectedly asked me to join him at his table and embraced me. I sat between Downey and Robin Leach who was drinking champagne from a woman's high heel shoe. Gossip columnists and paparazzi had a field day. Downey even offered me advice, saying, 'If you really want to get famous, you should put one of your paintings up for auction at Sotheby's and arrange for people to bid it up to a million dollars.' Downey's show was soon cancelled apparently because advertisers thought it was too violent."

"A few years later Downey called me and said he was filming a pilot for a new show and wanted to use some of my other portraits of

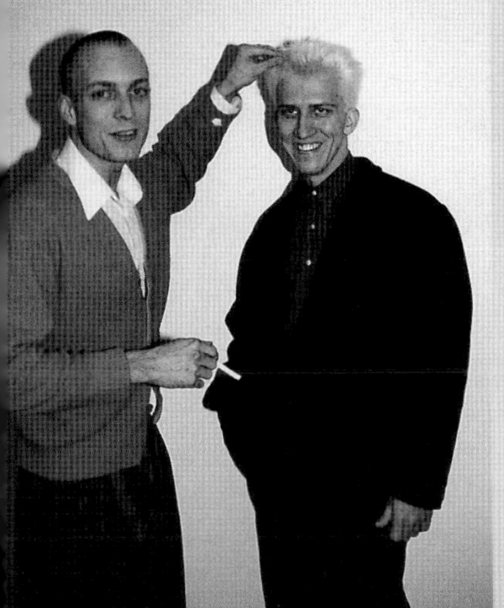

Painter Craig
Coleman.

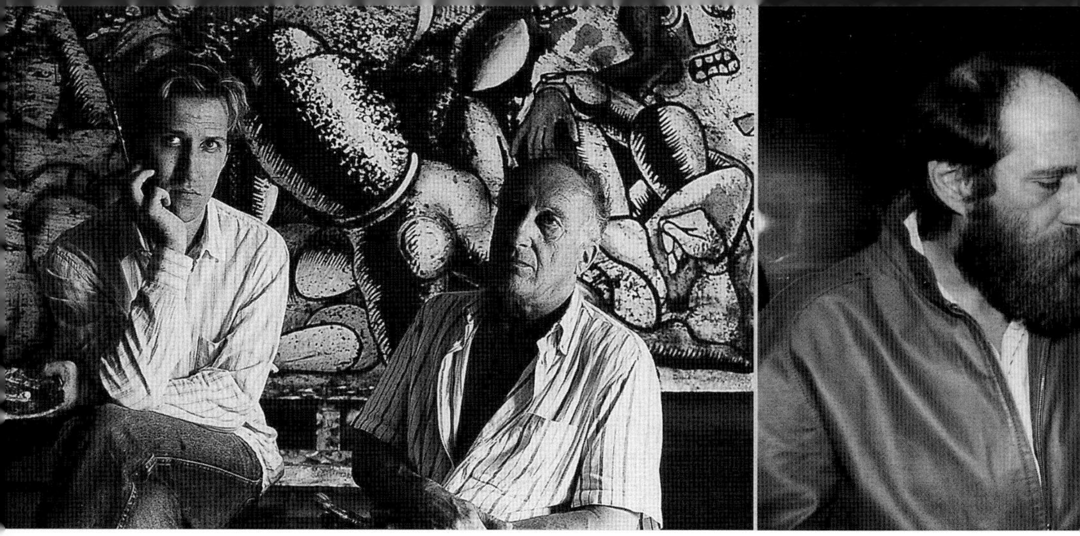

Painter Enrico Baj, who was praised by Marcel Duchamp and Andre Breton. Baj in turn praised the East Village scene and Mark in the Italian press. Eventually Baj collaborated with Mark on over 40 paintings and over a hundred drawings which were exhibited in European galleries and museums.

him as part of the set. Downey claimed that he tried to get my other painting back for me but said the studio wouldn't release it because of the $10,000.00 camera damage. I fell for the trick and sent over the two new paintings he requested. The show never happened. Months went by while I called either to get the artwork back or to get paid since Downey started to claim that he wanted to buy them. I encountered Downey wearing a fur coat while he was shopping for jewelry with his 'fiancé' at Tiffany's. He claimed, 'Don't worry, the show is definitely happening and your paintings

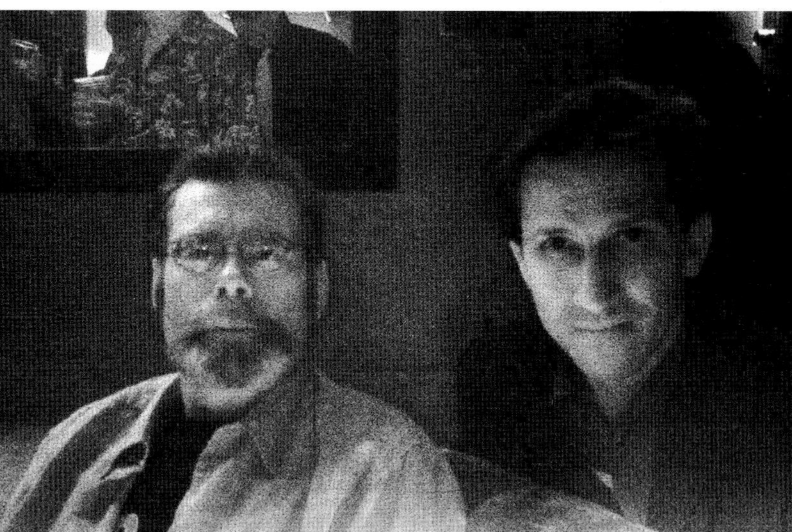

Novelist Stephen King.

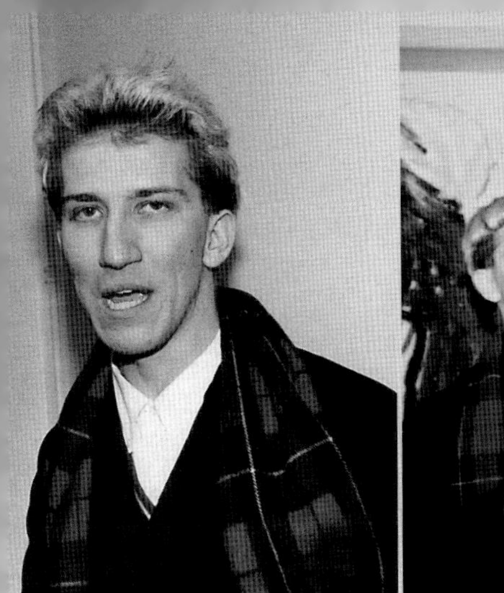

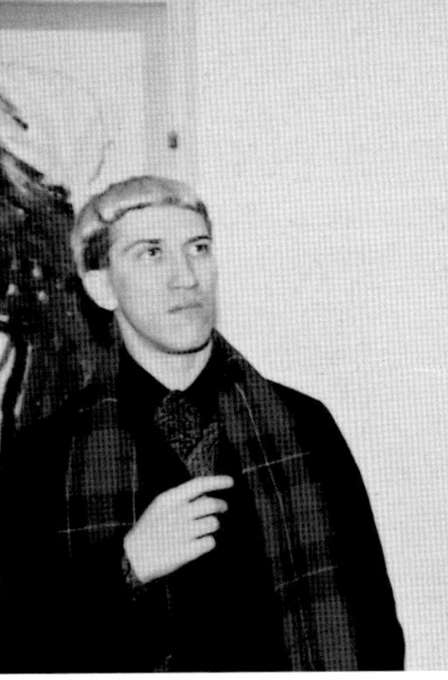

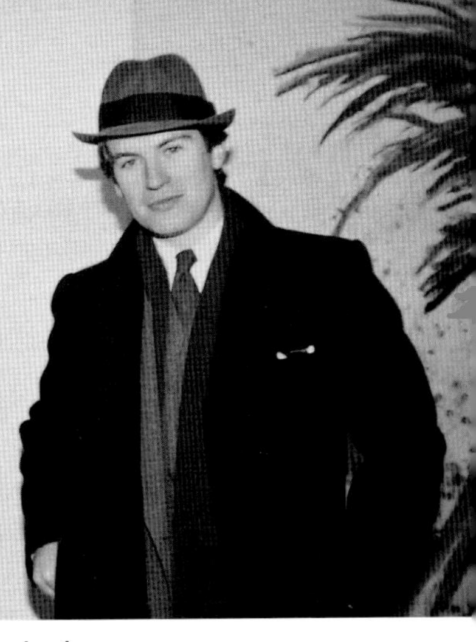

Conceptual artist
Lawrence Weiner.

SoHo gallery owner John Good who now
works for Larry Gagosian in Chelsea.

look great on the set.' I kept calling until my patience started running out." Mark woefully concluded at the thought of yet another ripoff, "I thought about pressing charges after I had called dozens of times but then he died of cancer from his chain smoking."

A few years later when I was working as a gossip columnist at the Daily News I interviewed Morton Downey Jr. when he had only one lung left. He had become a devotee to painting ("My favorite colors are red, yellow and magenta.") and acting. He told me that he wanted to play Mark Kostabi ("I would like to present Mark Kostabi genius-twitched in a Vincent Van Gogh way.") Downey's short-lived hope to play Kostabi in an indie film had been abetted by a NY Post mistake. Troubled thespian Robert Downey Jr. had been briefly interested in a Mark Kostabi biopic and the NY Post misattributed the project to Morton Downey Jr. which caused the Hollywood rumor mill to spin overtime for a few days. But Kostabi's run-in with Morton Downey Jr. only made Mark more popular with the media cognoscenti who had turned on Downey's browbeating ways.

Within days Mark was booked on Oprah Winfrey in Chicago. Mark had first gained attention for being talented, then for being famous, now he was getting publicity for being rich, a whole new niche for him. Mark said, "I was invited to be on the Oprah Winfrey Show not because I was a famous or a controversial artist, but because I was a 'millionaire bachelor who gets hit on a lot by women.' 'Gold Diggers' was the show's theme. I was one of a few millionaire bachelors along with some authentic gold diggers, replete with fur coats and dripping with flashy jewelry. I took part in a heated debate about marrying for love versus money. I was on the love side, claiming that true wealth was knowing how to enjoy life even with limited means. One of my arguments was that you can enter the Metropolitan Museum for one penny, as I did in my early New York days, and be surrounded for as long as you wish by an abundance of art treasures. I continued defending the merits of true love against a huge wave of loud materialist cynicism from most of the other guests and most of the audience until my frustration finally led me to spontaneously take $500 in cash out of my wallet and flamboyantly tear it up. I threw the torn money up in the air in a grandiose manner. Suddenly the entire audience fell silent. Oprah's jaw dropped. After a few seconds of silence the show started up again. Later in the show I announced that the money would be taped back together and donated to charity. When the show was over I left the torn up bills lying on the floor and Oprah's staff agreed to tape it back together and donate it to a charity. For the next two weeks, everywhere I went it seemed that I was recognized and complimented for being on Oprah. Cab drivers, deli workers and people on the street said, 'Hey, you're the guy who tore up money on Oprah!' Then after two weeks, no one mentioned it again.

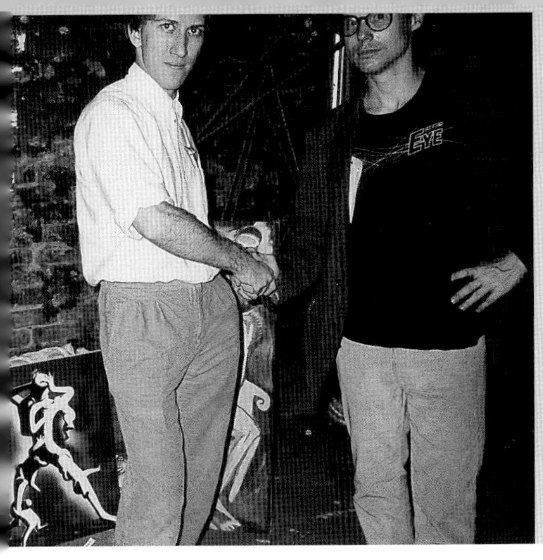

The garden at ABC
No Rio, Baird Jones
and Mark Kostabi?

I concluded that unless you're a regular TV personality, Oprah-type fame lasts exactly two weeks."

The TV camera seems to love Mark. Mark had wild success on TV even when no one knew who he was! He told me this anecdote: "One day in 1987 I had just dyed my hair extremely bright yellowish-green. An attractive girl stared at me on the street so I started up a conversation. We started going out. She was an actress and model and she soon introduced me to her agent. Her agent was currently sending actors on Levi's auditions. She thought my bright green hair signified extreme self-confidence, which was what Lesley Dector, the innovative Levi's commercial director, was looking for. I got the job and while waiting to shoot one commercial I flirted with an actress/model, Rebecca Glenn, who had also got the job. After the shoot we left together. Then the agent called me and said the director saw Rebecca and I leaving together and that gave him an idea for another commercial. He had thought of me as this strange-but-confident nerd with green hair. The last thing he expected was to see me walk off with the most beautiful actress on the set. So they scripted a commercial featuring this conventionally handsome hunk who does all these sexy things to impress Rebecca but in the end she walks off with me and my arm around her, to the surprise of this dumbfounded hunk. This was the commercial that played during the Super Bowl. I did a total of three commercials for Levi's and they never knew or acknowledged that I was a well-known artist.

They hired me entirely on my appearance and personality. I ended up dating Rebecca in real life for a few months. Later she dated the gallery owner Larry Gagosian for a few years, and had a part in Woody Allen's movie *Husbands and Wives*. My Levi's commercials aired extensively, including during the Super Bowl. It turned out that the Levi's commercials were the final convincing reason People Magazine ultimately wrote their article on me."

Mark even seemed to lead a charmed life with the hostility of his collectors. The Corcoran Gallery in Washington, D.C. is a major museum which has one of the toughest permanent collections to get into. One day an agitated collector came into the curator's office, unknown to all, carrying one of Mark's paintings which had been slashed with a knife, possibly by the collector himself. He said that he couldn't stand the painting any longer. "It was driving him crazy" according to Mark. The painting, called *No More Half Steppin' It*, is a large colorful work in which a woman floats over two seated figures, one of whom cradles a bunch of electronic appliances and the other holds a goblet of wine. The anonymous collector just had to get rid of it and then stomped out. The Corcoran curators, looking at an expensive restoration project, nonetheless liked the work, so they contacted Mark who restored the painting at his own expense, and then returned it to them. The painting is now proudly in the Corcoran's permanent collection.

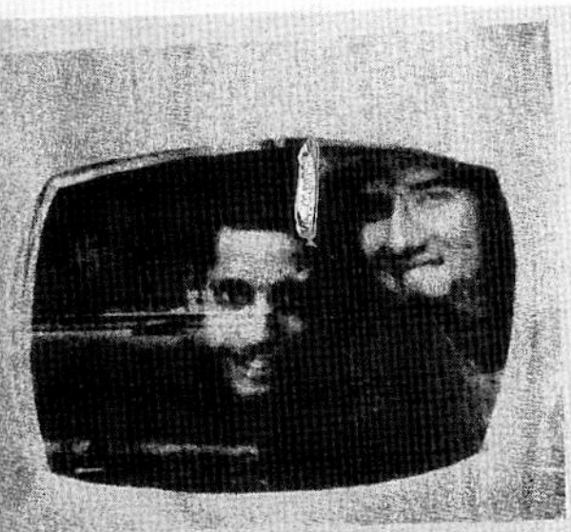

an exhibition
of photographs
of the
EAST VILLAGE
SCENE
by
BAIRD JONES
at the

TODD CAPP GALLERY

223 East 10th Street   YU2-4444

New Year's Eve, Dec. 31st, 6-9
(runs thru January 3rd)   (free admission)
refreshments and music

PHOTOGRAPHS

by

Baird Jones

at

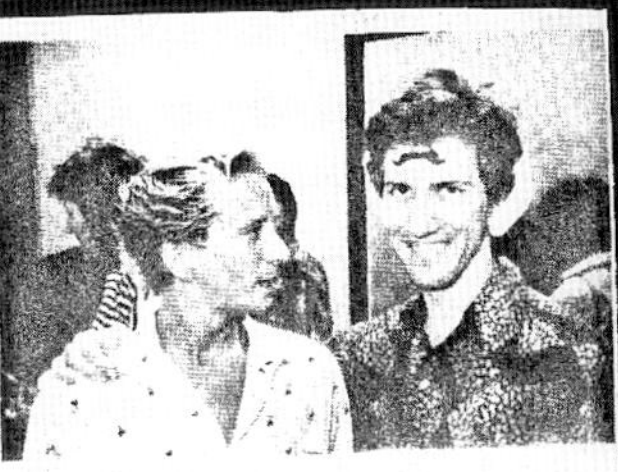

CIVILIAN WARFARE

at 155 Avenue B   Friday, January 24th
(free admission)
475-7498   refreshments and music   5-8

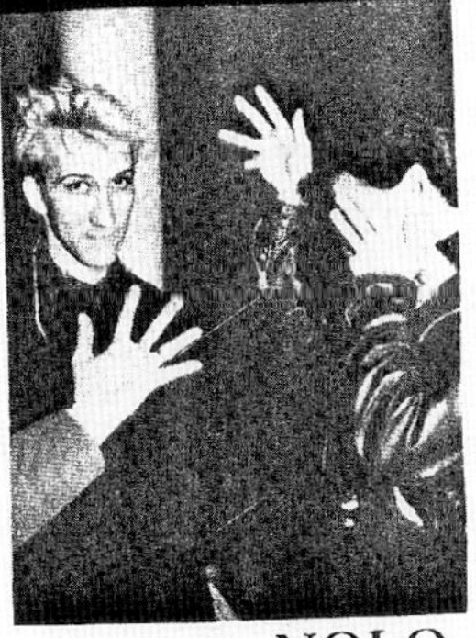

EAST VILLAGE

PHOTOGRAPHS

BY

Baird Jones

Saturday,

January 4th
5-8

at

NOLO CONTENDERE

520 East 11th Street
(free admission)   982-1394
refreshments and music

Photographs by BAIRD JONES

at Nada Gallery, 40 Rivington Street

Opening:

Saturday November 30th, 3:00 - 5:00

Free Admission   Refreshments

Nov. 30th thru Dec. 5th, Nada: 777-2756

PHOTOGRAPHS

by

Baird Jones

at the

Ground Zero Gallery

473-5995   339 East 10th Street
Friday, January 10th,   5-8
(free admission)   refreshments and music

You are cordially invited to an exhibit
of photographs by

BAIRD JONES

Saturday. November 23rd,
1:00 to 3:00 in the afternoon

at FASHION MODA,

2803 3rd Avenue, Bronx (148th St.)
located one block from the no. 5 subway
stop at 149th St.and 3rd Ave. (The no. 5 is
the Manhattan Eastside express line)

free admission   refreshments
Nov. 23rd to 29th, Tues. thru Sat., 2-7
for further info, Fashion Moda 585-0135

Throughout the mid to late 80s, Mark had been consistently making an enormous profit. In a 1984 Art in America review of Mark's solo show at Hal Bromm Gallery, the reviewer noted, "One large oil by Mark Kostabi, still wet but carried uncovered from studio to gallery, was reserved by a Soho passerby and wait-listed by two other passerbys." Mark's 1986 solo show at the Ronald Feldman gallery sold out with prices averaging $20,000 per canvas. Ronald Feldman told me that his sales of Mark's canvases netted over a million dollars a year at that time, "The money sure came rolling in." Autograph auction catalogs started to sell Mark's signature, a sign of his growing fame. Yet, nonetheless Mark moved on and would soon easily duplicate his Soho gallery net again with his controversial Kostabi World cloning inspiration. Mark's unique system of having his assistants paint his artwork and broadcasting it to the public as a kind of conceptual performance art, turned out to be his salvation, for all the nay-saying of his critics. The October 1987 crash of the economy completely flat-lined the New York art market. Even the best galleries had sales put on hold. Most never recovered. By the time the "last hope" of the Japanese bubble economy burst three years later, almost all of Mark's peers from the East Village glory days had already disappeared as commercially viable art players. Yet, in the relative critical isolation of Kostabi World, Mark's elves had efficiently kept cranking out his product, as they have right down to the present.

Finito di stampare nel novembre 2002
presso la S.V.E.T.
di Dosson di Casier (TV)
per conto di Matteo Editore